T0285265

THE SEX OBSESSION

SEXUAL CULTURES

General Editors: Ann Pellegrini, Tavia Nyong'o, and Joshua Chambers-Letson
Founding Editors: José Esteban Muñoz and Ann Pellegrini

Titles in the series include:

The Sex Obsession

Perversity and Possibility in American Politics

Janet R. Jakobsen

NEW YORK UNIVERSITY PRESS

New York

NEW YORK UNIVERSITY PRESS
New York
www.nyupress.org

References to Internet websites (URLs) were accurate at the time of writing. Neither the author nor New York University Press is responsible for URLs that may have expired or changed since the manuscript was prepared.

Library of Congress Cataloging-in-Publication Data
Names: Jakobsen, Janet R., 1960–   author.
Title: The sex obsession : perversity and possibility in American politics / Janet R. Jakobsen.
Description: New York : New York University Press, 2020. | Series: Sexual cultures |
Includes bibliographical references and index.
Identifiers: LCCN 2019043226 | ISBN 9781479846085 (cloth) | ISBN 9781479839421 (ebook) |
ISBN 9781479806737 (ebook)
Subjects: LCSH: Sex role—United States. | Women's rights—United States—Political aspects. |
Homosexuality—Religious aspects—Christianity. | Homosexuality—Government policy—
United States. | Gay rights—United States.
Classification: LCC HQ1075.5.U6 J35 2020 | DDC 305.30973—dc23
LC record available at https://lccn.loc.gov/2019043226

New York University Press books are printed on acid-free paper, and their binding materials are chosen for strength and durability. We strive to use environmentally responsible suppliers and materials to the greatest extent possible in publishing our books.

Manufactured in the United States of America

10 9 8 7 6 5 4 3 2 1

Also available as an ebook

For Christina

One would do a lot for her words

CONTENTS

Introduction

Why Sex?

What does sex have to do with social justice? Specifically, what can the politics of gender and sexuality—sexual politics—contribute to the broad project of making a better world?[1]

In order to think about the possibilities of sexual politics and social justice, I begin by asking, Why? Why are gender and sexuality such riveting public policy concerns in the United States? Why do questions about sex echo through statehouses, dominate political campaigns, and fill the halls of Congress? Why do we care so much about who has sex with whom, or how people embody their genders, or how people organize their households, or which bathroom anyone uses, or whether some workers use health insurance to cover contraception? Why are sexual politics so explosive, quickly mobilizing major voting blocs or requiring special legislative sessions and driving seemingly endless "culture wars"?[2] What's going on here? Why go to "war" over gender, over sex?

The usual answer may be summarized: "Because religion." Because in the United States religion is a powerful force dedicated to the moral regulation of sexuality. This common sense is at work across the political spectrum. Here is an example from the liberal *New Yorker* magazine in 2012:

> An elemental question kept crossing my mind as I browsed dozens of volumes of gay history and theory: Why has this small part of the population caused such vexation across the centuries? What inspires such profound contempt, contempt that is inscribed in the texts of several world religions? I grew up in the Greek Orthodox Church, serving for a time as an altar boy, and attended an Episcopalian high school. Although I don't recall hearing denunciations of homosexuality in either place, I certainly became aware of the most vehemently anti-gay passages in the Christian

tradition, and they both scared and mystified me. St. Thomas Aquinas could be found saying that the "sin against nature" was among the gravest of offenses, because it entails "the corruption of the principle on which the rest depend." The response is disproportionate, as if Aquinas were carpet-bombing an elusive target. There is much evil under the sun, and Rosie O'Donnell's gay-family cruise is not the prime cause of it.[3]

In other words, the Christian heritage of the dominant culture drives a punitive moral discourse about sexuality that is also to be found in "the texts of several world religions" (a conflation of Christianity and religion *tout court* to which I will return).

The Sex Obsession contests almost every part of this standard account. To begin with, sex is not necessarily under the purview of religion, nor do the "texts of several world religions" present unvaryingly punitive sexual ethics. Instead of the usual story, I put the politics of gender and sexuality in relation to other driving social forces: economics, health-care, war, peace, immigration, education, disability, the environment (a list that is expansive, but in no way exhaustive of the issues that might be canvassed in a book about sex and politics). And I follow the many schools of thought that make for what Linda Burnham has termed "social justice feminism," which recognize that gender and sex are also raced and classed and embedded in nationalism and citizenship.[4]

Religion is part of the story, but the standard account of religion and sex is not only misleadingly simplistic, but also damaging to both ethical and political possibilities. The usual story cannot include religious people whose values are not conservative, or who favor sexual freedom, or who may even favor sexual freedom as part of religious freedom.[5] Nor does this story include those who support religious freedom as crucial to an inclusive democratic polity, one open to people with many types of religious commitment—including none at all. As a result, this story sets up a binary choice that is part of a zero-sum game. One is either for sexual liberation or committed to religious regulation. A gain for sexual freedom must be a loss for religion. With this story, there is no possibility of expanding religious freedom and sexual freedom simultaneously.

Instead of focusing only on religion, *The Sex Obsession* traces the effects of movement among the complex social relations in which sexual politics is embedded, movement that may be highly energetic, may, in fact, be so explosive as to boil over into "war," but that nonetheless repeatedly entrenches existing political formations, especially hierarchies. Ultimately, the analysis shifts from the question of "why" to that of "how." How are arguments over sexuality part of maintaining existing social relations, even or especially in terms of unequal power relations? And how might it be different?

In considering these questions, *The Sex Obsession* takes up a seemingly intractable debate. The two sides of this debate, most commonly understood as between sexual conservatives and gender/sex liberationists cannot seem to agree on anything. In 2009, for example, President Obama hoped to build a compromise by advocating "abortion reduction": perhaps most people could agree that it would be better if public policy supported conditions that would reduce the need for abortion. But, instead of creating the opportunity for a new opening in public discussions of contentious issues, Obama was criticized vociferously by conservatives and faced a public protest that he should be the graduation speaker that May at Notre Dame, a Catholic university. It seems people could *not*, in fact, agree on abortion reduction. Abortion became the focus of intensifying disagreement throughout the Obama administration. Among the most vocal constituencies in the 2016 elections to choose Obama's successor were sexual conservatives who it seems (given that the conservative nominee turned out to be Donald Trump) would have voted for anyone who would promise to appoint abortion opponents to the Supreme Court.[6]

Given this state of affairs, I don't expect much of anyone to agree with what's in this book, but for those looking for a way out, I can offer an alternative. The common sense of sexual politics is created through intersections among issues and a tangle of interrelated stories. I begin to untangle these threads through readings that follow a dynamically intersectional approach that attends to movement between and among issues even as it recognizes their interconnection.

The basic claim of *The Sex Obsession* is that most of the assumptions that contribute to this never-ending argument are both factually wrong and set up to ensure that the argument goes on and on, intensifying as it goes. The argument over sex in public debates is drawn into a dynamic I call "mobility for stasis," which means that the more it goes on the less likely it is to go anywhere. The "two sides" are set up to ensure that never the twain shall meet, as anyone who doesn't fit on a "side" and might offer a different approach is thrown out of bounds as inauthentic, as religious people who support gender justice often are, or simply ignored, as reproductive justice activists or queer and trans parents so often are.[7]

Importantly, this set of assumptions also creates inducements for people to intensify, rather than lessen, their investment in the opposition between religion and sex. For example, the intensification can be seen in the development of sexual politics in the United States since the 1970s. As the usual story tells it, abortion politics brought conservative Protestants back into political activism after the Supreme Court legalization of abortion in *Roe v. Wade*. As historians of religion document, however, this story is misleading in a number of ways. It was not the Supreme Court decision on abortion that led to new waves of conservative religious activism, but rather decisions limiting prayer in public schools and in support of busing students for racial integration. These issues fed into a growing movement of white Christian nationalism that developed throughout the Cold War period of US politics, involving issues of both foreign policy and economics. Despite this complex of issues, abortion politics and other issues of sexual politics, including gay and trans rights, have come to represent all of conservative Christian politics.[8]

In fact, the only thing people on all sides of political debates, whether a liberal writer in the *New Yorker* or a conservative activist in the heartland or an objective journalist (of which we will see many herein), seem to agree on is that religion is the obvious focus of sexual politics. *The Sex Obsession* explores this commonsensical understanding precisely because it informs the limits of what's possible—of what can become policy and even of what can be imagined.[9]

For instance, tracking the intensification of conservative Christian concern with sexual politics suggests that the narrative need not be framed as one in which religiosity per se *causes* sexual conservatism. Rather, the main narrative thread could be that in the current configuration of public debate, one way to show one's commitment to religiosity is to display sexual conservatism.[10] In other words, the very narrative that religious identity and gender conservatism correlate can lead to the idea that one should articulate one's religious identity through gender conservatism. And, in turn, this presumption narrows the field of conceivable reality—this version of reality does not encompass religious people whose values are not conservative nor, importantly, does the story account for the sexual conservatism of secular actors—particularly the secular state.

The 2016 elections proved to be a flashpoint for many of the issues considered in *The Sex Obsession,* and the Trump presidency that followed has intensified the conflicts around them in important ways. But the dynamics traced here have also developed over decades, if not centuries. And these dynamics are formulated such that once set in motion, they tend to keep going. Change in elected officials alone has rarely interrupted the underlying dynamics. Many of the approaches to sexual politics that I document are shared across party lines. As chapter 3 will show, certain issues related to sexual politics are the site for some of the deepest divisions between parties, but others are the site of remarkable consistency across them. While it is important to follow shifts and changes in political formations, one of the points of the analysis offered in these pages is that many of these shifts follow lines laid down into the deep grooves of political common sense, and following those paths ultimately reinforces existing hierarchies.

The book argues that religion is both progressive and conservative and that secular freedom is part of sexual regulation in the United States; that religion is found in unexpected places and that secular morality is intimately entwined with material questions; that all kinds of issues drive sexual politics and that sex has its own material force.

Why sex? Because religion, because sex, because everything.

Because Religion, Because Values

In the usual story, religion is understood as the source of ethical values, and gender and sexuality are taken to be privileged sites for the enactment of those values. Religion drives values, values are about sex, and sex is worth fighting over. For example, when the *New York Times* reported on the influence of "values voters" in the 2004 presidential election, the *Times* named only two "values," both of them reflecting conservative sexual ethics: opposition to abortion and opposition to "recognition of lesbian and gay couples."[11] This conflation of values and sexuality is particularly important because the poll on which the claim was based did not name any specific values, but just asked people to rate "values" in relation to other issues like war and economics. In addition, the share of voters choosing "values" in this poll had actually fallen from a high point in 1996, when Bill Clinton was reelected. But the *Times* was willing not only to accept and promote the idea that values voters had swung the election, but also to promote the idea that the "values" these voters cared about were sexual in nature and conservative in force.[12]

This story also flatly conflates "values" with "religion." Consider Senator Robert Byrd's speech on behalf of the Defense of Marriage Act in 1996.[13] Byrd, a Democrat, was not a member of the identified "Christian right," and yet when he stood on the Senate floor to defend the value—the sanctity, really—of marriage between one man and one woman, he brought his family Bible to the Senate floor and in his peroration reached for archaic language to declare, "Woe betide that society, Mr. President, that fails to honor that [biblical] heritage and begins to blur that tradition which was laid down by the Creator in the beginning."[14] A decade later, the Values Voters Summit was founded by a conservative Christian organization, the Family Research Council, to promote precisely this idea—that "values" are religious and signified specifically by sexual conservatism.[15] This narrative, in which religion is the basis for all values, but most importantly for sexual values, is so commonsensical that it seems clear to a US senator that his personal, religious commitments are the appropriate basis for debate over public policy, and his family Bible the right book to flourish on the Senate floor.

Epistemological Questions

Once one begins to question the "obviousness" of the obvious connections between religion and sexual politics, however, there are a number of points at which the commonsense narrative wears thin.[16] The first such point is the conceptual framework—the epistemology—for the narrative itself, which as the *New Yorker* essay shows tends to merge "religion" and "Christianity." Take, for example, the debate over "religious freedom" in the United States, a debate that can assume the congruence among religion, Christianity, and the nation. "Religious freedom" is most commonly invoked, for example, in order to "protect Christianity," as Donald Trump said in 2016 in his campaign speech at Liberty University.[17] How did "religious freedom" come to refer only to the freedoms of "religious people," which is to say Christians, and only certain Christians at that, but not to the freedom of those Americans who are either differently religious or simply not religious? In our current political context, Muslims, for example, find freedom to practice their religion not only curtailed, but actively denied. Indeed, if we take liberal political theory seriously, one does not have to be religious at all to have a claim to religious freedom, to freedom *from* the religious claims of others.[18]

The invocation of "religion" to mean "Christian" in US public discourse extends well beyond Trumpian nationalism. The idea that "religion" is synonymous with Christianity extends throughout popular culture, which means that Americans live with a certain Christian hegemony—Christianity is just assumed as a given. As a number of religious studies scholars have argued, the very idea of "religion" *as a category* is historically entwined with Christian presumptions about what religion "is."[19] This Christian hegemony requires us to attend not only to the effects of Christianity in public life, but also to any general invocation of "religion."

As I consider in depth in chapter 1, positioning religion as a special motivator of sexual conservatism implies that there is an alternative, nonreligious or secular, realm free from, or at least with less propensity for, unreasonable conservatism. Within this framework, if religious repression is supposed to be the root of the problem of sexual politics, then freedom from religion is the answer to the problem. This traditional view plays into a larger Enlightenment narrative in which freedom from religion brings about human liberation.

The epistemological framework that separates religion from secularism allows religion to serve as an explanation for anything (and everything), particularly anything that seems irrational and beyond the bounds of science.[20] If a widespread secular way of thinking supports sexual liberalism—even sexual liberation—an idea of religion that is separate from and even opposed to secularism can seem like an adequate explanation for sexual conservatism, even if many religious people are sexually liberal. Within the conceptual framework separating religion from secularism, religion can become a self-evident explanation for everything that does not make sense from a secular point of view.[21]

In contrast to this view, however, I argue that the problem is as much secular freedom as it is religious regulation. Across its chapters, *The Sex Obsession* documents the ways in which secular policies and interests drive sexual regulation, including not just economic interests but also investments in white familialism, national borders, and the allocation of healthcare. It is not that religion might not also be part of these interests, but they are certainly not solely religious (as sexual politics is sometimes assumed to be), and so the intertwining of religious and secular concerns is at the base of my analysis. Moreover, I show the ways in which the predominant idea of secular freedom in the US remains grounded in Christian and specifically Protestant ideas of the free individual. The relation between—the intertwining of—religion and secularism, rather than either religion or secularism, drives not just sexual politics, but politics.

In addition to these fundamental epistemological worries, there are also reasons to be concerned about the story so often told about religion, sex, and politics specific to the United States. As with the *Times* reporting on "values voters," the empirical basis is not solid for the idea that religion is the source of conservative sexual politics in the US. For example, the obsessive concern with sex in the United States is often attributed to the country's Puritan heritage, but historians of religion suggest that the influence of the Puritans on religious and political culture in the United States has been overemphasized as part of an idealized narrative of American history, while historians of sexuality Estelle Freedman and John D'Emilio argue that the Puritans were not as "Puritanical" about sex as is often presumed.[22] Moreover, the history of sexuality in relation to religious conservatism is not a uniform one. For example, historian Daniel K. Williams has demonstrated that the focus on conservative sexuality in the Southern Baptist Convention did not crystallize until relatively late in the twentieth century. As late as the 1970s, sexual ethics varied from Southern Baptist congregation to congregation, a fact that seems unthinkable now that the denomination is so tightly identified with a radically conservative sexual politics.[23]

Much has also been made of the complexities of Donald Trump's relation to evangelicals—although the presumption that in the past evangelicals have demanded personal sexual morality from their leaders is not necessarily borne out. Here's how Peter Wehner, a frequent Christian commentator in the mainstream press, puts the dilemma: "How can a group that for decades—and especially during the Bill Clinton presidency—insisted that character counts and that personal integrity is an essential component of presidential leadership not only turn a blind eye to the ethical and moral transgressions of Donald Trump, but also constantly defend him? Why are those who have been on the vanguard of 'family values' so eager to give a man with a sordid personal and sexual history a mulligan?" This way of posing the dilemma ignores the fact that during the Clinton era the political champion of both Clinton's impeachment and "family values" was Newt Gingrich, himself a thrice-married adulterer.[24]

As recently as the Obama administration, we saw an openly Christian president who connected his religious commitments to progressive policy, including to a progressive sexual politics on women's rights and eventually on LGBTQ issues. The Obama era also saw lots of stories on evangelicals, particularly those younger than the "family values" cohort represented by Gingrich, moving away from sexual politics and toward issues like poverty and the environment. Now those stories seem to have disappeared and evangelicals are (said to be) only about sexual politics. For some Christians, religion *is* the reason for conservative sexual politics. There are differences, however, even among evangelicals.[25]

But this fact—that religious people, including Christians, including evangelical Christians, have many different views on sexual politics— has very little impact on the conversation as a whole. For example, in another article Wehner says that 2020 presidential candidate Pete Buttigieg was "upending assumptions" about religion and politics by claiming his Christian faith as a basis for progressive policies.[26] Wehner makes this claim despite the fact that Obama did precisely the same thing a decade before. But this is how common sense works—its assumptions (for instance, that Christians favor "family values" and "sexual fidelity") form the parameters for debate despite even recent history that points in a contrary direction.

Ethical Possibilities

The Sex Obsession thinks through these more complex understandings of history in relation to the types of claims about ethics and values that drive public discourse about sexual politics. I am an ethicist by training, and by embedding ethics in less commonsensical and more accurate social analysis, I seek to realize possibilities for materializing the values of social justice feminism, ethical values that are articulated beyond the narrow parameters of mainstream assumptions about "values" and "voters."

Why did the last several decades of the twentieth century make it seem as though the only possible meaning of the word "values" was a combination of evangelical Protestantism and sexual conservatism? This story is certainly politically powerful, and it becomes more so in the repetition of the telling. When Donald Trump identified sexual conservatism as the site where he could make an alliance with conservative Christians, he wound the narrative thread more tightly, making conservatives more likely to see sex as the leading edge of their politics.

The suggestion of this book, however, is that conservatives have not been the only political actors to conflate religiosity and sexual conservatism, although, as the Values Voters Summit shows, powerful social movements and organizations have made this claim. Political liberals and even queer scholars and activists have often been quick to say in return that religion is the driving motivation of sexual conservatives.[27] And when liberals respond in this way, they too tie religion and sex more closely together, making advocacy for sexual conservatism synonymous with naming conservative Christian commitment.

Every time progressives say that sexual regulation happens *because* the conservative opposition is religiously motivated, they reinforce the likelihood that those who wish to express their religious commitments publicly will do so through support for and enforcement of sexual regulation. The relationship between religion and sexuality is variable over time, yet the story that both progressives and conservatives tell about religion as the cause of sexual conservatism erases this variability.

In that agreement across the political spectrum, a world of possibility is lost. Every time this common sense about religion and regulation is repeated, it seems that if one is religious one must of necessity favor sexual regulation (this is not true) and if one favors sexual liberation one must of necessity denounce religion (this is not true). In the apparent necessity, however, the parameters of the possible narrow.

The Sex Obsession thus takes a different approach. I am interested in pointing to the evidence that counters these "assumptions," but also in investigating how the assumptions themselves are produced. And, perhaps most importantly, I challenge the framing of the basic question itself. It is not, Is Christianity or are Christians or are religious people progressive or conservative on sexual politics? Nor, Is secular freedom the answer to religious regulation? But, rather, How can we shift the conversation?

This book is not, then, as might be expected from a book about sex and religion, a book about "the Christian right."[28] Understanding the role of these conservatives in US politics, including sexual politics, is very important, but a singular focus on conservatives can create a sense that liberalism bears no responsibility for the shape of sexual politics today.[29] I read liberal commentators in major media for their investments in certain forms of sexual politics.[30] I consider the role played by conservative Christian activists in the 1970s and by secular political commentators in the present moment (chapter 2), by both liberal and conservative politicians from the 1990s, by the different presidential administrations since that time (Clinton, Bush, Obama, Trump) (chapter 3) and by the Supreme Court of the United States between 2013 and 2018 (chapter 4). I refuse to choose either religion or secularism as the devil or hero of the story.

I envision a politics both hopeful and perversely committed to thinking against the grain. To that end, I follow the workings of power through an analysis of a number of different stories that are related to the idea that sexual politics is such a problem because of religion and that sex serves as a barometer for the morality of the body politic. These popular stories also sometimes treat sex as a frivolous distraction from or cover for more truly pressing issues. In other words, sex can be invoked as the most important issue of the day or as utterly irrelevant. Or, in a variation, pundits may claim that sex mattered once upon a time, but no longer does. I consider variants of each of these stories not so much to debunk them as to follow their effects.

Because Morality, Because Materiality

For example, consider the idea that religion only appears to be the driving force of sexual politics, in other words that it is actually a cover for material, or economic, interests that are the "real" influences shaping sex and politics. The "common sense" of this story is that religion is merely a political tool used by powerful interests to hook less powerful Christians into supporting their agendas. One of the most persistent versions of this story, reiterated over decades, is exemplified by Thomas Frank's 2004 book, *What's the Matter with Kansas?* Frank argues that since the 1970s the Republican Party has led working-class people (more precisely, the predominantly white working-class people of Kansas) to turn away from their economic interests and align with Republican conservatism on matters of gender and sex.[31] The white working class was so taken with the Republican defense of heteropatriarchy against reproductive justice, gay marriage, women's liberation, queer sex, queer collectives, trans lives, gay and lesbian couples with children, racy films, and general sexual libertinage that they did not see how Republican economic policies and practices were materially damaging to them. This analysis remains pervasive, as we see in accounts of the 2016 elections charging that the Democratic Party lost its commitment to the true interests of working-class people by attending to social, rather than economic, issues.[32]

The way of thinking that makes this story into common sense separates economic policy from sexual politics as well as from other social relations like race, effectively allowing an isolated focus on white working-class people as if they represent the working class *tout court*. Alternatively, I trace how gender and sex are imbricated with the social relations of class, race, nation, and religion, and cannot, in fact, be extricated from that complexity. In particular, the *interaction* among issues produces the profound effects of power, including the conservative power that Frank hopes to account for by naming sexual politics as a fundamentally distracting force. For example, in *The Twilight of Equality?* Lisa Duggan's excellent historical study of sexuality in relation to the political economy of the last several decades, often termed neoliberalism, she pursues a conjoint analysis of "love and money," and demonstrates how battles over sexuality in the 1980s combined with racism to mobilize a shift from a liberal redistribution of income through progressive taxation to a neoliberal redistribution *up* the income ladder.[33]

Duggan argues that the "fights" between liberal and conservative politics can obscure broader connections among policies agreed upon and instituted by both Republicans and Democrats. In this sense, the economic social formation of neoliberalism is an assemblage of liberal, conservative, neoliberal, neoconservative, religious, and secular positions that together create the parameters of possible social policy. These positions come together in such a way as to ensure that no matter who is president of the United States, "redistribution upward" will persist. I show how this works out in chapter 3 by analyzing government policies ranging across the administrations of presidents Bill Clinton, George W. Bush, Barack Obama, and Donald Trump. For instance, some commentators have understood Donald Trump's election as part of a populist protest against neoliberal globalization, and yet the first major legislative initiative passed during his administration was a tax cut favoring wealthy individuals and corporations—redistribution upward. In this regard, it seems that Trump's policies are not so much against neoliberalism as for combining isolationism and redistribution upward into a "nationalist neoliberalism."[34]

Most importantly, sex is not simply a function of the relations with which it is imbricated. An analysis that cannot account for the relative autonomy of sexual politics cannot account for much that happens in social life and public debate, including the ways in which people's commitments regarding gender and sexuality (whether conservative or progressive) may be the driving force of their politics and the ways in which sexual politics may be the leading edge and model for—rather than distraction from—other forms of political action.[35] Ara Wilson, for example, in an ethnography of "intimate economies" in Thailand has shown some of the ways in which sex has shaped capitalism in Thai society. From the familial and kinship ties that made possible the shift from personal shops to impersonal retail sales on a large scale, to sex work as a tourist industry, Wilson shows that it is just as much sexual relations that have made possible the development of capitalism as it is that capitalism has made certain sexual relations possible. And in the United States, commitments to gender complementarity and heterosexual familialism are formative to labor markets, to the structure of the welfare state, and to neoliberal political economies. In other words, the answer to "Why sex?" is sometimes "Because sex."

When it comes to social justice, an analysis that ignores or dismisses sexual politics cannot serve as the basis for mobilizing social change in a world where the frontline of injustice is the sometimes violent and often intimate enforcement of gender normativity and sexual conformity.

Sex Is Frivolous, Sex Is Over

Often entwined with this narrative about the "real" issues is the sense that sex *should* not be part of political discourse. Despite all the undeniably public attention given to evidently consequential sexual politics, sex is still often treated as if it should be a private concern, separate from the various issues that rightly populate public life. Those who focus on sex in public are accused of distracting public attention from supposedly more important issues.[36] Take, for example, remarks made by *New York Times* columnist Thomas Friedman in an interview with NBC's Katie Couric on September 11, 2002. Couric invites Friedman to reflect on the national significance of the date, and he replies, "The nineties were a decade of real silliness. It was a decade preoccupied with Monica Lewinsky, O. J. Simpson, and ultimately Gary Condit on the eve of September 11. So there is no question we took our eye off the ball as a country and a society."[37]

Each case Friedman names as an example of frivolous public concerns involves gender and sexuality, but none of them are "silly." After all, the investigation of Bill Clinton's sexual involvement with White House intern Monica Lewinsky led to his impeachment. The other two instances Friedman mentions involve not only gender and sex, but also murder and racism, as Gary Condit was briefly a suspect in the murder of his intern Chandra Levy, and the Los Angeles police were accused of planting evidence against O. J. Simpson to bolster their case that he had killed his wife, Nicole Brown Simpson, and her friend Ronald Goldman. Both the Clinton and Simpson cases have been important enough in popular culture to be regularly revisited in the intervening years.[38] The impeachment of a president, police violence, and the inability of US public discourse to hold simultaneously in mind the facts of *both* police racism (notorious among the Los Angeles police force) *and* the deadly realities of domestic violence (three women are killed by their intimate partners every day in the United States)—none of these are frivolous issues.[39]

In fact, even as Friedman was declaring gender and sex to be over as public issues, they were part and parcel of how United States military power was mobilized in response to the terror of the 9/11 attacks. George W. and Laura Bush were both suddenly concerned with the oppression of Muslim women, as "saving" Muslim women became part of the public discourse justifying war in Afghanistan.[40]

Even as sexual politics repeatedly returns to public life despite its supposed unimportance, commentators, both liberal and conservative, repeatedly declare sex too trivial to warrant serious political discussion. The aftermath of the 2008 financial crisis elicited claims that the country could no longer afford to focus on sex, just as Friedman had assured us that the events of 2001 and its aftermath moved the focus of public discourse from frivolous sex to weighty consideration of war and peace.[41]

Sexual politics was once again declared over after the 2015 US Supreme Court ruling in *Obergefell v. Hodges* that declared restrictions on same-sex marriage unconstitutional. Backlash against this decision began almost immediately with cases that posed the "religious freedom" of wedding vendors, like bakers and photographers, over the right of gay couples to nondiscrimination when accessing public accommodations. At the same time, major conservative organizations and legislators pivoted to reinvigorate fights against reproductive justice and initiate actions against transgender people.[42] This movement among issues of sex and gender is a form of mobility for stasis: the issues facing gay people, trans people, and those fighting for reproductive justice are not the same, but movement among them as if they are creates what legal scholar Mary Anne Case calls the "seamless garment" of sexual politics and holds together a set of conservative alliances. Most importantly, the seamless movement among issues related to gender, sex, and sexuality makes certain that sexual politics will never be "over."

After *Obergefell*, for example, "bathroom bills," which police trans people's use of gendered bathrooms, were introduced into several state legislatures, often aimed at overturning local nondiscrimination laws. Some of these bills passed state legislatures, notably in North Carolina, where, in March 2016, the governor signed into law a bill requiring people to use the bathroom associated with the gender assigned to them at birth. After protests, the North Carolina law was partially repealed, but the legal battle over gender nondiscrimination policies at the state and local level continues.[43] The lieutenant governor of Texas went so far as to declare that the "spiritual war" to police gender is "the biggest issue facing families and schools in America since prayer was taken out of the public schools."[44]

As Lauren Berlant and Lisa Duggan have argued, in US public discourse, sexual politics are both overvalued and devalued.[45] Progressives, as well as conservatives, contribute to the oscillation between these two poles. Those committed to progressive politics often display a squeamishness about sex similar to Thomas Friedman's, worrying along with him that gender and sex are truly unimportant or seeming to accept the conservative assumption that ethical values linked to sexual relations can only be deployed on the side of a conservative morality.[46]

There are notable exceptions—movements for free love, utopian communities, sexual liberationist Marxism—but progressives rarely articulate issues through the prism of sexuality, despite its centrality to many issues of justice.[47] To take just one example: despite the ways in which sexuality is repeatedly deployed to legitimate conservative opposition to anti-poverty programs (as will become evident in my consideration of "welfare reform" in chapter 3), anti-poverty activists who are not already part of movements for specifically gender and queer economic justice have largely been unwilling to consider (much less embrace) the ways in which sexual democracy might help to alleviate poverty.[48] This dismissal of sex in progressive politics has often left progressive movements open to attack when sex and gender are used to undermine progressive efforts on the supposedly "important" issues.[49]

And the dismissal of sex has also been a way to downplay certain forms of conservatism, locating them in a mainstream that eschews the passions associated with sexual politics. One can find such squeamishness in plenty of examples in which commentators claimed that Donald Trump's campaign in 2016 had fundamentally shifted away from previous iterations of the "culture wars."[50] The argument that sex had been moved aside by Trump's brand of politics minimized his extremes and made his campaign seem more reasonable, thus moving it toward the mainstream of public discourse.

For example, in the first year of Trump's presidency, *Vanity Fair*'s *The Hive* ran an article by T. A. Frank titled "What Democrats Can Learn from Trump's Culture War."[51] Proclaiming that "sexual morality" is no longer central, Frank declares that Trump's campaign victory offers an important lesson for liberals (after all, the article is about what Democrats can *learn* from Trump). In the first step of his argument, Frank positions the new "culture war" as "different, perhaps bigger" than when "sexual morality was more central to the culture war." He argues that now the cultural question at issue is much more consequential, for it is "Western civilization" itself that needs to be defended from those who belittle and criticize it: "The underlying idea is simple: we have a lot more to be proud of than we have to be ashamed, so we shouldn't be afraid to treasure and defend it."

Frank distinguishes this new and "bigger" culture war from the one named twenty-five years earlier when Patrick Buchanan invoked a "culture war" in his speech on behalf of George H. W. Bush at the 1992 Republican National Convention. Buchanan's war, however, seems not to be that different from the version Frank touts as so meaningfully new. Buchanan's speech begins with economic nationalism, moves on to anticommunism and the US "victory" in the Cold War, then to "sexual morality," school choice, prayer in school, religious nationalism, and the riots in Los Angeles after the acquittal of the policemen who beat Rodney King, only to conclude with a return to economic nationalism.[52] The global threat of communism has been replaced in Frank's analysis by the threat of globalism itself, but most of the other issues referenced by Buchanan remain central to Trump's agenda.

Despite these major similarities, Frank declares it "[n]otable that sexual morality, hardly a Trumpian forte, plays no role" in the culture war that Trump fights and Democrats must understand. He dismisses as unimportant Trump's banning of transgender people from the military. He says nothing about the significance of the appointment of conservative, antiabortion justices to the US Supreme Court. He lets pass unnoticed that Trump's administration argues for expanding "religious freedom" so that Americans with the religious conviction that homosexuality is sinful may be free to discriminate against queer people in the provision of goods and services. He ignores the clear evidence that misogyny, particularly as expressed in online communities, played a role in the crystallization of the white nationalist alt-right and in the support for Trump within this strand of right-wing political mobilization.[53]

Given this series of actions by the Trump administration and its supporters, why state (twice) that "sexual morality" is no longer part of the larger pattern? This movement among issues—where sexual politics is displaced from center to margin—allows Frank to claim that he is clearing away the cultural noise (so to speak) and to conclude that the issue underneath the fire and brimstone of culture warring is ultimately about the values of "Western civilization." In Frank's rendition, sexuality disappears, along with a host of deeply contentious political battles, in order to bring Western civilization front and center. Viewed that way, culture wars are not really about any kind of hot-headed misogyny or xenophobia; rather, for Frank the culture wars are about a reasonable "pride" in the liberal values of Western civilization, which is now dissociated from all of the other elements of the US culture wars, like Christian nationalism and police violence, that were invoked by Buchanan. Instead of addressing a hotbed of issues, analyses like Frank's swirl complex political conflicts around until they come down as reasonable disagreements between two simply drawn sides—globalists versus nationalists, for example.[54]

Frank's turn of the kaleidoscope shifts issues to create a new pattern with the pieces arrayed around a distinct division between one side and another. This movement among issues is one of the key mechanisms whereby political conflict can be realigned to keep longstanding hierarchies in place once movement settles. Not only do gender and sexuality move in and out of public focus, but also the push and pull of such analyses play off of each other. If, for example, we bracket Thomas Frank's claim in 2004 that sex is overly important with T. A. Frank's claim in 2017 that sex is no longer important, we can follow the effects of this dynamic. If it is progressive to argue that sex has been accorded too much attention (as Thomas Frank claims), how can it be anything other than similarly progressive to remove sex from the conversation altogether? And, yet, as we see from T. A. Frank's conclusion, the effect of such removal can be to make a conservative "culture war" seem more mainstream. Swirling the issues around allows Frank to disconnect a supposedly reasonable Trumpian nationalism from Trump's extremism.

The mechanism by which such arguments relate to each other is thus best understood not as a pendulum, in which the import of sex swings back and forth, but more like a spiraling kaleidoscope. Not only does turning the kaleidoscope change the pattern of elements, making some visible at certain points and not at others (even as those elements remain part of the pattern), but the center of the pattern also shifts as the kaleidoscope is turned.

Even when sex isn't the topic, it's the topic. One of the ways that sex can be so powerful in US public life is that when it goes away it remains embedded in policy areas ranging from healthcare (you can provide insurance coverage through your employer to those you marry) to economics (marriage is seen as a major route out of poverty) to war and peace (the sense of the US as a good actor and humanitarian agent in its global military adventures is deeply entwined with the sense that the US is a morally good nation with gender equality and the right kind of sexual freedom).[55]

One way to think about the last forty or fifty years of sexual politics is to analyze sex both when it is at the center of discussion and to understand how sex remains consequential even when it is shifted to the side. If we don't take sex seriously, it is harder to see how the social infrastructure remains remarkably stable and hierarchical, despite all the moving parts.[56] Denying the importance of sex in public does not diminish the cultural and political effects of sexual politics, but it does make those effects more opaque and less open to critique.

The refusal to take sexual politics seriously also undermines important possibilities for organizing, alliance building, and social change. Sex materializes social relations of all kinds, not only the intimate relations of love and family with which sex is routinely associated, but also the economic relations, race relations, and international relations from which sex is routinely distinguished. Sex is neither the truth of ourselves nor a frivolous concern of the privileged. It is rather a social relation constituted by and constitutive of the various social relations that have made this historical moment possible.

Mobility for Stasis

Social analyses that move the public import of sex and gender in and out of view have an effect not just on sexual politics, but on the overall shape of political discourse. Political actors, scholars, and commentators across the political spectrum declare at one point that sex is politically meaningless, and at another that it is what matters the most, producing a range of rhetorical and political effects that I explore in the chapters that follow. This rhetorical mobility allows commentators on the left to declare that religiously committed people who take sexual politics seriously are missing the point or misunderstanding their own interests, even as it allows commentators on the right to charge those who would liberalize or liberate sexual practice with denigrating religion and religious ethics. It allows sex to stand in for other issues, such as those of race and class, even as it also allows those other issues to be invoked so as to push gender and sexuality toward conservative ends or out of view altogether.[57]

As examples throughout the book will show, the movement from sex to race to gender and back again weaves together a social fabric that is flexible enough to sustain some shifts in social relations without substantive change to the whole. I explore how the US Supreme Court released a "progressive" ruling on same-sex marriage, which led to intense media coverage of the social and political progress toward full equality for gays and lesbians; that same week however, the Court released deeply regressive rulings on affirmative action and voting rights that were largely overlooked in the hubbub over gay marriage. Progress on sexual politics came to the fore, sidelining discussions of structural racism in education and the ruling that dismantled part of an important legislative victories of the Civil Rights Movement, dismantled part of an important legislative victory of the Civil Rights Movement. Yet only a year later, the Court reasserted its commitment to racial justice in a decision that dismissed claims for gender equality as "vague." Through this movement among issues, the basics of the social text remain unchanged.

It is not just movement among issues that can reassert social hierarchies. Other sets of intertwined relations, such as those among facts and feelings or facts and values, can also reassert social hierarchy while seeming to appeal to what is only reasonable. Consider a discussion of the issue that the election of Donald Trump made signally pressing: immigration. Turning once again to a liberal critic who wants to put Trump's ascendance and the importance of immigration into the broader context of political economy, economist Jeffrey Sachs invokes facts, but ultimately depends upon values as the basis for his analysis of the ascendancy of Donald Trump in the US and the "Brexit" vote to leave the European Union in the United Kingdom. Sachs is a regular liberal commentator.[58] Yet, employing a common argument that could be found in the pages of the *New York Times*, *New Yorker*, and other mainstream publications, much like T. A. Frank urging Democrats to value Western civilization, Sachs produces an analysis in which facts, feelings, and ethics shift positions in relation to one another to make deeply conservative positions seem to fit his liberal outlook.[59]

A few months before the 2016 general election, Sachs made the case that the movements propelling both Brexit and Trumpian politics are part of a "deep trend" based on the "deep and pervasive problems in our approach to globalization."[60] Political movements supporting Brexit and Trump share core beliefs, he argued, including "that immigration is out of control, culturally destabilizing, and adverse to their economic interests. They believe that the political and financial elites have joined forces to abuse power, evade taxes, and twist globalization toward narrow ends." He continued, "These attitudes are not racist, xenophobic, or fascist (despite claims to the contrary, and despite enough racists and xenophobes in our midst). They are based on facts on the ground. In the past half-century, the United States and Europe have experienced a massive surge of migration, both legal and illegal. The foreign-born share of the US population soared from 4.8 percent in 1970 to an estimated 13.9 percent in 2015, and in the UK the share of foreign-born surged from 5.8 percent in 1971 to 13.1 percent in 2015. At the same time, inequality of income has soared; the top have made off with the prize. The rich countries lost effective control of their borders, or at least much of the public feels that way."

Note that over just four sentences Sachs has moved from facts to feeling.[61] Specifically, he moves from the "facts on the ground" that document the increased percentage of US and UK populations that are "foreign-born" between roughly 1970 and 2015 and the supposedly widespread feeling that these "rich" countries have "lost effective control of their borders." This shift from facts to feelings is important for two reasons. First, it allows a shift from a focus on an increase in the number of migrants to a claim about lost control of national borders, which is on much less stable ground empirically. While migration to the US and the UK has increased since 1970, it is not at a highpoint, and the specific increase to which Sachs refers is hardly the same as a loss of border control.[62] To make this argument, Sachs is lumping together legal and illegal immigration, thus implicating not "lost control," but legislative choices to allow more legal immigration. Border control has actually been heightened. The US-Mexico border (Trump's specific site of concern) has been increasingly militarized since the 1990s and the development of a post-9/11 security apparatus has intensified this effect. In other words, immigration *control* has increased since the 1970s.[63]

Sachs's move to feelings is the point at which moral evaluation of immigration indirectly enters the discussion. Given its somewhat loose factual basis, the "feeling" of "lost control" also brings to bear the ethical and political question of how immigration is valued. Is immigration the moral good proclaimed by the Statue of Liberty ("Give me your tired, your poor, your huddled masses yearning to breathe free"), or is it indicative of a "problem" in "our" approach to globalization as Sachs suggests?[64]

To reinforce the idea that immigration is an ethical problem, singularly symptomatic of deep trends, Sachs connects the immigrant/native-born opposition that he sets up to one between "elites" and "older, whiter, less educated, and working class" members of society. In doing so, Sachs invokes an implied ethical argument in which "elites" are the beneficiaries of unjust and uncaring social relations, since they profit from surging migration and globalization is in their interests. In order to bolster this moral argument, Sachs then recruits sexual politics through a longstanding moralizing narrative about poorer countries' demographics, a narrative that carries implications about both uncontrolled peoples and uncontrolled sexuality: "Populations in the source regions surged, leading to huge pressures for out-migration. . . . The economic elites took little interest in this. Companies made profits on low-wage immigrant labor, while richer consumers enjoyed the low-cost services supplied by the immigrants. The elites turned a blind eye to the falling wages of the working class, who were also being hit by increased trade competition, offshoring of jobs, and automation."

In addition to the moralized invocation of population "surges," which has nothing to do with the indictment of corporate profits and practices in the following sentences, Sachs further invokes the assemblage of issues that became so prevalent in analyses of 2016. Immigration is inextricably tied to increased trade competition, offshoring of jobs, and automation, even though there is no direct connection between immigration and automation, for example. And, in focusing on immigration, Sachs is effectively connecting all recent economic shifts and transformation to "globalization," rather than to, for example, the shift from industrial to finance capitalism or from Keynesian welfare policies to neoliberal austerity. Morality is brought into play with the language of "elites" who "turn a blind eye" and so an argument that is supposed to be based on "facts on the ground" becomes one that carries and is carried by strong moral implications.

The turning of the kaleidoscope among "facts," "beliefs," "feelings," and "elites" brings certain pieces of the argument to the fore while others recede to the background. And, in that shift, parts of the argument are connected together in unexpected ways. Immigrants and people of color are not among the most affected by economic injustice, but rather they are shifted to the side of the elites; morality is brought to bear to constitute facts on the ground, specifically that immigration increases are a "problem" of "our approach to globalization." On the other hand, the argument against Sachs's position is based precisely in the assessment that the movements in support of Trump and Brexit use racial, ethnic, religious, and cultural differences to stand for an array of economic and political problems associated with globalization, or what with different moral valences might be called "neoliberalism," "economic austerity," or "intensified inequality."[65] Linking economic problems to people's racial and ethnic identities, to their national origins, to their reproductive practices (as part of "population surges"), or to their religious commitments is xenophobic. It blames entire groups of people for something that is the result of social forces which are not driven by members of those groups, much less by the groups as a whole. Instead of arguing that rich nations have lost control of their borders, one could argue that rich states have lost control of corporate power.

What are the relations among economic inequality, deindustrialization, wage stagnation, and other effects of neoliberal economic policies? By recognizing the combination of empirical and evaluative claims that go into discussions of contemporary global relations, we could put together these pieces in a different way. We could acknowledge the problems of militarism, elite corruption, and losses to the working class (not just the white working class), while also acknowledging the racism involved in movements supporting Donald Trump and Brexit. By tracing the relationship between colonialism and neoliberalism, we could study how "rich nations" became "rich," and analyze the global economy that continues to produce riches that flow to the Northern metropoles, even after the dismantling of formal colonialism.[66] In other words, we could produce an analysis that takes seriously economic deprivation *and* the racism of white nationalism *and* the sexism of blaming sexual practices in immigrant communities for demographic shifts.

I am intent on following the movement among interests and values, economics and sex, fact and feeling, morality and materiality, religion and secularism, social and cultural analyses, and any number of related oppositions so as to embed thinking about values in a range of dynamic and interactive materialities. I want to know how sex contributes to social value, to the building of relations and communities, to the enlivening of potentially dire situations, and to material well-being. I want to understand how values regarding gender, sex, and politics are embodied by individuals and materialized in institutions. In this sense, sexual values are real, material, and powerful.

Power and Possibility

Sexual politics is part of a set of patterns through which many powerful political forces run, including nationalism, race, and economics.[67] These vectors of power form a crosshatched, flexible network that holds in place the idea that religious values and sexual politics are necessary to a well-functioning polity or economy or—as Senator Robert Byrd claimed—to "the nation." The assemblage formed by these relations is extremely mobile and unafraid of contradiction—sometimes the same politicians promote the idea of the United States as a secular beacon of freedom and as a Christian nation. For example, I provide a reading of policies promoted in the name of Christianity by the sexually conservative Bush administration, an administration that also aggressively proclaimed the "freedom" of the United States as the basis of the war on terror.

Intersectional feminism has named many of the problems with single-issue analysis and activism, and here I focus on the *dynamic interaction* of intersecting issues.[68] The chapters trace the ways in which political groupings are brought together and divided from each other in shifting, kaleidoscopic patterns that make it seem as if social change is happening all the time, while social hierarchies rarely undergo fundamental change. These kaleidoscopic shifts generate "mobility for stasis."[69]

One of the reasons I follow examples over several decades is to undo the idea that whatever is happening in contemporary sexual politics is either an unvarying historical reality or utterly new and different from what has happened in the past, even the recent past. Traversing the decades also raises questions about the progress narrative in which it seems that sexual politics can be adequately represented as a simple story of movement from a repressive and regulatory past toward a freer future. Like the story of Puritan origins, the progress narrative is part of the idealized narrative of the United States. In this story, movement occurs along a single path. While there may be moments of backlash leading to regression, the direction of progress is a straight line going forward into the future. Instead, I tell a story of sexual politics that is multidirectional, as I pay attention to unexpected continuities and discontinuities across the decades.

For example, in the timeline version of history, religious conservatives effectively stepped back from public life after the battles over "fundamentalism" and scientific secularism that had preoccupied US public life in the 1920s. In the 1970s, things change with the formation of the "new right." This new political formation returns religious activism to the public sphere with the formation of the Moral Majority. That organization, and others like it, opposed the liberalization of sexual politics (notably, the rise of women's liberation and gay liberation) and advocated a conservative sexual ethics. This story of the "return" of religion to the public sphere in conjunction with the rise of the "culture wars" is now understood as *the* story about sexual politics in the US. In contrast, I revisit histories of the 1970s, and follow the movement of sexuality in and out of public focus—which actually involves a much more complex and shifting movement among multiple issues, including race in public schooling, reproductive rights and justice, economic policy, and the global politics of the Cold War.[70]

"Culture wars" over sexual politics are often treated as *the* site for political polarization, but if one reads the politics that follow from the 1970s without presuming such a division, one can see similar forms of sexual politics recurring across partisan divides, whether in the 1990s in the Clinton administration's move to "end welfare as we know it" by focusing on "teenage pregnancy," or when the Republican Party drew up its Contract with America and Contract with the American Family, or in George W. Bush's AIDS policy of the 2000s, which focused on exporting monogamous familialism throughout the world as a means of "winning the war on terror," or when Obama's Office of Faith-Based and Neighborhood Partnerships was charged with both promoting "responsible fatherhood" in the US and moderate religion internationally as part of post-9/11 national security policy. To follow the complex play of intimate, domestic, and transnational politics is like looking through a kaleidoscope in which both sex and religion repeatedly appear, then move out of view. That political interplay is certainly not adequately represented by a static binary division between religious regulation on one side and secular freedom on the other that is then plotted onto the progressive timeline of history and partisan divisions.

In tracing the kaleidoscopic relations of sexual politics, I focus on the United States as an area of study, even as I place the country in a transnational context, including the context of the political and economic formation known as "neoliberalism."[71] Neoliberal policies and practices displaced New Deal Keynesian economics and its compromises among labor, industry, and government with policies and practices focused primarily on building corporate power and shareholder wealth. While I use neoliberalism as a heuristic device to articulate political economic relations, as with other concepts I draw upon, I see neoliberal relations as produced through an entangled set of policies and practices, rather than as the structure or framework for any and all social relations.[72] Analysts need both a view of processes and phenomena that exceed national boundaries and an understanding of state power as not simply a symptom of those processes.[73]

My particular understanding of the specificities of the US case in relation to transnational processes was developed in a set of conversations conducted over five years under the auspices of a research project sponsored by the Barnard Center for Research on Women—Gender, Justice, and Neoliberal Transformations, which I co-led with Elizabeth Bernstein.[74] This project involved thirteen scholars working in different areas of the world engaging in a conversation about similarities, differences, and interconnections in neoliberal politics and practices so as to develop a comparative and synthetic understanding of neoliberalism and some of its transnational characteristics and effects. Among these different sites we did not find a single set of policies or universal set of stages through which all political formations move, but rather a set of complex interrelations.

In attending to variation and paradox, the scholars in the project developed a feminist and queer materialism that makes connections with schools of thought like racial capitalism and social reproduction theory.[75] It is clear, for example, that the racialized systems of colonialism and imperialism are enacted and extended in important ways through neoliberal policies and practices, such that Kamala Kempadoo has argued that neoliberalism should not be considered a new formation, but rather yet another episode of neocolonialism.[76] As such, any study of neoliberalism must take into account the imbrication of capitalism and these racialized systems of violence. And it is also clear that social reproduction theory's critique of traditional Marxism (along with liberal political economy) remains relevant. In both classical economics and Marxian theory, it often seems as though human beings arrive in the world fully grown and ready to work. Social reproduction theory seeks to make visible the labor necessary to reproduce those workers. But, as José Esteban Muñoz has pointed out in *Cruising Utopia: The Then and There of Queer Futurity*, not all futures are reproductive futures, and not all gendered and sexualized labor is for reproductive purposes. A feminist and queer materialism focuses on nonnormative economic relations—not just those, like housework, that don't fit into waged labor, but also those that do not fit with the usual understanding of production or reproduction. In other words, connecting queer as well as feminist and antiracist approaches to materialism attends to labor that is often treated as a threat to, rather than a necessary (if unpaid) part of, society.

In developing this analysis, I critique two key parts of what is commonly identified as the narrative of "American exceptionalism": that the United States is profoundly Christian and exceptionally religious, and that the US is a beacon of secular freedom, as proved by its liberal, even cosmopolitan, treatment of both gender and sexuality.[77] Rather than idealizing the US as either a "shining city on a hill" or the nation bequeathing freedom to the world, I begin with what historian Allan J. Lichtman calls "white Protestant nationalism" and consider sexual politics in relation to this nationalism.[78]

Importantly, this commitment to a white Christian nation may involve a commitment to a *national sexuality* more than concern about any individual's sexual practice, challenging commonsense assumptions about the ways in which Christianity, sexual politics, and white nationalism intertwine. As Frank Rich repeatedly pointed out as a *New York Times* columnist in the heyday of debates over "family values," markers of sexual practice, such as the flourishing of sexual commerce, were much the same in the Red states as in the Blue, even as these states continue to differ greatly in their policies with regard to gender and sexuality.[79] Thinking about these debates in domestic politics as also transnationally effected and effecting underscores the interest in claiming a national sexual ethics as part of US actions abroad. And, indeed, I will trace the relations among an intimate politics of gender and sexuality, and domestic nationalism and US foreign policy in the George W. Bush, Obama, and Trump administrations.

As I argue throughout this book, synthetic analysis does not produce a new, complete view of the world—a new "theory of everything." Rather, reading these different approaches in relation to each other highlights both connections and disjunctions.[80] The purpose of pursuing such an analysis is to provide a critique that makes conceptual openings for analyses of difference that don't quite fit, social relations that don't make sense, and gaps between perspectives that create not so much lacunae in the scholarship as openings for possibility, including for possibility that might be realized through nonproductive, nonnormative, disjunctive, and potentially perverse practices.

Thinking Differently, Acting Differently

I pursue this analysis of policies and practices, facts and feelings, ethical values and economic value, so as to create possibilities for thinking and acting differently. The chapters that follow connect analytic rigor to hopeful political possibility.

I pursue a purposefully activist approach that moves among theoretical frameworks rather than trying to contain the world's complexities within a single frame or choose one side or the other of what too often become oppositional debates.[81] For example, I take up a queer approach to identity, refusing the modern presumption of a coherent identity as an accurate representation of material life, even as I also track the social power of identity categories.[82] I follow the interrelations among categories of race, gender, sex, class, and nation, recognizing that these categories are *both* fictions that misrepresent the complexity of material life *and* that they have material effects (particularly when deployed through the law) that are all too real.

I have developed this approach in part through what I've learned from participation in a series of transnational collaborative research groups, including—in addition to the aforementioned Gender, Justice, and Neoliberal Transformations—Interdisciplinary Innovations in the Study of Religion and Gender: Postcolonial, Post-secular, and Queer Perspectives, a working group established by Anne-Marie Korte; and Religion and the Global Framing of Gender Violence, led by Lila Abu-Lughod, Rema Hammami, and Nadera Shalhoub-Kevorkian.[83] The different theoretical engagements by participants in these projects—postcolonial, post-secular, feminist, antiracist, queer, and social justice—sometimes conflicted. But the discussions enabled by the projects also explored how the interaction of perspectives could inform each other.[84] Over the years, I began to see real possibilities for theoretical alliance without simply erasing the disjunctions among these perspectives and took up a "theoretical promiscuity."[85]

Given the complexity of the world, applying only one approach to the question of sexual politics seems likely to oversimplify any understanding of interlocking political forces.[86] Moving among theoretical perspectives allows me to articulate (both describe and bring together) realities that are likely to be obscured by orthodoxy—even as fissures will undoubtedly remain. Theoretical promiscuity, then, is different from what used to be called the "toolbox" approach to theory. Rather than pulling out one tool here and another tool there, promiscuity is a relational undertaking. It can build and expand relationships among theoretical perspectives.

One might think that an approach associated with promiscuity, even of a theoretical variety, is the result of my participation in queer studies, and in one way this is true.[87] Queer studies is concerned with the ways in which social differences are too often rejected, obscured, or excluded because they cannot be wrangled into place for the sake of coherence. But the need to engage with and move between theoretical frameworks is also influenced by my participation in religious studies and especially by the critique of secularism. Specifically, in the predominant version of the secularization narrative, modern secularism provides a single framework for all knowledge.[88] The critique of secularism suggests, alternatively, that secular modernity is not the framework for all views, but rather one viewpoint among multiple possible views. In other words, not everyone organizes their lives in relation to a secular framework, and we do not have to eject people such as religious actors from our vision of social life in order to project a coherence that doesn't actually exist. Just as there is no single, secular framework to hold all religious worldviews, there is no single theory that can encompass the world in its diversity and complexity.

Decentering secularism produces a world with multiple lines of ethical authority and ways of knowing that are not contained within a single frame, but rather that require movement between and across different realms.[89] While such formations are not coherent in the traditional sense of "the social," one can still develop tools to approach the complexity of social life. I argue for a multiplicitous moral and empirical universe that can consider "productive incoherence."

Overall, I question whether the idea of a "framework" is the best metaphor for social analysis, or whether alternative imaginations can importantly contribute to analysis and possibility.[90] I work with metaphors that can provide a sense of the ways in which gender and sex are categories with specific social effects, producing discontinuous (and even contradictory) relations, which nonetheless come together to produce a hegemonic social fabric. A colleague suggested a Wittgensteinian image of a rope mooring a boat to a dock. "What ties the ship to the wharf is a rope, and the rope consists of fibers, but it does not get its strength from any fiber which runs through it from one end to the other, but from the fact that there is a vast number of fibers overlapping."[91] As you have seen, I also find it helpful to think of a kaleidoscope in which patterns are formed from disconnected pieces of glass of different sizes, shapes, and colors. Analysis of a single piece or even a single pattern tends to tell one very little. Kaleidoscopic effects can be analyzed only by tracking relations in the large and shifting patterns.

Possible relations and reconfigurations among approaches are not infinite, however, but are rather limited by the context and histories of social relations. To ground my analysis, I embed it in activist alliances as well as in academic collaborations. Throughout *The Sex Obsession*, I present readings of a series of projects addressing a range of issues produced by the Barnard Center for Research on Women in conjunction with activist knowledge producers, including Queer Survival Economies, with Amber Hollibaugh; Responding to Violence, Promoting Justice, with Tiloma Jayasinghe; Valuing Domestic Work, with the National Domestic Workers Alliance; Reproductive Justice in Action, with the New York Women's Foundation; No One Is Disposable: Everyday Practices of Prison Abolition, with Dean Spade, Tourmaline, and Hope Dector; I Use My Love to Guide Me, with CeCe McDonald, Tourmaline, and Dean Spade; and Poverty and Public Housing Working Group with Pamela Phillips.[92] These projects seek to promote thinking differently and acting to make a difference. I turn to these projects as the materialization of an ethics of the possible.

Ethics can provide a catalyst for social solidarity, can pull us forward toward a world that we desire. *The Sex Obsession* looks at the contribution that sexual politics can make to social change as a means of producing and materializing values. We value something by making it real. We make what we value. Although gender and sexual relations are practices through which values emerge and communities are made, sex and desire, gender and embodiment are rarely taken to be the basis of ethical possibility.[93] That is no reason not to do so now.

1

Because Religion

Why is sexual politics so central in the US, anyway? If sex is a private matter, why does the federal government spend over $100 million every year on "marriage promotion" as part of its antipoverty programs?[1] And, if marriage is supposed to be so helpful in addressing poverty, why was there such long-standing resistance to opening marriage to gay and lesbian people or trans and gender nonconforming people, particularly when queer and trans people experience poverty at such high rates?[2] There are, of course, all kinds of reasons to doubt its effectiveness as a means of ending poverty, including the fact that most data produced about marriage promotion doesn't support the idea.[3] I will explore the queer critique of marriage in more depth in chapter 4, but if support for intimate and caring relationships could help to reduce poverty, it is not hard to imagine public policies that would support all kinds of arrangements, including children caring for parents, cooperative childcare, and community support that might be more effective than marriage promotion. So why should a relationship—marriage—that is imagined primarily as a sexual relationship be a focus for antipoverty policy and, if it is such a focus, why should the types of marriages allowed be restricted in any way?

We hear the same answer to both parts of this question. Religion is a primary reason why marriage promotion is part of antipoverty efforts in the US.[4] And, we also hear over and over that religion is the appropriate site for defining what marriage is and can be. Even after the Supreme Court legalized same-sex marriage in 2015, debates and litigation over "religious freedom" continue to tie the politics of marriage to religious imperatives.[5] In this story, religion drives sexual politics and is the primary force behind sexual regulation.

Leaders of both major political parties in the US have declared that religion makes sex a keenly moral question, and that the state has an ethical responsibility to regulate sexual relations. For example, although both President Obama and Secretary of State and presidential candidate Hillary Clinton "evolved" on the issue of same-sex marriage, before their views changed they subscribed to a version of this story. Clinton called upon a nebulous, but eternal sense of religious sexual regulation: "Marriage has got historic, religious and moral content that goes back to the beginning of time, and I think a marriage is as a marriage always has been, between a man and a woman."[6]

Clinton was in no way alone in calling on "religion" as the grounding for US marriage policy. When presidents or candidates for the office have said that their opposition to same-sex marriage was because of religion, they may have been expressing a personal religious commitment (George W. Bush).[7] Yet politicians have also made such claims even when they themselves weren't particularly religious (Howard Dean),[8] or when their religious denomination supported same-sex marriage (Barack Obama).[9] As a candidate, Donald Trump made contradictory statements on this issue, including a statement that he supports "traditional marriage" and also that he is a "real friend" to the "LGBT" community.[10] His actions on "LGBT" issues as president, however, including the appointment of Supreme Court justices assumed to be conservative on sexual issues, reinstatement of a ban on transgender service in the military, rescinding of protections for transgender students, and advocating rules to allow government contractors to discriminate against LGBT people, indicate that he thinks his conservative Christian supporters should set the terms for policy regarding gender and sexuality.[11]

And, make no mistake, these politicians seem to have only Christianity—and one version of Christianity—in mind when they speak of the "religious" imperatives of sexual politics. It is not the case, as Clinton claims, that marriage has always been "between a man and a woman" since "the beginning of time." Religious sexual ethics have varied across time, place, and religious tradition, and they have also varied within Christianity, giving Christians what Mark D. Jordan calls "contradictory counsel," including the counsel that marriage is a fallback for those who cannot sustain the morally superior practice of celibacy.[12] So, in ascribing their political positions to unchanging "religious and moral content," these politicians are invoking the common sense of public discourse, a sensibility that may be common enough to cross the lines of political parties but is not necessarily based in the traditions that are claimed as its source.

And, in arguing that religious teaching about sexual life—or, more accurately, the teaching of some versions of Christianity—should become the law of the land, whether for reasons of personal commitment or political effect, these politicians declare themselves bound by a religious ethical imperative that they mostly do not extend to other areas of life.[13] The idea that religion is legislatively authoritative on questions of gender and sexuality but not on other issues runs deep in the popular culture of the United States. When Pope Francis released a papal encyclical on environmental justice, a number of commentators suggested the pope should attend to the real business of religion and leave politics alone.[14] It is difficult to find similar suggestions from commentators at any point on the political spectrum when statements from religious authorities concern sexual relations and public policy.[15]

Similarly, political actors are often more than happy to engage with religion when the issues involve sexual politics and reticent to do so when religion is entwined with other issues. For instance, the US Supreme Court refused to hear a religious freedom case focused on environmental issues brought by nuns from the Adorers of the Blood of Christ.[16] On the grounds of their religious commitment to protect the earth as a matter of religious freedom, the order sued the Federal Regulatory Energy Commission in the hope of stopping a natural gas pipeline that was to be built on land they owned that had been seized by eminent domain. On the other hand, the court has taken up multiple religious freedom cases with regard to gender and sexuality, including more than one on the regulations requiring institutions that provide health insurance to their employees to provide coverage for contraception (or request an exemption) and one on the right to deny customers seeking to purchase products and services like cakes, flowers, and photography for gay weddings.[17] In producing a compromise decision in a case about whether even an exemption from the provision of contraception resulted in an undue burden on religious actors, the Court's decision noted the "gravity of the dispute" in the case, a stark contrast to the apparent lack of gravity attributed to a dispute over land taken by eminent domain—supposedly for the public good—being used for a purpose that the Adorers of the Blood of Christ saw as violating their religious commitment to protect the environment.[18] We are returned to the idea that religion is about sex and sex is about religion.

My hope in writing *The Sex Obsession* is to break open the political stalemate that produces this story as common sense in the US—to break open the idea that issues related to gender and sexuality are the defining points of religiosity and that religious ideas of gender and sexuality are always conservative. In doing so, I hope to make space for more, and more varied, ways of inhabiting both religious and secular ethics; to break open the presumption that religion equals Christianity and thereby open space for more, and more varied, religious voices in public policy. Gender and sexuality are entwined with any number of issues in public policy, not just those that are religious, and religion is similarly broad in its concerns. Recognizing these facts opens up the public space that has been boxed in by the commonsensical story of religion and sexuality, space that might allow for alternative alliances and action across the usual boundaries between and among religion, secularism, and political affiliation.

In this chapter and those that follow, religion, sex, secularism, freedom, race, gender, capitalism, nation, and state form kaleidoscopic patterns in relation to one another. One turn, and we observe the same social forces, but arranged in a new pattern that shifts how we see the pieces. Movement among issues makes it hard to understand that the complex intertwining of religion and sex in public policy is not because they are locked away in a social bubble with just those two elements; rather their intertwining is an effect of multiple elements, each with its own force. I am committed to following elements of social, cultural, and political life in their multiple patterns. Each one has something to tell us about how hegemonic power is sustained by creating what I call mobility for stasis, movement that does create real social change but that does not fundamentally shift the prevailing order of things.

For instance, the multiplicity of intertwined social relations and their movement in relation to each other allows for the formation of what Ann Pellegrini and I call "Christian secularism." This oxymoron, Christian secularism—wherein secularism, considered to be the opposite of religion, is instead *modified by religion*—offers a way to think about both the direct influence of religious groups and organizations on American politics, and the secular political and cultural institutions of American public life that have developed historically out of Christian contexts and which presume Christian norms and values.[19] Christian secularism is part of the structure of everyday life, where, for example, the Christian calendar forms the basis for global financial transactions and for school calendars in the United States. And, as Ann Pellegrini and I showed in our book *Love the Sin*, Christian secularism also structures the values of the US legal system, particularly with regard to any case dealing with gender and sexuality.[20] Tracy Fessenden has traced the development of this presumption in American culture from Puritan ideas of God-given dominion over Native Americans as foundational to the United States to a larger project of "equating American Protestantism with American culture," such that "those religious sensibilities that do not shade invisibly into 'American sensibilities' fail to command our attention as foundational to our national culture, while those that *do* shade imperceptibly into American sensibilities fail to command our attention as religious."[21]

Christian secularism is not religion in disguise; it is a specific social formation, with specific sensibilities, affects, practices, and norms.[22] Religion and secularism are not coextensive in Christian secularism, but they are profoundly interrelated. In fact, religious regulation and secular freedom are interlocked in the shaping of sexual politics. Seeing these pairs of supposed opposites (religion and secularism, regulation and freedom) as entwined could make for social change—and perhaps justice.

Writing the Usual Story

In this chapter, I consider the habitual ways of thinking that make the opposition between sexual freedom and religious commitment seem commonsensical. In writing the usual story, religion is first separated from other social relations (nationalism, race, and economics, for a start) that organize sexual politics in the United States. Once religion is disembedded from these intertwined relations, it can be consolidated to represent a single thing—sexual conservatism—and placed in opposition to sexual liberation. Disembedding religion allows it to be the "cause" of sexual conservatism, so that politicians from both major political parties can attribute their more or less conservative stances to religiosity (whether based on their own commitments or the conservative politics attributed to voters). And both religious conservatives and sexual liberationists can focus on religion as the appropriate framework for discussing sexual politics.

If religion is the cause of sexual regulation, this implies that there must be a nonreligious or secular realm free from religion and its regulation. This common sense is reinforced by the fact that the idea of secularism is historically rooted in an idea of freedom—of freedom from the church and from its strictures. This idea is part of a larger narrative, often called the "secularization thesis," which Ann Pellegrini and I describe in *Secularisms* as follows: "The secularization thesis makes for a narrative that connects a number of elements—most notably, modernity, reason, and universalism—into a network that has strong moral as well as descriptive implications. . . . Implicit within the narrative is the idea that each step forward in time also marks a moral advance: a move away from religious authority and toward greater intellectual freedom and more knowledge, leading eventually to governance by reasoned debate and ultimately to democracy and peace."[23] Those who resist the moral claims of secularization can thus be read as resisting freedom, progress, modernity, democracy, peace, and even reason itself.

The traditional view of religious repression as the force behind America's obsession with sexuality creates a dichotomy that has been extensively exploited by the political right. Jerry Falwell notoriously blamed the September 11 attacks on gays and secularists. Bill O'Reilly framed the 2015 Supreme Court decision on gay marriage as a triumph for secularists and posed a polarizing question: "Are religious Americans in danger?"[24] Freedom becomes a zero-sum game in which any expansion of freedom must also mean a loss of freedom in another area.

The dichotomy makes it seem as though there are two (and only two) types of people—religious people who favor sexual regulation, and secular people who favor sexual freedom. This way of thinking is tempting to progressives, of course, who can easily believe that progress itself depends on protecting the freedom of citizens from the imposition (or even the expression) of religion in public life.

Disembedding religion from its context in multiple social relations thus makes it easier to isolate the dichotomous relation between religion and secularism. Specific religious views on sexuality, like those of Christian conservatives, come to stand in for "religion" as a category. As religious studies scholar Heather Shipley argues, gender and sexuality provide sites for presumptive religious convergence across difference—*all* religions are understood to be focused on sexual morality.[25] This presumption of unity is advanced both by progressive advocates resisting sexual regulation and by religious conservatives who hope to naturalize this connection, thereby making opposition to sexual regulation the same as opposition to religion.[26]

Yet the binary can also shift its axis, retaining its force, in order to mark a sharp division between *this* religious tradition and *that* religious tradition.[27] Thus, the traditional secularization narrative creates not just a boundary between religion and secularism, but a three-way division among (a) secularism, (b) good, reasonable religion, and (c) bad, unreasonable religion that is intolerant and unenlightened.[28] Good religion and secularism are often understood as allied against an intractable, unreasonable religion, often called "fundamentalism."[29] Unreasonable religion is dedicated to dogmatic regulation, whereas secularism and its good religious allies produce a modern freedom that is organized by self-discipline and so is supposed to be neither overly regulatory nor licentiously free. When it comes to narratives about sex and gender, all religions can be presumed conservative, even as distinctions can be made to separate out those religions that take this conservatism "too far" or, on the other hand, distinguish those religions that are "bad" because they do not share dominant sexual ethics.[30]

For example, political scientist Samuel P. Huntington's critique of US immigration policy in *Who Are We?* makes the reproductive practices of Latinx Catholic immigrants a critical part of his argument that some immigrants are fundamentally different from the national, supposedly Protestant, culture of the United States. This argument about religion and sexuality then becomes central to Huntington's claims that Catholics cannot be assimilated to US culture and to his overall call for a radical defense of Protestant culture in the United States.[31]

As Huntington's argument shows, once religion and sex are locked into the narrative of regulation and freedom they can easily be invoked for political effect on other issues, like immigration. Subsequent chapters in *The Sex Obsession* consider how sexual practices, including marriage and reproduction, have been linked to everything from ending poverty and fixing education to preventing crime, providing healthcare, and securing international relations.[32] But when isolated as a polarized binary, sex/religion fuels political campaigns and creates seemingly endless opportunities for politically potent simplifications. If, however, social analysis returns both sex and religion to their dynamic context, ethics and politics can address the complex circuits that constitute social relations.

Sex, Ethics, and Secular Freedom

Together in their interrelation, religion and secularism become a crucial part of the matrix of heteronormativity in the United States.[33] For the scholars Roderick A. Ferguson and Amy Villarejo, "heteronormative" names a dominant set of sexual arrangements that are embedded in relations of race, gender, class, and nation.[34] Understanding sexuality as situated in a dynamic matrix allows for an analysis in which specific social relations are at once relatively autonomous and also incorporated into an active social field.[35] On this understanding, normativity names the incoherent and yet connected affects, materials, and ideals that make a hegemonic formation, what Lauren Berlant terms the "internally contradictory promises (of acknowledgment, amelioration, protection, retribution, balancing, delegation, discipline, and enabling to thrive)" that tie people to social formations.[36]

Rather than simply invoking a long list of related categories, the conceptual power of "normativity" becomes its ability to index kaleidoscopic interrelation. Ideas about sexuality, imbricated in a matrix of power relations that includes nation, race, and religion, are all part of a social pattern that is strengthened by movement among the pieces. Religion and secularism appear as separate pieces that move in and out of the center, while the pattern remains trapped between glass within the kaleidoscope. In this sense, the back and forth between religious regulation and secular freedom maintains both existing patterns of sexual politics and the overall power relations of normativity. Sometimes religious regulation is at the center, sometimes secular freedom, and sometimes both are sidelined as nationalism or class move to the center, even as religion and secularism remain part of the pattern, perhaps providing crucial background pieces. Normativity, then, is not some static "structure" but is dynamic movement held together—often very tightly—by the interrelation among the pieces. Understanding social relations involves both tracing the movement and following the relation between this movement and the overall pattern.

A critique of normativity suggests that not only can the relations among the pieces in the pattern change, but the kaleidoscope can be broken open and a different type of pattern—a different set of relations— could emerge. The critique of normativity is often associated with queer studies, but has multiple genealogies and is important in several fields.[37] For example, this critique is also important in fields like disability studies, in which justice for people whose bodies do not reflect social norms and ideas of what is normal is central to the field.[38] Ferguson develops a critique of normativity that draws upon women of color feminism, crystallized, for example, in Audre Lorde's essay "Age, Race, Class, and Sex: Women Redefining Difference." Lorde argued that the idealized social norm of white, wealthy, and powerful masculinity is really a myth that even men that fit the description have anxiety about maintaining: "Somewhere, on the edge of consciousness, there is what I call a mythical norm, which each one of us within our hearts knows 'that is not me.' In america, this norm is usually defined as white, thin, male, young, heterosexual, christian, and financially secure. It is with this mythical norm that the trappings of power reside within this society."[39]

The critique of normativity is particularly important for ethical analysis in that it directly addresses the relation between ethical norms, epistemological claims about what is normal in society, and power in social relations. Much of the work on normativity has focused on the subjectivation of individuals: the way that individuals live out power relations, particularly through the practice of self-discipline. Discipline and subjectivation are certainly part of the story, but here I am interested in social relations so as to draw out how normativity articulates relations among ethics, knowledge, and power.

Michel Foucault argues that in European modernity the central moral problematic is the connection among ethical norms, discourses about what is normal (particularly statistical discourses), and power. How do ethical norms relate to a modern epistemological understanding of what is normal? The normal can be simply the average, the everyday, or the commonsensical, whereas norms engage the language of morality.[40] Modern understandings facilitate a slide between the statistically normal and the ethically normative. In an essay on the combined statistical and moral work done by surveys on sexual practice, for instance, Mary Poovey shows how a central statistical claim that most people have sex with persons like themselves (except in terms of gender) turns into a moral claim that most people *should* have sex with people of a different gender but otherwise much like themselves (of the same age or race, for example).[41] Michael Cobb has argued persuasively that the moral power of normative sexuality tends to censure even those who choose to be single or celibate.[42]

Disability studies has importantly refocused attention on how moral evaluation and the idea of that which is statistically normal come together in public policy. Susan Schweik has traced nineteenth-century legislation that targeted disabled mendicants who supported themselves by begging or selling their formulaic "autobiographies." What came to be called "ugly laws" responded to these public displays of difference by legally sequestering the maimed, the halt, and the blind in charitable institutions, out of sight.[43] This idea that a nonnormative person is deviant, troublesome, and of uncertain character is crucial for understanding how moral norms work together with knowledge and power.

As the institution of the "ugly laws" makes vividly clear, norms are embedded in power and are far more than cultural conventions. Norms shape social possibility. As a result, some lives are made vibrantly livable, some troubled, others fundamentally at risk. For instance, the interaction between norms and institutional power allows for a dynamic interrelation between legal and extra-legal violence in which norms shape the parameters of legal force and even support extra-legal violence in the enforcement of norms. In the case of CeCe McDonald, a trans African American woman who was attacked on the street and fought back, the police responded by arresting her, and she was imprisoned. After an extensive activist campaign, McDonald was released, but her case is all too indicative of the ways in which violating gender norms puts one at risk for both legal and extra-legal violence.[44] In a similar case, Ky Peterson killed an attacker who was raping him, but was told by a police officer, "You don't seem like a rape victim to me." He was convicted of manslaughter.[45] Gender, race, and class all shape powerful norms governing who "seems like a victim," which affects how the criminal justice system polices the population. These cases show the power of norms to constitute a double bind for those living nonnormative lives, since they face both the danger of extra-legal violence and the violence of the state.[46] Interaction among norms, knowledge, and power ensures that many whose lives do not fit the statistical norm become morally and politically marginalized.

The critique of normativity analyzes the interaction of ethical norms, methods for producing knowledge that make some ways of living seem normal and others not, and the regime of power that is normativity. This critique is not reflexively "antinormative," but is rather a critique of how ethical norms and ways of knowing work together with modern power relations.[47] Norms shape and sustain all social practices and are always an exercise of power, but different norms—and the practices with which they are associated—are differently related to power, including both cultural and institutional power. Moral norms need not align with what's normal, and they need not reinforce or be reinforced by the modern institutions that create contemporary power relations.[48]

To create substantive social change requires radical shifts in the relation between norms and power. The critique of normativity that I am exploring in this book considers how activists, artists, and thinkers work to subvert, challenge, or break connections to prevailing power relations and imagine—and enact—life differently. I am sustained by the knowledge of work being done for social justice that creates new social relations governed by refashioned norms. This work is necessarily both highly imaginative and acutely practical.[49]

Freedom as Normativity

Queer studies has often emphasized the critique of normativity because the matrix of norms, knowledge (in the form of statistics, say), practices (sedimented in institutions), and power relations makes sex a central and much-contested aspect of modern life, into a singular shape a set of relations that have varied considerably over time, even within Christian traditions. Considered statistically, marriage might be the norm (although marriage was not always institutionalized—it could be simply an arrangement between the parties involved—and was not consolidated as a sacrament until the twelfth and thirteenth centuries). And, even if normal, marriage was *not* necessarily the ethical ideal in premodern Christian societies. For many Christian communities, the sexual ideal for religious life in Christianity was celibacy, an ideal that changed again through the upheavals of the Protestant Reformation. Thus, in much of this history—the supposedly unchanging background of contemporary sexual politics—what is normal in the sense of what most people did and what is ethically ideal might well be distinct.[50]

This understanding of ethics as historically variable entails that sex has not always been the central site of moral concern. Both Caroline Walker Bynum and Rudolph Bell have argued convincingly that during the medieval period in Europe, food, not sex, was the primary site for the embodiment of morality. Gluttony was the gravest sin, not adultery, homosexuality, or other sexual perversions of ethical law.[51]

In modern ethics, however, ideal and norm converge: ideal as norm/ norm as ideal. Most people are married, and marriage is the ethical good par excellence. This consonance between ethical ideal and statistical norm is also a move toward the particular understanding of individual freedom that reaches full flower in the Enlightenment. In works he wrote in the eighteenth century, the philosopher Immanuel Kant proposed an ethic in which to be free the rational individual gives ethical Law to himself, internalizing it so that it governs his behavior (a gendered term I use advisedly here, for Kant is philosophizing about abstract, putatively universal Man). The Law is itself transcendent, but discoverable by Man's reason. To be truly free, to have the liberty to make autonomous decisions, individuals internalize and act on this moral system, and in so doing set the disciplinary boundaries for themselves.[52]

Foucault argues that in this modern understanding, self-discipline—rather than, for example, the cultivation of virtue—becomes the foundation of moral life. Self-discipline also requires knowledge of the self, and this need for self-knowledge coincides with the rise of fields of knowledge that fall under what is broadly called the "human sciences," making what is considered normal for human beings crucial to moral understanding and action. In contradistinction to Kant, Foucault is thus arguing that both freedom and autonomy are effects created by modern disciplinary practices that come not from transcendent law but from common sense about what is normal for the average individual. This sense of the normal becomes morally normative.

The Kantian ideal of freedom induces people to produce themselves through the norms of autonomous individualism, in which we understand ourselves as most free when acting separately from others, each determining their own actions rather than allowing their activity to be determined by others. Self-discipline becomes the hallmark of modern freedom and individualism. The inducement for individuals to be normal contributes to a biopolitical governmentality that connects large-scale institutions and power relations (including state and corporate power) to relations and practices across a range of sectors (medicine and healthcare, education, cultural production). So, for example, the freedom of American mass culture is the freedom of individuals to choose, particularly through consumption, to be like everyone else.

Just as normative discipline constitutes a particular, modern form of freedom, the practices of the security state are also in the service of the moral ideal of freedom. In a security society like that of the United States, certain forms of social control are presented as if they not only keep the nation safe, but also ensure the freedom of the nation. Without the control of such security, we are told, freedom would be threatened at every turn. Both self-discipline and the control of populations are thus part of the apparatus of modern freedom, but freedom is experienced differentially. Some populations manage themselves through inducements to be normal. Other populations are actively controlled through extensive security measures organized along the lines of race, class, and citizenship.[53] The interdependence between individual freedom and biopolitical governmentality creates an oscillation between the disciplining of subjects and the control of populations.[54]

Biopolitics works by denying these relations, obscuring the connections between one "population" and another. An example of this biopolitical denial would be the way in which public discourse in the US tends to focus on the hard work of American individuals to explain American economic success rather than on the way in which the US economy was constituted through slave labor and the labor of populations across international divisions. The fact that the life of any individual—even a hardworking one—is dependent on countless others living under very different conditions disappears from ideas of both freedom and moral agency.

Sex is one site for the interaction between freedom and control on which biopolitics depends, an interaction that is represented in public discourse as a battle between sexual regulation, often at the level of the state, and sexual licentiousness, often at the level of commercial culture.[55] An analysis of biopower suggests, however, that the two sides of this argument represent the oscillation between outright control and the incitement to produce sexual freedom as a component of biopolitics. The state may be a site that works to control the sex of nonnormative populations and commercial culture can then be the site at which people "choose" to have sex like everyone else. What these arguments do not acknowledge is that commercial freedoms often depend on government regulation, just as individual freedoms are constituted by the actions of the security state.

One can see the parceling out of freedom or control to different groups of people in the ways in which middle-class white women and poor women of color are often treated with regard to reproduction.[56] As reproductive justice advocates have long argued (and as I will track further in chapter 3), public debates and government action have varied dramatically in the treatment of white women's reproductive concerns and those of women of color, particularly when the discourse is refracted through class and focused on white, middle-class women and poor women of color. Specifically, white women have been encouraged to reproduce and government enforcement has been focused on blocking them from *not having* children (through both restrictions on abortion and renewed controversies over the use of contraception).[57] In contrast, US history includes numerous examples in which women of color have been directly blocked from *having* children (through both forced sterilization and court-mandated contraception), as well as indirectly through economic barriers to supporting children. Hence, reproductive justice requires support for women who face different types of unjust obstacles in their reproductive lives.

Despite a vibrant reproductive justice movement, the oscillation between promoting childbearing for some populations while promoting contraception for others continues in contemporary mainstream media commentary in the United States.[58] In December 2018, for example, an opinion piece in the *New York Times* advocated long-term contraception for poor women as a means of fighting poverty, even as the availability of contraception for women who have workplace healthcare insurance was also under attack.[59] Such oscillation continually recurs in US public life because the connection between freedom and control—between, for example, the freedom to "choose" with regard to one's reproduction, and control of populations whose choices are either restricted or directly denied—is obscured by the biopolitical discourse of sexuality, which posits "choice" and "control" as opposites. Instead, both choice and control are elements of modern freedom. Those engaged in public debates often take up one side or the other, just as abortion rights advocates took up "choice" as a primary metaphor, rather than intervening in the dynamic itself. Such intervention would require acknowledging both the relation between choice and control and the effects of oscillation between the two.

Because sex is the site of the literal production of bodies and also a potent site for figuring control of one's body, normative self-discipline and biopolitical governmentality flow through both body and mind by making sex central to one's very being. Sex becomes an increasingly important site of moral concern, as the human sciences (not priests or kings) are authoritative at the nexus of power, pleasure, and knowledge, producing modern individuals for whom normative sex is at the center of their ever more complex inner selves. Psychological depth and affective introspection are increasingly required of the modern subject and are managed by comparing the self to what is known about the "general population." American culture is suffused with sexuality, and the modern ethical subject has the task of freely choosing sexual activity, and of leading a well-regulated and law-abiding life.

In US political life, sexual ethics are thus an object of fascination. Public debate always turns on whether the ethic is a conservative one, focused on regulation, or a liberal one, focused on sexual freedom. There is no way in this oscillating debate to question how sexual ethics is sutured to the operation of power, yet a focus on sexual liberation, in which sex is thought to be the route to freedom, is as much an operation of modern power as state regulation. Modern normativity disciplines subjects with both state regulation and market imperatives to freely choose a sexual lifestyle. Sex is one of the most important ways in which people become socially recognizable. Each individual must "have" a sexuality, and even more, this sexuality is the "truth" of that individual. Without a sexuality—freely chosen and/or state regulated—one is not fully recognizable. In this system, regulation by the state through marriage is configured as the "freedom to marry," because the combination of freedom and regulation is actually at the center of modern morality.

Crucially, this ethic makes marriage and the family the central social formation for the autonomous individual. In the family, a number of the elements of the heteronormative matrix come together. So, for example, race and sex are entwined in policy discussions of marriage and family: family structure is repeatedly appealed to in policy debates about poverty, as when Senator Marco Rubio said on the floor of the Congress that marriage is "the greatest tool to lift people, to lift families and children out of poverty."[60] Since marriage is the social institution in which sexuality is supposed to be contained, it becomes the imaginary resolution of the intractable problem of poverty: if only men and women were faithful to each other, they would have the strength of character and discipline to get and keep jobs that would somehow support a family.[61] Despite a lack of evidence that this is the case, policy initiatives to promote marriage have been central to both Republican and Democratic administrations (I analyze these initiatives in chapter 3). These efforts are hardly effective in promoting marriage, much less reducing poverty. They do, however, reiterate and confirm social hierarchies—of race, of class, of gender, of sex—within the existing matrix of power relations.[62]

Religion *and* Secularism, Sex *and* Ethics

Modern governmental power—governmentality—involves both state and corporate power. As we have seen, this power is constituted within a normative matrix in which religion, secularism, sex, freedom, and regulation are historically interlinked. In order to follow this set of interrelations, I turn to a genealogical reading of the Protestant reformers Martin Luther and John Calvin, and to their influence on modern conceptions of the autonomous individual.[63] The Reformation and the Enlightenment, religion and secularism, states and markets are together responsible for the idea of a modern individual who makes both moral decisions and market choices. Ethical values and economic value are fundamentally entangled, and freedom is one site for this entanglement.

Martin Luther, in the preface to his translation into German of Paul's Letter to the Romans, offers a significant commentary on a Christian and specifically Protestant understanding of freedom.[64] According to Luther, Christianity gives to Christians a new form of freedom. Such freedom does not mean that Christians do not follow the law: "Our freedom is not a crude, physical freedom by virtue of which we can do anything at all. Rather this freedom is a spiritual freedom; it supplies and furnishes what law lacks, namely willingness and love."[65] Christians follow the law, but they do so because they want to.[66] For Luther, spiritual freedom is wanting to do the right thing. It is a discourse of desire.

The disciplines of this form of freedom become apparent in Luther's next paragraph, which is a reading of a biblical analogy between the position—and freedom—of a wife after the death of her husband and the position of Christians who have "died to the law" through a transcendence above earthly things that Luther understands to be offered by Christian faith. This is a strange analogy in many ways. First, if Christians were in the position of the wife, the law would have died to them, not they to the law. But Luther's gloss adds another twist: "The point is that [the widow] is quite at liberty for the first time to please herself about taking another husband."[67] The Pauline text is not worried about the widow pleasing herself.[68] The only concern that the biblical text expresses is that the wife would be an adulteress if she lived with another man while her husband was alive, and now she can marry again without fear of adultery. Luther, however, nowhere states whether the woman will or will not take another husband. In fact, he explicitly states, "The woman is not obliged, nor even merely permitted to take a husband," but rather she is at liberty to please herself. Yet, in Luther's conclusion to the analogy, Christians are free to "really cling to Christ as a second husband and bring forth the fruit of life."[69] With this conclusion, Luther reveals his conviction that, free to please herself, the woman will not only certainly choose conjugal relations again, but she will also procreate with her new husband, bringing forth "the fruit of life." Once free to please herself, the faithful Christian desires nothing more than to fulfill the law.

In other words, Protestant freedom is desire for self-discipline. Importantly, for Luther, desire is turned explicitly toward marriage and reproduction over against the celibacy of priestly and monastic life. Luther advocated marriage for clergy as a major distinguishing characteristic of the Reformation. Clergy and those with religious vocations are now free to marry, and for Luther this freedom produces a directed—a disciplined—desire toward marriage and the law.

This freedom opens a social space that Luther clearly desires, but there are also losses of social possibility. As a number of feminist historians have noted, the Reformation's opposition to monastic life closed down an alternative prospect for some women.[70] The options of marriage and the celibacy of religious community may not offer an expansive vista of social possibility, but convents offered an alternative way of life, one that allowed some women access to education and empowerment within the Church.

The Reformation's shift to marriage as both norm and ideal is also then a shift from communalism to individualism. Monastic celibacy was itself a communal way of life; further, each convent was part of a broader network of religious communities. In the reformed world, however, the Christian who clings to Christ and the widow who chooses a new husband are alone, free to make a choice to please themselves alone. Yet choice is limited: marriage or not. Other forms of affinity could have been possible, including those that were neither communal as the religious orders were, nor individualistic in the modern sense, but not to Luther's way of thinking.

The elevation of marriage as both norm and ideal is a crucial shift, part of the tectonic changes brought about by the Reformation and providing a background to broader developments in European modernity. Modernity brought individuality, self-discipline, and the normative understanding that the institution of marriage is fundamental to both social order and the reproduction and rearing of children. Marrying requires a license, for marriage is a contract two parties make that is enforced by the authority of the state, which is understood to have a clear interest in marriage and reproduction. A democracy like the United States might tout its own sexual liberation, but we learn (through common sense) that only one specific sexual relation—marriage—is desired by responsible individuals. The freedom these individuals enjoy depends on responsibility for its proper social order and defense. This is one reason that the movement for "gay liberation," initially understood by many as freeing gays and lesbians from the oppression of the family and pushing back against the regulatory state, has led so inexorably toward both gay marriage and service in the military.[71] Free to marry and join the military, gay people join the adult world of individuals who give the law to themselves.

A genealogy of value and values also includes John Calvin, another major figure in the Reformation that remade Europe. Like Luther, Calvin is highly critical of the Church's communalism in which, for example, monks and priests follow the ritual and edicts of the Church rather than reading the Gospel for themselves as Protestants do. Calvin takes a step beyond Luther when he connects freedom to marry to economic relations. In enumerating his "considerations against ancient monasticism," Calvin is clear that monasticism is a problem for Protestants not because of its self-denial, but because it is spiritually and materially excessive.[72] All monastics, he says, display a "perverse zeal." He goes on to elaborate, "It [is] a beautiful thing to forsake all their possessions and be without earthly care. But God prefers devoted care in ruling a household, where the devout householder, clear and free of all greed, ambition, and other lusts of the flesh, keeps before him the purpose of serving God in a definite calling."[73]

The ideal of the moderate householder is, of course, the connecting point between sexual life and economic life, showing the interdependence of the two. For Calvin, Protestant marital life ensures that the individual will not be perversely excessive in his relation to God or in relation to worldly goods. By choosing marriage, devotion to a family, and labor in a vocation (that is, understanding the work that one does as praise of God), the individual is freed from "greed, ambition, and other lusts of the flesh."

Calvin then develops an extended critique of the vow of chastity, at the end of which he declares, "I shall not stop to assail the two remaining [monastic] vows [of poverty and obedience]. I say only this: . . . these vows seem to have been composed in order that those who have taken them may mock God and men. But lest we seem to criticize every little point too spitefully, we shall be content with the general refutation that has been given above."[74] Forbearing further critique "lest we seem to criticize every little point too spitefully" is an odd statement to make in a text that in its modern English edition is over fifteen hundred pages long. Yet Calvin makes perfectly clear that sex alone comes to stand for right relation to the material world and right relation between God and humanity. The Protestant relation to God is defined by the individual freedom to marry rather than by obedience to a community, and the ideal of the individual married householder is central to the whole world of reformed social relations.[75]

We see here a profound articulation of Protestant individual freedom of conscience with the right kind of sexual relations. Freedom is accomplished in part through the elevation of marriage to a normative ideal.

This was, as we have seen, a major shift in Christian understandings of the ideal of sexual relations. Both Luther and Calvin took the position that everyone should enter a married state, and Luther, who had himself been part of a religious order, was especially adamant that clergy should marry. Those who choose marriage and who discipline themselves accordingly are more, not less, free than those who do not. "Earnest enforcement" by the Protestant community affirms this discipline as what everyone *should want*. Neither discipline nor regulation per se make one unfree. Rather, the normative enforcement of marriage is the very sign of freedom itself.

Sex literally produces the autonomous and free individual. Sex replaces food as the sin extraordinaire, the sign of gluttony and dissolution, and it also replaces the vows of poverty and obedience as the sign of right relation to both God and the world. Sex becomes the premier site of morality.

Luther and Calvin do not encourage those with a religious vocation to leave the monastery and convent and live alone in their faith, as pure autonomous individuals. Luther and Calvin encourage them to get married, and this is because, as feminists have long pointed out, autonomous individuals do not actually exist autonomously.[76] Rather individuals depend on the labor of others, and in what is now called the traditional family, they depend on the labor of wives and servants. The progress that modernity is supposed to provide by which more and more people can become autonomous individuals, until eventually all are equal, will always be a contradictory movement, because there is no such thing as an autonomous individual, a person who is free from all dependence on others. For Luther and Calvin, however, the free individual is a householder whose freedom is expressed through the combination of the freedom to marry and the freedom to respond to God by doing the work of a calling.[77]

When Enlightenment thinkers like Kant make the individual central to secular freedom, this type of regulated activity—marriage and a calling—also becomes internal to secularism. And the individual becomes a site at which religion and secularism do not represent two different domains but are, rather, definitively fastened. As Mark D. Jordan has documented, these articulations have made what is actually a complex and contradictory genealogy of Christian thought on sex and marriage appear to produce a singular and universal position on marriage.[78] This supposedly singular Christian view, constituted in relation to commerce and the state, is then reiterated by both public discourse and lawmakers as the justification for the secular vision of state-regulated marriage *as freedom.*

Sex thus works in particular ways within the development of governmentality. Sex produces modern individuals, both literally and subjectively. And modern freedom has become the offer of becoming "normal." So, for example, when the US Supreme Court ruled that states could no longer deny same-sex couples the freedom to marry, Justice Kennedy's decision repeatedly asserted that exclusion from marriage is a fundamental insult to human dignity, saying, for instance, "It demeans gays and lesbians for the State to lock them out of a central institution of the Nation's society."[79] No more. Now homosexuals face the same normative pressure to marry that heterosexuals have felt all along. They may choose whomever they wish to love, but if they want to be normal, they will need to become intimate not only with a lover, but with the state. (There is more to say about this decision; I analyze it in detail in chapter 4).

Normativity ties together a particular form of governmental power and a specific way of becoming a recognizable human subject. Modern normativity enables a politics of sexuality that conflates freedom and individual discipline and then ties them both to governmentality and the control of populations. Sex becomes politically central to modern freedom and hence to the conduct of modern democracy. In other words, the modern problem of sex, the problem that makes sex so obsessively the focus of American public life even as that obsessive focus is denounced, is the problem of modern freedom itself.

Placing the moral problematic of secular modernity at the center of an analysis of why sex is so profoundly powerful in American life shifts the usual understanding of why sex is a public problem and how that problem might be solved. Biopolitics and the modern moral structure of normativity are deeply imbricated with the religious heritage of Christian secular societies, meaning that the *intertwining of the apparent opposites, religion and secularism, constitutes the social power of sex.*[80] The cause of America's sexual obsession is as much secular freedom as it is religious regulation.

The Protestant Reformation marked a major change in Anglo-European sexual relations that instituted a particular form of sexual freedom.[81] The Protestant Reformation is also a sexual revolution. Charles Taylor has likewise argued that the Catholic response to the Reformation in the form of the Counter-Reformation made sex, and sexual regulation in particular, central to modern Catholic morality.[82] Most importantly, the reverberating strains of this sexual revolution tie the idea of individual freedom to the institution of marriage: the free individual is the individual whose sexual activity is regulated in marriage. This idea of freedom in marriage is also intimately entwined with the market, for the responsible householder understands that exchanging his labor for a wage is the way to fulfill his calling.

The secularism of the Enlightenment did not so much end the centrality of the religious regulation of sexuality as extend the relations between freedom and regulated sexuality. Secular freedom from religion (whereby the individual, freed from religious dogma, is directly responsible for his own moral life) is imbricated with the Protestant vision of freedom as autonomy (the individual, freed from the mediation of the Church, stands alone before God). Enlightenment thought is supposed to represent a fundamental break with religion, but the autonomous individual remains central to the Enlightenment. And this individual is the bearer of the discourse of sexuality, which combined an emphasis on regulation, an incitement to sexual liberation, and an implication in the management of populations. Most importantly for the analysis I develop in this book, in a United States dominated by Christian secularism, religion is not just responsible for our ideas of sexual repression. Religion has also shaped our understanding of sexual freedom.

Writing a Different Story

If the usual story about religion and sexual politics depends on the contrast between religious regulation and secular freedom, then there are real problems with that story. While the root of American sexual regulation may be religious, salvation is not to be found in simply seeking freedom from that religion. Such a search is based on the imagination of freedom from the Church sought by the reformers and by Enlightenment advocates of individual freedom, the very imagination that fuels the unspoken assumptions of Christian secularism.

The problem is not a failure to be secular enough. If religion and secularism are intertwined and sexual politics is one of the points at which they interlace; if freedom from the Church, market freedom, and individual autonomy are all central nodes in this entanglement, then the idea of moving from religious regulation to secular liberation that has been such a force in US sexual politics actually leads back into the tangle of relations from which secularism is supposed to cut us loose.

Because both religious regulation and secular freedom suture gender and sexuality into normative power relations, they together create an oscillation in US political discourse between the religious regulation of sexuality and the secular demand for sexual freedom. When the idea that religion is the cause of sexual regulation is constantly reiterated, sexual conservatism becomes a way of distinguishing religious life worlds from the predominantly secular public sphere. Secular social formations can also depend on this dynamic for their own constitution. Literary critic Michael Cobb has traced the ways in which focusing on religious "hatred" of homosexuality has helped to constitute gay "liberation."[83] And repeatedly invoking this story means that gay liberation becomes a presumptively secular undertaking.

Public discourse pings back and forth, and with each movement, sexual conservatism becomes more and more a part of what it means to be a "religious" person, obscuring religious commitments to liberation of all kinds and reinforcing the presumption that to be free is to be secular, to be secular is to be free. Not only do religion and secularism become entangled in their mutual, if oppositional, definition—religion needs sex as part of its identity; sex needs religion to make it free.

But also, both religious conservatism and secular freedom are sutured into the prevailing normativity. In the three-part division among secularism, good religion, and bad religion, good religion serves as the moral basis of secularism—as Hillary Clinton's remarks about the religious basis for marriage law show. Christian secularism here works to keep sex within the framework of the freedom to marry, even as that freedom moves to become available to homosexuals, and it keeps gender within a binary framework even if that framework might allow for equity between supposedly complementary genders. And, although bad religion takes sexual conservatism "too far," the normative story also repeats in a seemingly unending refrain that "religious morality" has always been sexually conservative, so that the common sense of and about good religion is that it must be conservative if also tolerant. Secular freedom meets good religion in the "freedom to marry." What disappears from this picture is religious morality as potentially liberatory, a disappearance that belies the history of liberation theologies and of sexual spiritualities. Instead, secular freedom demands that each person "have" a "sexuality" and a "gender" in order to be an individual, thus making sexual politics a key to modern politics itself.

In another turn of the wheel, this tangle of relations, with its two commonsensical ideas—that religion is the site of conservatism and secularism the site of freedom—is deployed as part of the apparatus of national power by the US government. Specifically, Christian secularism allows for the seemingly contradictory claim that the United States is both a Christian nation and a secular nation, both a paragon of values and a beacon of freedom. For example, the idea that "religions"—most recently Islam—are more conservative than the secular US government on issues of gender and sexuality can be invoked to promote American global interventions on behalf of freedom, including women's freedom, even as the US also promotes its own sexual conservatism through foreign policy (as discussed in Chapter 3). The seemingly unending argument back and forth between "Christian nation" and "secular nation" is an oscillation that reaffirms normativity and actually restricts possibilities or substantive change.

The intertwining of regulation and freedom contributes to the power of Christian secularism. In the pages of the *New York Times*, conservative columnist Ross Douthat explains and praises the ways in which modern, secular liberalism depends on underpinnings from those very things liberalism supposedly supersedes, including religion and conservative sexual politics. For Douthat there are only two choices: a secular liberal order that understands itself as entirely separate from religion or an acknowledgement of their interaction that requires an acceptance of religious conservatism. Fortunately, there are other possibilities, and I will conclude this chapter by highlighting a few creative ways in which rethinking the categories of religion and secularism can create new ethical possibilities.

Here's how Douthat describes Christian secularism and the choice he thinks it poses:

> [L]iberal societies have always depended on an illiberal or pre-liberal substructure to answer the varied human needs—meaning, belonging, a vertical dimension to human life, a hope against mortality—that neither John Stuart Mill nor Karl Marx adequately addressed. In American history, that substructure took various forms: The bonds of family life, the power of (usually Protestant) religion, a flag-waving patriotism, and an Anglo-Saxon culture to which immigrants were expected to assimilate. Each of these foundations often manifested illiberalism's evils: religious intolerance, racism and chauvinism, the oppressions of private and domestic power. But they also provided the moral, cultural and metaphysical common ground that political reformers—abolitionists, Social Gospellers, New Dealers, civil rights marchers—relied upon to expand liberalism's promise. . . . [For many human needs] a deeper vision than mere liberalism is still required—something like "for God and home and country," as reactionary as that phrase may sound.[84]

The combination of Christianity and secularism he describes—*Christian secularism*—names the contemporary social formation in the US more fully than "secularism" alone. Unsurprisingly, though, I do not think that "something like 'for God and home and country'" is the best way forward.

But there are hopeful intellectual and activist efforts to bring together religion and secularism without activating the powerful binaries of modern freedom, wherein one oscillates endlessly between religion and secularism. Instead, it is possible, as Josef Sorett suggests, to see religion and secularism as "both distinct and entangled."[85]

Sorett argues that African American religions are often positioned as providing a counternarrative to that of white Protestant hegemony in the United States, but that this positioning works to reinforce the power of the normative. Simply appealing to religion as the nonnormative other to modern secularism, or to African American religion as the contrast to White Protestantism, reiterates the back-and-forth movement that holds normativity in place. Even the idea that some religions are nonnormative sites of fluidity across the religious-secular boundary can reaffirm normative hegemony. In making this argument, Sorett points out that a narrative focused on a nonnormative "Black sacred/secular fluidity" positions African American religion as "other" to both normative religion and modern secularism. Sorett suggests that a traditional narrative of Black religiosity can account for distinctness but not entanglement, and a counternarrative of "fluidity" at the boundary between religion and secularism can account for entanglement but loses track of distinctness. An analytic emphasizing either distinctness or fluidity alone can thus participate in "a form of racial politics that conforms to the logics of a Protestant hegemony."[86] Change in these relations requires a both-and approach that recognizes distinctness *and* interrelation.

In *Spirit in the Dark: A Religious History of Racial Aesthetics*, Sorett explores how an oblique approach to thinking about religion, such as his focus on aesthetics, allows a narrative that articulates both specificity and fluidity in understanding religion and its relation to secularism.[87] In a related argument, Max Strassfeld has presented the possibility of "transing religious studies," meaning taking up thinking and practice that shifts the study of religion away from its assumption that binary gender is the basis of human being. Strassfeld argues that this project is crucial to undoing the assumption of a division between religious commitment and trans lives, the same assumption that, for example, drives conservative legislation restricting trans lives.[88] Strassfeld makes clear that transing is taken as liberatory by many trans activists, including religious activists who work in their traditions and do not position "trans (bodies, people, cosmologies) as external correctives to religion."[89] Trans liberation thus need not be oppositional to religious lives or communities. Developing such an approach shifts possible ways of thinking religion, secularism, *and their relation.*

Happily, there are many different practices that disengage from the oscillating narratives of modernity, in other words, that exist in modernity queerly. Thelathia Nikki Young argues that the intersection of queerness and religion creates precisely such a space, because religion in any given time period can both contribute to hegemonic relations and have "the queer capacity of standing outside of and counter to the society for which it was dictating hegemonies."[90] Melissa Wilcox argues, for example, that the activist group the Sisters of Perpetual Indulgence takes up and reconfigures traditional religious practices as a way to engage in "serious parody," a practice that is neither precisely religious nor precisely secular. Such a practice "simultaneously critiques and reclaims cultural traditions in the interest of supporting the lives and political objectives of marginalized groups."[91] Melissa Sanchez argues that one can read the promiscuous intertwining of religion and secularism in the "queer faith of the secular love tradition," from the texts of Augustine and Petrarch to the popular music of Beyoncé, George Michael, Madonna, and John Legend.[92] Sanchez takes up this reading in part to show how recognizing the promiscuity within religious texts and popular culture can put pressure on the presumption that respectability and Christian monogamy are mutually supporting beams in the structure of white supremacy.[93] Mark D. Jordan sees queer possibility in creatively engaging religious practices that protect and promote a heteroglossia, a multilingual, multitemporal approach that does not see religious practices as individual instances of the timeless entity called "religion" to which politicians so often appeal.[94]

There are, indeed, many ways to undo the sense that there is only one way to be religious and everyone from politicians to pundits knows what that is and what moral values follow from it. Drawing on Black feminist readings of the Haitian divinity Ezili as "the Iwa who exemplifies imagination," Omise'eke Natasha Tinsley produces a set of readings directed toward divine imagination as a source of not so much religious difference as a different system of values: "As a principle of both femininity and imagination, Ezili calls out a submerged epistemology that has *always* imagined that black masisi and madivin as well as black ciswomen *create our own value*, through concrete, unruly linkages forged around pleasure, adornment, competition, kinship, denial, illness, shared loss, travel, work, patronage, and material support."[95] The possibility of multiplicitous value systems undoes the tight connections between religion and conservative values on one side and secularism and freedom on the other.

How might sexual politics shift, for example, if we thought of the US public sphere as not simply secular? As both secular and religious? Jonathon Kahn has written movingly about the ways in which religious acts in public spaces might be acts of secular, as well as religious, freedom. Specifically, such acts might break open the secularization narrative in which the secular public sphere is built by freeing itself from religion.[96]

A public sphere that is understood as simultaneously religious and secular might, for example, be more open to religious acts of support for queer lives than is the current conception of a secularism devoid of religion. Such an understanding of public life could break open the religion-sex/secularism-freedom matrix so as to make possible a more expansive sense of religious freedom, one concerned with freedoms other than those of sex. And such a public sphere might also be open to forms of secular freedom other than the modern freedom of individual autonomy. Secular freedom itself might be reconceptualized, in part, by reconfiguring its relation to religious freedom and dissolving the opposition between the two.

Kahn illustrates this point by describing a counterdemonstration that he and his students imagined in response to an antigay demonstration at Vassar College where he works. Members of the notoriously homophobic Westboro Baptist Church had come to the college to proclaim their Christian hatred of homosexuality, and he and his students thought to offer a specifically religious example to answer their hate by enacting in public the ritual of foot washing. He writes, "[I]n wanting to perform an illicit act [foot washing] with obvious Christian roots, students were not issuing a call for greater religious freedom, or more religion in the public square. They were issuing a call for greater, as it were, secular freedom: for a more complicated way of making sense of uncertainties in the interplay of bodily histories on campus." Kahn and his students were hoping to acknowledge the fact that Christianity continues to be publicly active in the US by explicitly engaging the politics of that history in their counterdemonstration, not to enforce "tolerance" by privatizing religion, but to make religious claims for sexual possibility a more direct part of public conversations.[97]

The freedom that Kahn imagines, then, would be open to acts that could not be classified as either religious or secular. And one can, in fact, find such secular religiosity/religious secularism throughout public culture in the US. Such expressions include both expressly religious practices that exceed the bounds of institutionalized religion and popular culture that engages with religion but is presumed to be secular because the engagement is undertaken within the context of the arts or of commerce.[98] Such freedom might best be understood as neither religious freedom nor secular freedom or as both religious and secular.

Historian Ann Braude argues for an active openness to seeing religion in sites that are generally considered secular.[99] In an essay in an anthology analyzing secularism and gender, Braude argues that too often analysts focus on progressive activism as if it is only secular, when in fact religious actors play key roles.[100] She suggests we look instead to unexpected sites and sources where we might see religion in action. For example, the struggle for basic labor protections for domestic workers is often conceptualized as a secular struggle on behalf of excluded workers. Worker centers, however, have been a promising development for domestic workers, day laborers, and restaurant and retail workers who have been excluded from traditional labor movements, and these centers are often supported by religious activism. Some are loosely networked through Interfaith Worker Justice.[101] Jews for Racial and Economic Justice, a community-based organization in New York, has supplemented the work of the National Domestic Workers Alliance by developing standards for fair employment and testifying for more expansive legal protections.[102] But the religious acts associated with worker organizing are rarely counted as representative of "religion."

Braude's approach to recognizing religion in unexpected places also opens possibilities for analyzing unexpected relations and interconnections, including those between religion and secularism, as well as those between religion and sex. And expanding where religiosity is taken seriously could shift what is meant by "religion." When religion is no longer defined by its opposition to secularism, what understandings become available?

Kahn's vision of secular freedom certainly shifts possibilities for religious freedom and how it is imagined in US public discourse. When Ann Pellegrini and I wrote *Love the Sin*, we argued that if the reasons for sexual regulation in US law were truly religious—as so many politicians of both parties argued—then sexual practice was necessarily a matter of religious freedom. If sexual politics is organized by religion, then when the state establishes sexual regulation, it is also establishing religion—a violation of the First Amendment. Instead, we advocated the free exercise of sex as part of the free exercise of religion. One didn't need to see sex as secular for it to be free from state regulation.

Since the initial publication of *Love the Sin* in 2003, much has changed. Possibilities for sexual freedom, particularly when framed as the freedom to marry, have opened. But, perhaps most significantly, the possible meanings of religious freedom have narrowed in the intervening years. Religious freedom has usually applied only to Christianity in US law and policy, even as activists have advocated that many types of religious practice should be the subject of freedom. And, indeed, secular practices are also the subject of religious freedom in that they should be protected from the state's establishment of religion. In the last decade, however, the idea has intensified that religious freedom applies only to the freedoms of "religious people," specifically Christians (and only certain Christians at that), and not also to the freedom of those who are either differently religious or simply not religious.[103]

In a 2017 US Supreme Court decision about government funding for a religious school playground, Chief Justice John Roberts stated explicitly that the case was not one of protecting religious freedom by ensuring that the government did not use its power to establish religious practice. Rather, he said, "This case involves express discrimination based on religious identity."[104] Justice Sonia Sotomayor responded directly in her dissent by pointing out that religious "identity" and religious "institutions" are two different things. Religious freedom is not the purview only of religious people, of those with religious *identities*, and it is protected by not entangling the state in funding for religious *institutions*.[105]

What has become apparent since 2003 is that if one values social possibility, then both religious freedom and secular freedom, like that imagined by Kahn, are needed and both religious freedom and secular freedom need to change. In particular, the recent political narrowing of religious freedom makes it imperative to take seriously religiosity outside of the bounds of traditional authority structures.[106]

Lucinda Ramberg addresses similar questions from a different angle when she writes about the implications of thinking through practices that exceed both the category of religion and the category of secularism. Ramberg has written an impressive ethnography of South Indian devotees known as devadasis, who marry the goddess Yellamma. The marriages Ramberg describes both "exceed secular reckoning" and "do not qualify as religion, as a modern category of human experience and practice."[107] Dedication in marriage involves both sexual practices (not sanctioned by state-recognized marriage) and alternative models of gender and kinship, so devadasis married to Yellamma live lives dedicated to neither widely sanctioned religious practice nor secular family-formation. Instead, the practice of families dedicating the lives of their daughters to the goddess has long been "subject to reform . . . as illicit sex and superstition."

Reform movements trying to end this practice refuse to see an intertwined religious and sexual practice as valuable or even viable for women's lives: "[O]ne thing seems clear from this story about devadasi lifeworlds and their eradication. Sex cannot count as religion, at least not as modern religion."[108] In response, Ramberg suggests that scholars refuse the singular sense of modern religion as only regulating sex and instead take seriously the sexuality of religion: "My point is that not only the ecstatic rights surrounding a South Indian devi, but all rites and religions have a sexuality: they mobilize and organize sexual economies, distributions of fertility, the limits and possibilities of public pleasures, and the shape of our desires. Forms of secularity and religiosity both invest themselves in bodies and pleasures; they shape the possibilities we are given over, or give ourselves, to."[109]

By highlighting the sexuality of religion, Ramberg's reading also shifts possible understandings of the relation between religion and secularism away from the powerful binary instituted by modernity. The work helpfully demonstrates how queer practices need not refer to a sexual identity, but rather to a way of acting to create values that are not wholly contained within modern categories or contemporary structures of power.

Religion, Secularism, and Possibility

Social movements and activist practices that challenge the division between religion and secularism demonstrate new ways to build possibilities for social change. As with sexual politics, gender-based violence is another point at which the division between religion and secularism is enacted. And, as with the narrative of sexual conservatism, when religion is taken to be a cause of gendered violence, the correlative implication is that secularism frees women from that violence.[110] As a result, the secular state is often positioned as the solution to gendered violence, whether through the enactment and enforcement of laws against domestic violence or, at the international level, through the type of military action that the US has undertaken in Afghanistan (and much of the world). What is left out of this narrative as it moves from cause (religion) through problem (gendered violence) to 'response (intervention by the secular state) is that the solution offered—intervention by the secular state—involves the use of violence.

Community-based organizations and social movements are working to challenge the narrative that religion causes gendered violence, and in doing so they are not only contesting the supposed division between religion and secularism, but also building sites for articulation among movements that are sometimes separated from each other. For example, the Barnard Center for Research on Women (BCRW) worked with activist fellow Tiloma Jayasinghe, former executive director of Sakhi for South Asian Women in New York City, on a project called Responding to Violence, Restoring Justice.[111] The project draws upon feminist and queer ways of responding to violence that have been produced by movements like INCITE! Women of Color Against Violence (including their collaboration with Critical Resistance) and Generation Five.[112] Focused on the intersections among intimate violence, state violence, and histories of colonialism and slavery, these movements have produced ideas of transformative justice that neither restore a preexisting and romanticized community nor invoke violence to create a new revolutionary community.[113]

Responding to Violence, Restoring Justice involved convenings and interviews to document how anti–domestic violence organizations, like Sakhi, are continuing to develop alternatives to calling on the violence of the state to respond to intimate violence. For a project focused on South Asian immigrant communities in the United States, ideas about religion, violence, and the secular state must be actively challenged. Sakhi is an important site for such efforts because it takes up organizing in the midst of narratives that presume the predominance of religious conservatives among immigrant communities. The presumption is that religious traditionalism will hide and even promote violence while the state will protect women and prevent violence. In recognizing that this story is not true, Jayasinghe's project shows that the religion-secularism binary creates an oscillation between religious and secular authority, in which South Asian women disappear into a choice between the secular state or the presumed masculine authorities of the community. The oscillating demand to choose one side or the other of the binary does not, for example, allow for any kind of complex identification that might oppose violence and also recognize the value of religious commitment. Jayasinghe seeks alternative ways to address violence without turning to the police. Sakhi is working toward a future in which religious tradition, beliefs, and practices are not excluded, but are emboldened to summon a future simultaneously vividly local and exuberantly South Asian and universal in its claims to safety from violence. In the midst of this activist approach, religion is not automatically considered a source of violence and may very well provide the resources for restoring justice. Perhaps most importantly, restoring justice does not require separating the religious from the secular or vice versa. Making such a distinction is no longer the key to ending violence. When one takes Braude's advice in looking at putatively secular organizing, one can often find religious acts that are often not counted as such, including in feminist acts that refuse traditional religious and community authority but nonetheless take religion seriously.

Along with shifting the lens for analyzing religion, Responding to Violence, Restoring Justice documents a range of activities to end violence that suggests the capacious possibilities created when sexual politics is not contained by the religion-secular and community-state binaries. In a section on community-based alternatives, the project documents activities already undertaken by organizations like SisterSong, Beyond the Bars, Manavi, the Center for Women's Global Leadership, INCITE!, Korean American Family Service Center, Threshold Collaborative, and Creative Interventions. Activists develop community education projects through translation services, economic empowerment, projects at local restaurants to raise awareness, and healing through storytelling. Such practices can piece together different aspects of social possibility, including a world free from anti-Muslim bias that allows for prison abolition, affordable housing, and economic sustainability.

Reframing gendered violence involves taking seriously both the pragmatic and local work of responding to violence that is done by organizations like Sakhi and the expansive work of envisioning a world beyond the framework of secular modernity. As the slogan of the World Social Forum once proclaimed: "Another world is possible."[114] And building an-other world requires both new analyses of this world and creative imagination about possibilities that summon social justice.

2

Because Morality, Because Materiality

Political struggles over sex and gender in the US evoke claims on behalf of religion. Sexual politics is taken to be a matter of moral regulation with religion located as the ground of moral value. *The Sex Obsession* argues instead that religion is not the sole or primary force behind sexual politics, and offers a dynamically intersectional analysis of the intertwining of sexual politics with a range of issues, including race, economics, national boundaries and immigration, access to housing, environmentalism, and mass incarceration.

Such expansive understanding is obstructed by mainstream analysis across the political spectrum, however. Conservative commentators certainly do invoke religious regulation as the front line of sexual politics. But possibilities for political action can also be constrained by the invocation of the usual divisions between and among issues as they are articulated by liberals, progressives, or radicals. Even for progressives, issues like gender and sex are often deemed to be related to morality rather than materiality, values rather than interests, identity politics rather than kitchen-table issues, culture wars rather than social struggles. The commonplace association between religion and sexual regulation reinforces the placement of sexual politics on the moral side of these ledgers, keeping political possibilities within long-established boundaries.

In this chapter, I track the effects of divisions among issues and of their subsequent recombination, which can be as pernicious as the division itself. I am particularly interested in the ways in which political issues are brought together and divided from each other in shifting, kaleidoscopic patterns. The movement among issues works by sometimes aligning issues with each other (religion and sex, for example) and sometimes by dividing issues from each other (sex and immigration, for example). I focus on the division between moral issues and those that are considered to be of material import, a division that is deployed by conservatives but is also often invoked as a key to progressive political possibility. For example, Thomas Frank, in an analysis of the 2016 election in his book *Listen, Liberal,* explicitly contrasted the focus on "morality" at the Democratic National Convention with the Democratic Party's willingness to embrace corporate power and unwillingness to address the economic interests of working people. Frank argued that Hillary Clinton's "one overarching cause during the campaign was opposing discrimination, the unfair 'barriers' that kept talented people from rising." Frank does not say where he gleans this as Clinton's overarching issue, but it fits with his narrative divide between morality and materiality: "The official slogan of the Democratic convention in Philadelphia was 'stronger together,' a jab at Trumpian divisiveness. But the real theme of the gathering was moral goodness."[1] Frank admits that some of the moral claims were meaningful: "There was a necessary and healthful aspect to all this. Trump richly deserved to be called out for his bigotry and racism." But for Frank any claim to morality on the part of the Democrats was undercut by the contradictory facts on the ground and those facts involved economic inequality: "For the generation coming up now, the old social contract is gone—or at least the part of it that ensured health care and retirement for blue-collar workers."

One can, of course, agree with this critique of economic precarity without also buying in to the set of divisions that Frank attaches to it— including that between opposing "bigotry and racism" and the needs of working people. Note that the division between morality and materiality allows concern about racism to become the purview of those who are at the top of unequal economic relations, rather than of people who have been systematically excluded from power and privilege in the United States. In other words, the moral-material division allows for opposition to racism to be placed on the side of morality *over against* materiality and then to be aligned with "elites" *over against* working people, even as those for whom discrimination is most threatening are those who are economically precarious. This movement among issues allows Frank's argument to seem serious and progressive, but it does not offer any analysis of the relation between racism or sexism and economic inequality. If one agrees with his critique of economic policy over the last several decades and the ways in which these policies have increased economic precariousness for many people, then one particularly needs a powerful, intersectional, and dynamic analysis to create effective social change.

The movement among issues has other effects as well. Frank's argument highlights healthcare as a lost part of the old social contract, when the expansion of access to healthcare is the signature achievement of the Obama administration, and the repeal of this achievement was a major component of Trump's 2016 campaign.[2] It seems that making healthcare available through the Affordable Care Act is on the "moral" side of Frank's central division. Healthcare would count as "material" only if it were provided through jobs as in the old social contract, even though this contract makes healthcare unavailable to many working-class people. The old social contract left healthcare out of reach for people who work in service industries rather than factories, and may well face barriers in their working lives, in their health, and in their access to healthcare and other forms of social support because of racism and sexism. Frank's division between morality and materiality thus allows for a recombination of issues such that opposition to racism and government support for social goods like healthcare are bundled together as a set of issues that can be placed over against the interests of working people. As I explore further below, this alignment of issues does not create a bulwark against politics like that of the Republican Party post–Donald Trump (as Frank claims it does), but is instead part of the constellation that provides a pattern for Trump's political base: white workers (those positioned as not facing "discrimination") are promised that they can receive benefits through jobs, even if those benefits are unavailable to most people as a result.

In the end, Frank's argument supports the type of conservatism that his analysis hopes to prevent—if liberals would only listen. But, despite this incoherence, it continues to be taken as making sense, and many commentators on subsequent elections have taken up the same tack.[3]

Reading binary divisions from unexpected angles, like the angle engendered by not simply dismissing the import of religion in politics or by seeing sexual politics as central to economic policy, opens new ways of understanding how economic injustice is created and maintained. The reason to refuse divisions is not to move away from materialism, but rather to develop a materialist analysis that can adequately engage the complexity of social relations and the material world. Through such engagements economic issues might be addressed more effectively.[4]

The Productive Incoherence of Value and Values

The need to disrupt political common sense arises from the ways in which traditional habits of thought and analysis so often take expansive realities and reduce them to either-or divisions, such as those between morality and materiality or cultural politics and economics. In particular, much political analysis still depends on an assumption of coherence in the formation of policy, whether that coherence is based on presumptions of rational choice based on the interests of political actors or the sociological coherence of social relations.[5] One of the reasons (and there are many) that single-issue analyses remain so persistently difficult to displace despite the power of claims for intersectionality among scholars and activists is because single issues provide analytic coherence.

In this chapter, I employ the concept of "productive incoherence" to illuminate the complexities of social relations.[6] The idea of productive incoherence allows for a tracking of both the conjunctions and disjunctions that create kaleidoscopic patterns of interrelation. And the concept also highlights how, somewhat counterintuitively, incoherence may actually reinforce existing social formations and make them difficult to dislodge.

The practice of separating moral and material concerns in political discourse, for example, constitutes a productive incoherence with wide-ranging effects. As with the story of religion as the "cause" of sexual conservatism, the idea of a division between morality and materiality forms a common sense shared across the political spectrum. Not only is it appealing to progressives like Frank, but conservatives also deployed this division as part of their campaign to take over the House of Representatives in the 1990s after decades of control by the Democratic Party after the New Deal. The Democrats controlled the House for all but brief periods from the 1930s until 1994; in order to win a majority in the House and tip US politics further to the right, the Republican Party produced two campaign documents: the Contract with America and the Contract with the American Family.

The two contracts were deliberately split by Republican Party strategists so that the Contract with America could be pitched as fiscal policy, while the Contract with the American Family was presented as addressing social issues. The split between the two contracts created options for managing the potential incoherence necessary to persuade both fiscal and social conservatives within the electorate, a split that continues to have effects.[7] Because the two contracts are divided, fiscal conservatives can support initiatives for a balanced budget, tax cuts, and small business incentives without having to actively identify with an agenda focused on privatizing public education, restricting abortion rights and access, and cutting support for the arts and public television. Social conservatives, on the other hand, could support these latter measures while distancing themselves from the economic elites at the top of the Republican Party and their pursuit of complete freedom for the market.

The explanation, then, for the persistence of the Republican Party alliance between fiscal and social conservatives is that these two approaches *work together*, and they continue to do so even as they have been stretched by the deep incoherence of policy during Donald Trump's presidency. One could say that Trump's incoherence on policy actually ensured that (with only a few exceptions) both fiscal and social conservatives got enough from his administration's scattershot approach to policy (whether in the form of tax cuts favoring the wealthy or the appointment of socially conservative Supreme Court justices) to remain in the Republican coalition.[8]

To understand how sexual politics is produced in the United States, one needs to trace not only the complexity of social relations, but also how the incoherence resulting from that complexity is managed so as to constrain social possibilities. As religious studies scholar Catherine Bell has argued, common sense is sustained by a "loosely knit and loosely coherent totality."[9] The looseness of coherence allows slippage in the network. And this slippage can actually reinforce the overarching social formation by providing a shifting site of reference in the face of counterevidence. When one claim is challenged or insufficient, it is possible to discursively slip to another, thus protecting the network as a whole. When fiscal conservatives express concern about the increasing politicization of the US Supreme Court, the Trump administration can be defended by focusing on tax cuts or the rollback of regulations.

Simply pointing out incoherence will not unravel the fabric. It may be easy to poke holes in a particular aspect of the dominant common sense, but the multiplicity of connections makes it hard to effectively unravel the whole cloth. The density of the network ensures the possibility of myriad interactions that nonetheless hold the fabric in place. This density is aptly illustrated by the binaries that Eve Kosofsky Sedgwick details in *Epistemology of the Closet* as having been marked by the "modern crisis of homo/heterosexual definition." The binaries intersecting with this single social relation include: "secrecy/disclosure, knowledge/ignorance, private/public, masculine/feminine, majority/minority, innocence/initiation, natural/artificial, new/old, discipline/terrorism, canonic/noncanonic, wholeness/decadence, urbane/provincial, domestic/foreign, health/illness, same/different, active/passive, in/out, cognition/paranoia, art/kitsch, utopia/apocalypse, sincerity/sentimentality, and voluntary/addiction."[10]

In listing these binaries, one can begin to see how interwoven they, in fact, are. The work of making social change is so difficult precisely because the social fabric is made up of these densely networked relations that simultaneously allow for slippage. Yet while the network tilts toward existing power relations, it does not create an unchangeable or unchanging latticework. Engagement that draws threads together differently has the potential to support change.

Finding ways to intervene in a productively incoherent social formation requires keeping track of the disjunctions, as well as the connections, among social relations. Disjunctions add to the resilience of the social fabric, as one thread can unravel while other threads are drawn together to become the center of the pattern. Slippage from one point in the pattern to another thus protects the individual threads from having to bear the full weight of potentially contradictory social relations. Disjunctions also provide openings for engagement, however, and with active engagement, opportunities for change.

Sex, Religion, and Materiality

Common sense stories about sexual politics both invoke and constitute the division between morality and materiality, family values and economic value. In order to explore the productive incoherence of narratives that separate moral and material interests, as well as analytic alternatives, I turn to a focus on the social formation known as "neoliberalism" that has become powerful over the past several decades.[11]

As Elizabeth Bernstein has helpfully summarized, "neoliberalism" names a set of political and economic policies and practices that can also be understood as a political project or as a period in the history of capitalism that encompasses the last decades of the twentieth century and the first decades of the twenty-first: "Of late 'neoliberalism' has become a rather fraught term within contemporary social analysis—not because of its sparseness as a signifier but because of its capacity to signify so many different processes and entities."[12] In the Gender Justice and Neoliberal Transformations research group, which Bernstein and I co-convened and which included scholars from both the global North and the global South, we found that neoliberal policies and practices vary across different areas of the world. Neoliberal formations can include some combination of the following elements: a move from industrial to finance capitalism; a shift from direct domination of those marginalized by race, sex, and gender to a redeployment of social hierarchies and violence via a politics of diversity and assimilation; a shift from the welfare state to the carceral state; and, for those countries that have social safety nets, a reduction of social protections and an increased emphasis on personal responsibility.[13] Through our conversations across sites, we came to understand neoliberalism as a *concatenation* of differential projects—some political, some economic. Some places are the direct subject of structural adjustment policies imposed by transnational institutions, some have moved beyond these direct policies toward new social and political formations, and some were never subject to structural adjustment directly but have nonetheless experienced a range of neoliberal effects such as the proliferation of nongovernmental and semigovernmental organizations. As these policies and practices both vary and are shared or travel across different locales, conversations in the Gender Justice group conceptualized neoliberalism as both specific and interconnected.[14]

Not only does neoliberalism name a bundle of policies and practices, but contemporary governmentality is also produced by practices that have been layered over time. Neoliberalism creates new forms of organization that build on old contradictions, introducing new, taxing levels of incoherence. In this sense, neoliberalism is both a new formation and an ongoing enactment of capitalism.

Because both policies and practices vary so widely, the question of whether neoliberalism is an accurate way to conceptualize contemporary political and economic relations is also a matter of debate.[15] In articulating the complexities of contemporary political possibility, for example, Mario Pecheny has argued that Latin America has oscillated between neoliberalism and "post-neoliberalism." Neoliberal policies have been instituted in many Latin American countries, shifting people's lives in ways that have continuing effects, and these effects now interact with newer policies and practices.[16] Many Latin Americans thus live in post-neoliberal conditions in the sense of both the period after the imposition of neoliberalism, and the period in which a formation after neoliberalism is taking effect. Pecheny argues that the resulting multilayered set of policies—drawn from time periods and policy formations marked by liberal modernity, neoliberalism, and post-neoliberalism— also produces a fracturing within the state itself, as the state simultaneously undertakes practices of direct state violence, normative discipline, and control and securitization.

Analysis of "neoliberalism" is crucial because the term names shifting forms of economic and political injustice that are the critical objects of many projects on behalf of social justice. However we understand neoliberalism, its lived effects have created a world marked not just by stark inequality, but also by increasing precariousness for a wide range of people.[17]

As is so often the case, these projects can also be articulated in ways that reiterate the long-standing contrast between economic and cultural politics, including those of religion and sexuality. In the early 1990s, Marxist David Harvey, for example, developed an influential analysis of the shift from industrial capitalism to the more "flexible form" of neoliberalism, with its emphasis on financial instruments, the gig economy, service work, and piecework.[18] Harvey remains committed to the idea that economic interests are fundamentally different than any other kind of interest or commitment. In holding on to the binary divide, Harvey faces challenges in tracking the movement among social relations.

In this narrative, Harvey ties this division between moral values and material value to a traditional secularization narrative and its assumption of a division between religion and secularism. In rehearsing the story of modernity as the philosophical framework for industrial capitalism, Harvey narrates: "[Modern] Enlightenment thought . . . embraced the idea of progress, and actively sought that break with history and tradition which modernity espouses. It was, above all, a secular movement that sought the demystification and desacralization of knowledge and social organization in order to liberate human beings from their chains."[19] He then describes the shift to flexible accumulation (and eventually neoliberalism), which produces the reappearance of religion so as to provide stability to a newly insecure secular/economic world:

> While the roots of this transition are evidently deep and complicated, their consistency with a transition from Fordism to flexible accumulation is reasonably clear even if the direction (if any) of causality is not. To begin with, the more flexible motion of capital emphasizes the new, the fleeting, the ephemeral, the fugitive, and the contingent in modern life, rather than the more solid values implanted under Fordism. . . . But, as Simmel (1978) long ago suggested, it is also at such times of fragmentation and economic insecurity that the desire for stable values leads to heightened emphasis upon the authority of basic institutions—the family, religion, the state. And there is abundant evidence of a revival of support for such institutions and the values they represent throughout the Western world since about 1970.[20]

Harvey is trying to trace a "consistency" or coherence between values and value. In this narrative, secularization, especially the "liberation" provided by secular freedom, forms the values to support industrial capitalism in modernity. Then, when capitalism shifts away from the industrialism of the modern period and toward more flexible forms (that came to be termed "neoliberalism"), no longer rooted in industrial factories and "fixed" capital, the response to the accompanying destabilization is a resurgence of religion and other institutions that provide a sense of stable values. Secularism is separate from religion, but when secularism becomes unstable, religion returns to supplement and stabilize it.[21] Note the effect of separating secularism and religion: capitalist values, including those of neoliberal capitalism, are secular values— those of flexibility and individual freedom.[22] And religious values are conservative values—stable and directed toward authority.

In a later book, *A Brief History of Neoliberalism*, Harvey argues that conservative Christians become part of the "construction of consent" for neoliberalism, even though their values are opposed to the flexible and consumerist "culture of neoliberalism."[23] In order to explain how conservative Christians become willing to provide supplementary support for neoliberalism, Harvey turns to a well-rehearsed narrative of false consciousness in which conservative Christians are brought into an alliance with the Republican Party through their commitments to "cultural and traditional values," rather than a certain brand of economics. These "values" are understood to "mask other realities," which Harvey later names as "capitalism and corporate power."[24]

Religion remains a crucial force in the construction of consent for neoliberalism, but just how it does so is much less clear than the first claim that religion, along with the state, provides stable support in the face of unstable and changing capitalist relations. The binaries that Harvey lines up in the first story—value/values, flexible/stable, market/state, secular/religious, individual/family, economic/cultural—begin to shift around as he works to tie his narrative to political events. In this follow-up narrative, the state is seen as moving from its position in the earlier narrative, on the side of conservative and authoritative institutions, to the side of "liberal elites" who use excessive state power. This negative perception of the state is reinforced by "a well-funded group of neoconservative intellectuals . . . espousing morality and traditional values."[25] Now the state is on the side of flexible capitalism and is identified with liberal forces rather than traditional authority.

It becomes hard to tell where exactly religion lands. The neoconservatives who support traditional values join conservative Christians in the Republican alliance by "supporting the neoliberal turn economically but not culturally." So on which side of the divide do conservative Christians fall? Do they, like neoconservatives, support neoliberalism economically but not culturally or, as social conservatives, culturally but not economically? Or is it the case that they support neoliberalism neither culturally nor economically, but are willing to join in the construction of consent for neoliberalism because they want to ally with neoconservatives in their opposition to neoliberal culture?

I would suggest that the fact that this narrative is hard to follow is not an accident. If, for example, we take up the last option—that conservative Christians support neoliberalism so as to enter into an alliance with neoconservatives in opposition to neoliberal values—then in Harvey's narrative a culture of consent for neoliberal economics is created by an alliance between two political movements, both of which oppose the culture of neoliberalism and one of which (made up of conservative Christians) has no material interest in the economics of neoliberalism. The original analysis depends on the cultural-economic divide to create a sense that conservative Christians forsake economics in order to protect their cultural commitments. But they forsake economics for a cultural formation that involves greater consumer and cultural freedoms, which they oppose. In other words, conservative Christians, it seems, support neoliberalism because they oppose both its culture and its economics.

The split between cultural and economic issues is utterly incoherent, and yet it is also productive. As we have seen, it produces the politics of left, right, and center. Not only is analysis across the political spectrum narrated through this split, but the split is also embodied and materialized through political formations that enact it—whether through left politics that focus only on class while ignoring other issues; or through the Republican split between fiscal and social conservatives, which allows Republicans to maintain an incoherent alliance within the party; or, as we will see in the next chapter, through centrist political campaigns like Bill Clinton's in 1992, which featured the slogan, "It's the economy, stupid."

Harvey's story lines up various binary elements to support his narrative so that market freedoms must somehow be aligned with and reflected in the culture of neoliberalism. But the relationships among these lined-up elements—between, for example, the state and the nation, or among religion, secularism, and culture, or, yes, the relation between economics and culture—are all shifting as Harvey moves through his narration.

This type of kaleidoscopic narrative is told as if particular elements line up on one side or the other of a divide, but as the productively incoherent narrative proceeds, the elements and the divide itself are not fixed, but mobile. Rather than undercutting the social formation, this shifting incoherence allows for different configurations to sustain complications and even contradictions. Accounts like Harvey's about religion and conservative Christian support for neoliberalism seem to make perfect sense when read as part of a loosely coherent whole—so clearly reasonable, so obvious that they need no further investigation.

The movement of the elements within the analytic narrative creates this sense of obviousness, and yet we end up with a narrative in which conservative Christians must be read as dupes at both the cultural *and* economic level.

The analytic alternative is to provide a dynamic intersectional analysis that recognizes and traces the intertwining and recombination of the elements that Harvey places on opposite sides of the moral-material divide. In Harvey's story, support for the free market from Christian conservatives and "the white working classes" is based on some kind of misdirection or mistake—the real interests of white working-class workers are in the welfare state. Their support for neoliberal policies that undercut the welfare state is a mistake.[26]

Another way to interpret the commitment to neoliberalism on the part of many conservative Christians and white workers, however, would be to understand that commitment as a real part of their "interests"— their intertwined cultural and material interests. In other words, Christian conservatives may understand their economic interests as a paradoxical investment in policies that make their lives harder but that also preserve a particular version of what they value about both family and economy. Specifically, the fundamental interest of those committed to the privatized family of Christian "family values" may be found in the hope to be saved *from* the social safety net, not *by* the social safety net.

Holding on to this hope for the private and traditionally gendered family as sustained only through "hard work" rather than support from the government may be their most abiding commitment. Part of the interest here can be named as maintaining a moral distinction between "earned" and "unearned" benefits, one that allows white, working-class families to understand themselves to be "separate" from government because they understand government programs directed to white families as providing "earned benefits" rather than "entitlements." Such programs include Social Security and Medicare, which are paid for by taxes on current employees' wages, and tax benefits like the mortgage interest deduction and the child tax credit, which benefit those in the lowest income bracket the least.[27] As journalist Chris Ladd outlines in detail, state policies with regard to employment make it seem as if those with good jobs "earn" a set of social benefits from the state that are otherwise simply "given" to recipients of direct state support: "Like most of my neighbors I have a good job in the private sector. Ask my neighbors about the cost of the welfare programs they enjoy and you will be greeted by baffled stares. All that we have is 'earned' and we perceive no need for government support. Nevertheless, taxpayers fund our retirement saving, health insurance, primary, secondary, and advanced education, daycare, commuter costs, and even our mortgages at a staggering public cost. Socialism for white people is all-enveloping, benevolent, invisible, and insulated by the nasty, deceptive notion that we have earned our benefits by our own hand."[28] Some of these benefits are tied to employment history, and the stratification of the labor market by race and gender ensures that access to these benefits follows that stratification, giving the white men with the best access to jobs more access to government benefits as well, while the racism and sexism involved in this system disappear from view.[29]

This sense of the distinction between "earned" and "unearned" government benefits means that Trump supporters identify with a distinction—grounded in race and gender hierarchies—between the state support that they receive and state support received through the social safety net. For those who understand themselves to have suffered socioeconomic losses due to deindustrialization and neoliberal policies, the political promise to "make America great again" is an animating one, as they hope it will return the United States to a system in which the distinctions between white men and other people, those with jobs and those without, and a moral distinction between earned and unearned benefits will be brought into line. In other words, they are willing to support the shredding of the safety net if they believe it has a chance of "bringing back" the jobs that allowed for a sense not just of economic well-being, but also of being morally "deserving." And so they may even be willing to risk losing some of their "earned" benefits if they believe there is a chance of "bringing back" the economic system that made this intertwined set of distinctions operative on their behalf.

Thinking of moral commitments and economic interests as a binary distinction, analytically separate from the start, is too simple.[30] Moreover, a narrative that traces the entanglement of value and values allows one to take seriously the commitments of various actors, including conservative Christians, rather than wishing those interests away or condescending to religious commitment as a mistake. So, too, beginning with the assumption of complexly intertwined beliefs, interests, desires, motivations, and commitments means taking racism and sexism as seriously as class interest and antagonism. As Ladd summarizes: "When it seems like people are voting against their interests, I have probably failed to understand their interests. We cannot begin to understand Election 2016 until we acknowledge the power and reach of socialism for white people." In this example, the analysis is not that racism drives people to mistake their interests, but rather that the intertwining of morality and materiality constitutes their interests and drives political action. People who vote on behalf of the idea that the material benefits of government support should be funneled through "jobs" do so because they identify with an interest in ensuring that the benefits are given only to those who are thought to be morally deserving. This moral interest is also a material interest in how the economy should be shaped, even as it is also entangled with racism and the history of white supremacy.

On this reading, social change is not a project of getting people to recognize their "true" interests over against "false" consciousness, but of working to create new possibilities for moral and material commitment. As historian Joseph E. Lowndes points out: "Politics is not merely the realm where preexisting interests and passions are given expression. Rather, it is in and through politics that interests, grievances, and passions are forged and new collective identities created."[31] Effectively undertaking such contestation depends on being able to articulate a different analysis.

Exploitation and Domination

As a way of thinking about interrelation differently, I turn now to an alternative narration of the dynamics of interrelation that produced neoliberalism in the 1970s and 1980s. Harvey is in no way alone in thinking that economics is of a different order than other social relations. Barbara Foley provides a feminist variation of this view, in which she highlights the importance of intersectionality.[32] But Foley also establishes a distinction between the "oppressions" of racism and sexism and the "exploitation" of capitalist alienation. For Foley, capitalist exploitation is the social relation on which all others depend.[33] Foley argues that the relation between exploitation and oppression is causal and that it is singularly so: "Oppression . . . is indeed multiple and intersecting, producing different kinds of experiences, but its causes are not multiple but singular."[34] Oppression and the categories through which it is experienced is "the product" of the exploitation of labor.[35]

In contrast, I argue that although exploitation and domination are, indeed, different types of social relations, they are also mutually constitutive in their difference. In this way, we can see how exploitation may be in dynamic relation with the oppressive forces of racism, sexism, homophobia and transphobia that are enacted through social domination.

Rather than assuming that domination is ideologically constructed solely as a function of exploitation, Gayatri Chakravorty Spivak, in her essay "Scattered Speculations on the Question of Value," broadens the analysis beyond the dialectics of morality and materiality to the full range of dynamics that create both value and capital.[36] As Spivak makes clear, economic profit is produced by a chain of value, a set of differential relations that move from labor through the production of goods to the exchange and consumption of those goods. She argues that, in most Marxian understandings of the labor theory of value, the origin of the chain is located through a naturalized concept of labor undertaken to satisfy basic human needs. Once one assumes that it is human nature to want and need to labor, to use the natural world to productive ends, there is no need for an explanation of why labor is the ground of value.

Spivak points out, alternatively, that this chain begins not with an already formed human being who labors, but with the formation of humans and their values. She denaturalizes labor in order to see how labor is (always already) *in* social relations. Labor is not just about the production of economic value; labor is to make something of social value.[37] So, labor is formed in part by what is valued.

By attending to the production of human bodies and beings, Spivak rethinks domination and exploitation by reading domination as both produced by exploitation *and* as preceding exploitation. She focuses on the question of subjectification: How are subjects created who not only *can* participate in capitalism, but who are willing and even *desire* to do so? Through the "predication of the subject," human beings become people who not only need to labor, but who "desire to consume the affect of labor itself." Desire and the values that it embodies are not only at the heart of capitalist *consumption* but are central to *labor*—to the process of producing value (economic and moral) and to the process of producing human beings who participate in that production. People do "socially necessary labor," but the sense of what is necessary is also socially produced, as is the conviction that working is a morally good thing to do.[38]

Exploitation is never value-free. It is both dependent *on* and structured *by* the values that make certain things "socially necessary." And these values are materialized through the normatively constituted—the dominated—body. Social and cultural values, including specifically ethical values, come into play at each point along the chain that leads to the production of economic value. And values come into play not just because of direct domination, but also in part because human beings want to make what they and others value as good. The desire to work and the desire to find one's work meaningful are recognizable emotions.

Cultural values also come into play at the point of exchange in which goods are valued and used within a cultural system of assessing the good. The desire for consumer goods is virtually unavoidable in capitalism. As Richard Ohmann charmingly writes in *Selling Culture*, when looking at his cats while writing his book, the cats can catch their morning and evening meals. The cat food Ohmann provides is not materially necessary to their survival, but "on the whole, the cats prefer to eat commodities."[39] The cultural values, those of taste or time, that make a commodity preferable (even to cats) or that give the idea of a material good a moral as well as functional meaning are part of what powers capitalism. The idea that labor itself is a moral good is contemporary common sense, as is the idea that commodities have a moral valence—are either beneficial or deleterious to the earth, for example.

Value and values are fundamentally interlinked. There is no way to extract the bare bones of either the practice of labor or the exchange of goods from the circuits of desire or the values that constitute them. Values make the act of valuing and hence the creation of value possible. Separating values from value, ethical commitments from economic necessity, culture from the market, all contribute to thinking that makes it harder, not easier, to critique the commitment to productivity that is in many ways fundamentally destructive to bodies and minds and the natural world.

Economic and cultural values are not the same, but neither are they wholly distinguishable. Domination and exploitation are not analogous, nor do they mirror each other. They cannot be lined up in opposing sets with moral values on one side and economic value on the other. They cannot be added up to form a coherent whole. Rather their relation is mutually constitutive and, as Harvey's narration shows, productively incoherent. Furthermore, one cannot be established as the origin or base to the other. This means that domination has its own base in cultural values and that there is constant exchange between these values and economic value. In the end, there is no origin, no base, beyond these relations. Dominative values—racism, sexism, homophobia, nationalism, Christian supersessionism—may work for capitalism, but they also make capitalism work in the way that it does. At each point along the chain of relation (from the production of human beings through labor to the production of value), one thing is desired, is valued, over another (whether consciously or effectively or both). And that valuation could change. The lack of causal necessity means that the world could be otherwise.

Kaleidoscopic Interrelation

I am committed to addressing value and values as intertwined realities. The intertwining of value and values also provides a new way to link politically the American obsession with sex to other issues. Sex is not a mere distraction from the real issues of economic interest.

Spivak's analysis of subjectification in relation to both exploitation and domination opens analytic possibilities that allow for new ways of analyzing the social, cultural, political, and economic interrelations of the 1970s (where Harvey began his story of the move to flexible capitalism). The 1970s are often marked as a crucial historical moment for both the development of neoliberalism and the political force of conservative Christianity in the United States. And, the 1970s were (as always) an active time for sexual politics, the fight for racial justice, and anticolonial liberation. There was a lot going on.

A number of political conflicts amid shifting economic conditions led in the 1970s to the displacement of Keynesian economics and the consolidation of neoliberal policies that favored market-based rather than state-based solutions to economic problems. One obviously anti-democratic event was in Chile, when in 1973 the CIA contributed to the violent overthrow of the recently elected president, the socialist Salvador Allende.[40] As Marcus Taylor and Naomi Klein have narrated, in a complex feedback loop, ideas incubated in the United States became part of a policy experiment in Chile variously aided and abetted by the US and its security forces.[41] The Chilean dictatorship of Augusto Pinochet then produced a set of practices and policies that helped to form neoliberalism in the United States, a shift that intensified with the 1980 election of Ronald Reagan.

This reading of the coup in Chile places it in the context of the panoply of anticolonial movements that spread across many areas of the world after World War II and picked up steam in the 1970s.[42] Lisa Duggan understands neoliberalism as in part a direct response to these movements as nations, international institutions, and transnational corporations from the global North responded to decolonization by working to maintain their power through both violent suppression and the imposition of neoliberal economic policies, like structural adjustment and indebtedness organized through the International Monetary Fund and the World Bank.[43]

Similarly, Roderick Ferguson places the development of racial and sexual politics in the 1970s in the context of radical liberatory movements, a history that includes interactions among Black Power movements, anticolonial liberation movements, and sexual liberation movements. Sometimes these interactions were among leaders of specific organizations and sometimes they represented the influences of multiple intellectual traditions. Ferguson concludes: "Part of why the history of these movements matters is precisely because that is a history in which groups such as Gay Liberation Front and Third World Gay Liberation insisted that sexuality and sexual freedoms be part of projects that worked to promote freedom *from* state and military violence, economic deprivation, and imperialism."[44]

There were also a number of mainstream cultural and political movements that reacted against the push for sexual freedom, including the campaign against the Equal Rights Amendment led by Phyllis Schlafly, Anita Bryant's antihomosexual Save Our Children campaign, the Briggs Initiative in California to ban gay men and lesbians from working in public schools, and the formation of the Moral Majority.[45]

The 1970s saw a major shift away from mainline Protestantism to conservative evangelicalism as the predominant public idea of religiosity, signaling not just shifts in church membership, but also the formation of explicitly political organizations run by conservative evangelical leaders.[46] Conservative Christianity has continued to be a force to be reckoned with in US politics, as well as in different national contexts and in transnational institutions.[47]

The story of the 1970s is often told with a singular focus on one, or at most two, of these phenomena.[48] As I've suggested throughout this book, maintaining separate analyses of these formations has allowed for various binary oppositions to dominate social analysis, including that between religion and sexuality, as if one is the expression of tradition and the other of change, as well as that between "culture wars" over issues of family values and the material shifts made by the force of economic value. We have seen how Harvey analyzes the coincidence of these different phenomena through an incoherent account in which movements for women's and sexual liberation helped create consent for the developing neoliberal hegemony by contributing to a culture of flexibility and individualism, while religious conservatives supported neoliberalism because they mistook their economic interests in the glare of their support for cultural conservatism (which is somehow also part of neoliberalism).

To explore alternative approaches to this bifurcated story, I would like to spend some time articulating relations that run across the scholarship on the 1970s but that are rarely brought together into an interrelated narrative. Taking a kaleidoscopic approach to the economics and politics of the 1970s allows for an analysis that follows movement among issues as it weaves together the social fabric of neoliberalism. Acknowledging the incoherence of the patterns that are formed allows not only for an assessment of the fabric's tensility, but of gaps in the weave, threads that might be pulled, and new patterns that might be produced.

I begin with Judith Stein's *Pivotal Decade: How the United States Traded Factories for Finance in the Seventies*, because Stein presents one of the more complex analyses of the economics of the 1970s—recognizing, for example, that the "working class" includes people of color and should not be invoked as a synonym for the "white working class."[49] But she also presents an analysis that tends to hinge on the division between the moral and the material. For example, she retells the story of the move from "old left" to "new left" in a traditional manner that depends on the contrast between the labor politics of the "old left" and a moral politics of the "new left."

As Stein tells it, "SDS [Students for a Democratic Society] embraced traditional left goals—civil rights law, reduced military spending—but its signature was the statement of values. Awed by the civil rights movement and embracing its moralistic language, the students cultivated the extra-economic goals of 'self-direction, self-understanding, creativity and human independence,' lives that were 'personally authentic' and a democracy that was 'participatory,' not simply formal. It was a New Left because it found the labor orientation of the Old Left limiting and in some cases irrelevant to their sense of America's ills."[50] We should note here that the self-actualizing goals of the SDS statement were hardly the same as those that emphasized the value of "beloved community" in the Civil Rights Movement, but Stein's move to group them together creates a division between the "extra-economic" world of values (no matter what those values might be) and the economic struggle over labor and value.

She follows this split analysis with a narration of much more complexity, showing the ways in which the increasing radicalism of the student antiwar movement "brought students into contact with individuals from the Old Left, religious left and veterans of the peace and civil rights movements of the early 1960s."[51] But the framework of division between the economic and the extra-economic ultimately structures the analysis, as Stein concludes the first chapter of her book by reiterating the sense that the new left was all about cultural politics. She questions whether "the Democrats' fractious components, which had honed their weapons on issues of war, race and culture, could retool when the economic tremors of the 1960s became a tsunami in the 1970s."[52]

One could read this history differently, however. One can, in fact, narrate the economic shifts of the 1970s by grounding them in the dynamic context from which they develop, rather than abstracting them out of those constitutive social—and cultural—relations. Telling this story in kaleidoscopic fashion, one could follow the example of Robin D. G. Kelley, who sees the Civil Rights Movement of the 1960s as, in part, an outgrowth of cross-racial alliances in the old left, particularly in its more radical wing of the Communist Party USA, rather than of just the labor unions upon which Stein focuses.[53] In this reading, the economic analysis of the left and the moral analysis of what has come to be called the Civil Rights Movement could be understood as connected in important ways. Historians like Kelley, Jacquelyn Dowd Hall, and Danielle L. McGuire, who have developed an analysis of the "long civil rights movement," have provided an expansive grounding for reading it as a movement involving issues intertwined across conventionally perceived divides like those Stein draws between morality and materiality, or between race and economics, or between race and gender.[54]

By thinking about events of the 1960s as intertwined and interconnected, we can understand more fully the social and cultural, moral and economic happenings of the 1970s. In this more complexly articulated understanding, economic shifts are not a move *from* "war, race and culture" *to* economics, but always and already in relation to militarism, nationalism, race, sex, gender, religion, *and* economics. Parts of this story can be read by attending to the details that Stein's text presents. She helpfully narrates the economic developments of the 1970s as a challenge to the Keynesian economic consensus, which held that fiscal stimulus could be employed to buffer cycles of inflation and recession. Over the course of the decade, economic stimulus by the US government lost some of its effectiveness.[55] An already far from robust economy was staggered by the oil crisis of 1973 and weakened by both persistent inflation and stagnating growth (dubbed "stagflation") with no clear sense of how government policy could address the difficulty.

Stein highlights a schematic tension between domestic industrial production on one side and global trade and finance capitalism on the other. There is much to be said for this analysis. One of the reasons that Keynesian stimulus was less effective in the 1970s than previously was that dollars spent by the US government were likely to move either into economic streams that led outside the United States and toward global chains of supply and production, or that moved from industrial production toward investment banking as the leading "industry" in the United States. These shifting economic flows meant that the intended "multiplier effect" of each dollar of stimulus was more likely to be significantly undercut, thus muting the effect of Keynesian fiscal policy.[56]

But, as with Harvey's analysis, Stein's history depends on lining up binaries—national/global, industrial/financial—so as to create a coherent narrative, even if financialization and globalization do not always act in coherent relation to one another. As a result, she is able to produce a clear narrative that valorizes the nationalist approach that has long been adopted by the US labor movement, in which globalization is the primary problem and nationalist politics the primary solution.[57] An analysis that questions the coherence of these binaries opens other ways of understanding—and of actively organizing—relations between and among workers across local, national, and global economies.

For instance, Stein gives an account of changes in "extra-economic" social relations that all had an impact on the development of neoliberalism. Although she does not follow this route, her account could provide some crucial signposts for an understanding that moves beyond simple versions of economic causality. She documents how regional changes, particularly changing political relations in the US South, Midwest, and West, contributed to the policy choices of the 1970s. Stein describes George Wallace's surprising strength in the 1972 Democratic presidential primaries as based in the interaction of white racism, economic populism, and antigovernment rhetoric. Opposition to school busing as a means of desegregating public schools crystallized this combination of factors, but Wallace's appeal was not just to white segregationists. As Stein says, "By now, Wallace had moved beyond his racialism to attacks on government for favoring the rich."[58] In this way, discourse about economic policy was constituted in part through a mobile assemblage in which "school busing" and/or "small government" could serve as the leading edge of contestation.

In the 1970s, the explosiveness of antibusing activism connected a discourse opposing government interference in local communities to deep conflicts over race, gender, and sexuality. As Jane Dailey has documented, Southern Christians understood school desegregation in response to the Supreme Court decision in *Brown v. Board of Education* as a challenge to racial domination and the established hierarchies of the South, and they linked the fight against school desegregation to claims for "state's rights" that justified resistance to the implementation of federal policies.[59] Dailey also notes how the claim of "religious freedom" was appealed to as the justification for protecting the private, all-white

Christian schools that expanded across the South as a way to build a seg-regated educational network and avoid sending white Christian children to integrated schools.

School desegregation was perceived as threatening, in part, because it might create societal openness to cross-racial relationships of all kinds, including sexual relationships. Dailey documents the ways in which conservative Christian theology in the first half of the twentieth century tied the human catastrophes recounted in the Bible (the Fall, the Flood, and Sodom and Gomorrah) to the sin of miscegenation, and sex across racial boundaries was in many ways understood as an existential threat to what conservative Christians understood "the nation" to be. Here, once again, sexual politics provides scaffolding for racism, and in the shifting kaleidoscope of issues, both sexism and racism become tied to "small government" as the basis for the conservative political realign-ment emerging in the 1970s that carried forward in subsequent decades.

Gillian Frank, like Stein, views Wallace's 1972 presidential run in the Democratic primaries as crystallizing a set of issues that actually became central to the Republican policy agenda.[60] Frank focuses on the primary in the state of Michigan, which Wallace won: "Against the backdrop of George Wallace's Democratic primary victory, the Nixon and McGovern presidential campaigns and the battles over busing students to racially integrated schools, Michigan voters debated whether to reform the state's abortion laws. . . . The [state] referendum on abortion, known as Proposal B, received scrutiny in particular from the Nixon administration, which aspired to achieve political realignment by using social issues such as busing and abortion to forge a conservative political coalition . . . reveal-ing the ways that resistance to abortion and the backlash against busing were not separate strands, as they are usually presented, but deeply inter-twined and central to an emergent conservative politics."[61]

Advocates for abortion had initially framed the issue as one of ra-cial and economic equality, arguing that it should be legalized because "'our [existing] law [restricting abortion] has not stopped abortions; it has merely sent our poor women to the back alleys and our wealthier women to other states at inflated costs.'"[62] By contrast, opponents of abortion framed the issue as one of sexual permissiveness that threat-ened not only "family life," but raised the specter of general licentious-ness and "sexual chaos."[63]

Against these threats, protecting the white family became a connecting node between antibusing rhetoric and the antiabortion movement.[64] While reference to Nixon strategists' use of the "Southern strategy" to drive a racial wedge between the Democratic and Republican parties is relatively common, this strategy is often analyzed separately from the similar wedge that Nixon used with regard to abortion: "Richard Nixon and his supporters deliberately connected Michigan's battles over race and sexuality to each other and viewed each as paramount in a quest to build a national conservative political majority."[65] As Frank makes clear, the "Southern strategy" was not a single-issue strategy, and it did not just involve the South.[66] The politics of the 1970s thus show a shifting articulation of the cultural, political, social, and economic issues of race, class, religion, sex, gender, and nation that cannot be schematically pulled apart.

An analysis of this mobile constellation of issues can show the ways in which tying sexual politics to race and economics made religious conservatism into a power that contributed to the realignment of American politics. Splitting off specific issues makes it difficult to address the depth and breadth of this realignment, and the interlocking causes that contributed to it. Joseph E. Lowndes points out the importance of attending to "the deeper legacy of the modern Right . . . and the racial exclusions stretching back through the New Deal that helped lay the basis for later confrontations."[67] As Marisa Chappell argues in her history of "welfare reform," in addition to racial exclusions of the New Deal, the presumption of a "family wage" established one of the limits to advocacy on behalf of welfare provision and to the political coalition supporting the welfare state.[68] Robert O. Self extends this point with a compelling history of the type of white familialism that tied antibusing and antiabortion politics together with economics.[69] He argues that "[o]nly by considering the politics of gender, sex, and sexuality in tandem with—and just as often embedded in—the politics of race can we understand how breadwinner liberalism over the two decades after 1972 became breadwinner conservatism. For some whites, racial animosity fueled their breadwinner politics—in debates over affirmative action ('the best man for the job'), crime and welfare. For others, struggles over gender, sex and family were enough to propel them rightward."[70] In other words, racial and sexual politics *together* imagine what it means to be a "breadwinner."

Connecting these historical analyses to the mutual constitution of domination and exploitation points to the possibility that "racial animosity" and "struggles over gender, sex and family" might be interpreted as primary—not secondary—propellants of political realignment. Specifically, hegemonic values in regard to "the family" constitute the social relations that also organize how economic value is produced.[71] The important thing for some people is that there should be families and that those families should be male-headed and racially white. In this scenario, labor—the practice of breadwinning—should be structured to make and enforce gender and race relations within the paradigm of white familialism. Work is structured to produce "the family," just as much as family is structured to produce work.

Even this familial framework is not sufficient to fully characterize the lived reality of sexual politics. The family is an assemblage that implicates gender, sex, race, economics, education, and the nation, but it is also articulated with other assemblages. For example, in his chapter on religion, Self puts conservative religious familialism in the context of the Cold War. He highlights the growth of evangelical Christianity after World War II and the role of anticommunism in motivating many evangelicals to engage politically. For many in the United States, and for evangelical Christians in particular, communism provided a potent symbol of the triumph of secularism over religious commitments: "Believing themselves to be spiritually obligated to oppose 'godless communism,' evangelicals found new purpose after World War II."[72] These fears and the purposiveness in fighting them may have been made more powerful by their global scale, but they were often fought out in battles over schools and education, placing the protection of children and the family at the center of a global struggle. The sense of global implication gave urgency to fighting postwar Supreme Court rulings that were understood to be expanding secularism in public schools by outlawing denominational school prayer and Bible reading. Within this context, the limiting of official Christian expression in schools was read not as creating a public space open to all students regardless of religious commitment, but as the dominating imposition of state secularism and oppression of Christians.

Daniel K. Williams, in his *God's Own Party: The Making of the Christian Right*, highlights the development of connections between local struggles to protect the family by fighting the spread of secularism and the global struggle opposing communism. Williams offers a way of thinking about how these histories dynamically interrelate, showing that they are not simply static stacking boxes moving from intimate through national to global scales. He describes how battles over integrated schooling in the 1960s moved in the 1970s to conflicts over scientific sex education.[73] And in some cases the connection to the fight against sex education revitalized and transformed the fight against communism: "The campaign against sex education transformed anticommunist organizations into defenders of a broader, socially conservative agenda. In 1969 when the John Birch Society launched the Movement to Restore Decency (MOTOREDE), an anti-sex-education affiliate, the society was in decline, unable to attract new recruits with dire warnings of a communist conspiracy. Sex education, which the society members believed was a product of a communist plot, offered a more tangible enemy for social conservatives."[74]

Familialism is not just anticommunism instantiated at its smallest, most intimate level, but a driving force that works actively with anticommunism. The exchange between the two helps to hold both commitments in place, and the exchange runs in both directions: shifting from anticommunism to familialism proved effective for conservative political movements, like the John Birch Society, just as shifting from familialism to anticommunism embeds family values in politics at the global scale.[75] Fighting against "sex ed" and fighting a battle against international "evil" were now conjoined.

In another turn of the kaleidoscope, part of the material basis for both familialism and anticommunism in the 1970s was accelerating suburbanization.[76] Sex and religion are deeply implicated in the narrative of suburbanization, as demonstrated by Lisa McGirr's book, *Suburban Warriors*, on the development of new right activism in Orange County, California, in the 1960s. The story of suburbanization can be told in a number of different ways—as white flight and racial segregation, as a story of the postwar economic boom, as a technological and global economic story in which the combination of cheap automobiles and cheap oil makes it possible to separate living and working spaces by long distances. Yet, for all these different accounts, the story of suburbanization is rarely told as one of a specific arrangement of and fantasy about sexual relations, despite the fact that suburbs are also often referred to as "bed-room communities."

Suburbs are, in part, about a reorganization of familial forms as people moved away from both urban and rural extended families. Specifically, the sexual form of the nuclear family in a bedroom community is differ-ent than the extended family urban or small-town formations in which many Orange County residents had grown up. It represented a new way of living the "American dream" that conservative Christians simultane-ously heralded and enshrined as "traditional." But the nuclear family did not become the "traditional American family" until after World War II, and Orange County suburban warriors wrapped their traditional focus on the family in the dreamy new life of Southern California.[77]

Moreover, many of McGirr's suburban warriors were fighting for a new form of capitalism to accompany the suburbs' new familial form. McGirr quotes from a Christian book popular among Orange County conservatives that specifically contrasts freedom with personal security, with religion on the side of freedom rather than security:

> The weapons of hate and fear by which collectivists have moved a genera-tion of Americans to sell their freedom and integrity for security would never have worked had American roots in basic Judeo-Christian tradi-tions not first been severed.[78]

She cites this passage to explain how "Judeo-Christianity" is simultane-ously rooted in tradition and supports a commitment to the freedom of the market over a "collectivist" security provided by the state as a specifically Christian commitment. The dual nature of this commit-ment—at once market-based and Christian, new and traditional, free and stable—is crucial to political realignment, allowing the new conser-vatives to embrace both families and the free market and to manage the ambivalences and tensions between the market and family formation.[79]

Note how different the role is that religion plays in McGirr's story than in Harvey's. His story presumes that conservative Christians in the United States do not support the economic agenda of neoliberalism, but being so taken up by sexual politics, they misunderstand their economic interests and accede to the "construction of consent" for neoliberalism. By contrast, McGirr argues that, in the 1960s through the 1970s and into the 1980s, Christian conservatives, especially early Reagan supporters, *did* have specifically economic interests. Moreover, these interests were to promote and extend *changing* economic theory and economic practices, leaving behind the Keynesian consensus that had dominated both major political parties in the United States since the Depression.[80]

Sexual freedom aligns with the free market "culture of neoliberalism" in Harvey's story, while sexual conservatism aligns with the market in McGirr's.[81] When these stories are read together, the incoherence in the binaries undergirding Harvey's understanding comes to the fore. His story is incoherent as he moves Christians back and forth across the line between cultural and economic support for neoliberalism, because the line itself is incoherent.

If the "culture of neoliberalism" coherently extends freedom, including sexual freedom (as one version of Harvey's story tells it), then it is unclear why conservative Christians would support neoliberalism at all. If, however, the "culture of neoliberalism" is a productively incoherent one, in which issues are discursively separated from one another and then relinked in ways that create a moving assemblage, in which concepts and actors shift about in relation to one another, then various actors, including conservative Christians, can shift their attention and their energetic engagement across and among issues and across different meanings of freedom to create a sense of coherence that produces and maintains hegemonic social relations. Power is produced and maintained not in spite of incoherence, but through incoherence.

Schematic analyses obscure precisely the crosscutting relations in which religion and sexuality play complex roles in producing, as well as responding to, changing economic times. The separations among and across issues created by schematic analyses, particularly the separation between morality and materiality, are part of what allows religion and sexual politics to be harnessed to support neoliberalism regardless of whether one is promoting sexual freedom or sexual conservatism. Thus, it is important not just to tell a different story about sexual politics in the United States—it is important to tell a different *kind* of story.

The account I am developing here is one in which it is necessary to consider multiple factors when thinking about political economy, and these factors play complex, crosscutting, and disjunctive roles: liberal, conservative, neoliberal, neoconservative, religious, and secular positions together create the parameters of possible social policy. These elements do not necessarily fit neatly or easily with each other. They cannot simply be added together or lined up in a structurally consistent series of binary oppositions. Rather, they are concatenated, contradictory, disjunctive, and dynamically interrelated. Such an analysis allows for an understanding of neoliberalism that is built up out of pieces of policy, intertwining and diverging in sometimes unexpected ways, but also articulating with each other to make surprisingly resilient formations. In this story, opposition to sexual freedom can be understood as part of a productively incoherent assemblage that is at once traditional and new, stable and flexible, cultural and economic.

Producing Change

From the standpoint of ethical possibility, an analysis that takes productive incoherence seriously also offers different ways of understanding social change. Political scientist Ilene Grabel takes up the concept of "productive incoherence" as a way of shifting understandings of major global events like the 2008 financial crisis: "Instead of comprehensive change, the global crisis has induced ambiguous, uneven, modest, and cross-cutting initiatives that reflect continuities and discontinuities."[82] And in response to productively incoherent events, social change can also be built out of "uneven" and "modest" elements: "[T]he small, the disparate, the seemingly trivial, the experimental—these must not be discounted in advance because they don't amount to much, because they are not the embodiment of some grand, over-arching plan, because they are not scalable. . . . The potential for change . . . is located here in the disparate, the unplanned, the experimental, rather than in a new 'ism' to replace the eroding neoliberalism."[83]

These uneven elements can be connected through a "transverse solidarity," as described by political economist K. Ravi Raman.[84] Raman studies politics and activism in Kerala, India, and he has done an in-depth study of rural activism to get the Coca-Cola company to stop using the community of Plachimada's water and cease operations there. Raman provides a detailed ethnography of what he terms "a plurality of contested issues and struggles at multiple sites of power" that eventually allowed a "water-based subaltern movement" to force the transnational

Coca-Cola company to change its plans. He argues that the movement was successful by connecting a set of nonequivalent actors into translocal networks.

The very unevenness of these networks allows for the creation of a patchwork of actions across sectors, simultaneously engaging the state and realms well beyond the state, and creating unexpected possibilities for justice. Participants in the Plachimada movement included "a curious mix of environmentalists and social activists: the Gandhians, the moderates, the radical Maoists, and a large number of NGOs."[85] To say that this is a diverse and uneven group of people is an understatement. But the ability of the movement to maintain some uneven and undoubtedly contentious solidarity across these groups created a form of popularity that eventually meant the local government had no choice but to cancel the factory license for Coca-Cola's operations.

To return to the beginning of my alternative narration, Stein tells a story in which economic globalization and the move from industrial production to the predominance of finance capital are coherently related phenomena that represent the central problem of the 1970s. Globalization is not always the leading edge of financialization, however.[86] But Stein's schematic analysis allows her to separate domestic policy from global trade and to prevent a nationalist economic policy that protects US labor as the moral choice. In other words, the lineup of binaries that undergird Stein's analysis reinscribes the nation-state as the site of moral good.

One could, however, tell a story in which globalization is not in and of itself the (moral) problem; rather, the ethical critique could focus on the ways in which both nationalism and globalization are enmeshed with domination and exploitation. One of Spivak's concerns in "Scattered Speculations" is precisely to keep the international division of labor central to materialist analysis. Globalization can, for example, be read as part of larger nationalist agendas of the United States, including that of exploiting cheap labor in the global South.[87] As many of the policies of the Trump administration have shown, a focus on nationalism may have as many—or even more—detrimental effects on workers as does a focus on globalization.

A kaleidoscopic analysis of social relations and the type of translocal solidarity documented by Raman together offer a way to critique and contest both exploitation and domination, both globalization and nationalism. The creation of solidarities that traverse the boundaries between national and global may be the best, if not only, hope for workers around the world, including in the United States, to gain more justice in the workplace and in their lives. Such an approach might allow those who seek justice to traverse the boundaries of not only the local and the global, but also those dividing the cultural from the economic, gay liberation from anticolonial struggle, gender justice from housing and education, or sexual politics from worker justice.

3

Because the Social

In 1992, when William Jefferson Clinton won the election for the presidency of the United States over the incumbent, George H. W. Bush, he famously organized his campaign around the slogan "It's the economy, stupid." The slogan announced that the Democratic Party was focused on economic issues that affect everybody, but particularly working people, and that, by contrast, the patrician Mr. Bush and the Republican Party as a whole were out of touch with anyone struggling economically.[1] In the aftermath of the 2016 election, the charges were reversed: the Democratic candidate, Hillary Clinton, was said to be "out of touch" with workers hard hit by neoliberal economic policies. Further, some suggested Clinton should have focused less on the "identity politics" of gender and race and more on strictly economic issues.[2]

Bill Clinton's slogan may have focused on "the economy," but how he addressed that issue demonstrates how "identity politics," specifically the politics of race and gender, shaped his political initiatives and subsequent public discussions. While African Americans were an important constituency of the Democratic Party and Clinton's campaign signaled a cultural openness to African Americans, he also famously singled out from the supposedly inclusive issue of the economy recipients of government aid as depending upon outdated social supports created in the context of an old economic order that was coming to an end.[3] To optimize conditions for the new economy, he promised to "end welfare as we know it" and played up generalized racist resentment of "welfare recipients" dependent on so-called government handouts. American popular culture imagines those on welfare as poor Black people residing in cities, despite the fact that more white than Black people receive support from the government.[4] Clinton's promise to focus on the economy in conjunction with his promise "to end welfare as we know it" was thus a strategic appeal to white working-class voters (the constituents to whom Donald

Trump later appealed) who would know that their concerns were being addressed when he invoked "the economy."

The legislation eventually passed in response to Clinton's promise to advocate "welfare reform" was called the Personal Responsibility and Work Opportunity Reconciliation Act of 1996. The "personal responsibility" portion of the title suggests the significance of racial and sexual politics to this major overhaul of welfare. As both the *Congressional Record* and media coverage of the debate over the act show, politicians repeatedly declared that welfare supported "teenage pregnancy," a term widely recognized as code for young, poor, unmarried women of color.[5] "Personal responsibility" was supposed to be the antidote that would mean young poor people would no longer need government assistance. As social ethicist Traci West has documented, in arguing for the legislation, Clinton claimed that policy changes could cut the poverty rate by over 50 percent, stating that a crucial component of realizing this possibility was that "teenagers who are unmarried [don't] have babies."[6] Even after the legislation was passed, Clinton hyperbolically stated that "none [of the problems in US society] stands in our way of achieving our goals for America more than the epidemic of teen pregnancy."[7] Race and sex are highlighted in this turn of the kaleidoscope, not economics. And yet all of this talk about personal lives and young people's sexual behavior was part of a congressional debate that ended up changing one of the most important parts of the New Deal, the Social Security Act of 1935, which had created Aid to Families with Dependent Children (AFDC).

Contrary to the idea that conservative Christianity is the primary source of sexual conservatism in US politics, conservative Christians were positioned in many different ways during the debate over "welfare reform." Some conservative Protestants supported the new law, but many other Christian organizations and authorities, including the US Catholic Bishops Conference, opposed "welfare reform" and were not swayed by the appeal to sexual morality and fear of "teenage mothers."

The directive force of the tracks laid down by the usual ways of thinking mean that an analysis focused on answering "Why is sexuality so important in the US?" with "Because religion" cannot tell us much about how sexual politics worked in this debate. Nor can a turn to some other issue—economics perhaps—that can be isolated as "*the* cause" that shapes sexual politics in America while other issues fade into the background. Bringing one issue—or another—to the fore (with a turn of the kaleidoscope) is part of the dynamic mechanism that obscures much of what's actually happening in social relations. When Clinton focused on the economy, it made it seem as though he was leaving identity politics aside, creating room for the perception that he was progressive on issues of race and sex even as many of his policies, including his economic policies, were quite conservative *on precisely these issues*.

Whenever an issue, like the economy, is pulled out of its context and isolated, other issues form a pattern around it. As we saw in the last chapter, isolating the issue of "small government" can be a means of articulating a program of fiscal conservatism separate from socially conservative issues like school integration through busing and opposition to abortion. But it also creates a pattern in which "small government" can invoke these very issues without explicitly naming them. When a Democrat like Clinton similarly wants to focus on economic issues, it also forms a pattern with race and sexuality.

These two patterns do not match up precisely. Clinton did, in fact, support certain progressive issues on race and sexuality, including affirmative action and an Equal Pay Initiative.[8] There are many ways in which the Clinton administration and the Bush administrations that preceded and succeeded it were different. But these patterns do contain many of the same pieces, and when they are presented as completely different from each other, it is easy to lose sight of the common sense upon which they both draw.

The turning of the political kaleidoscope makes it seem as if the political world is repeatedly changing, even as it holds in place many of the basic hierarchies that have constituted the US for centuries. Given that the patterns are actually shifting even as they maintain social structures (in other words, given mobility for stasis), the analytic challenge is to be able to follow the effects of the shifting patterns, including their disjunctions, while also bringing to the fore their dynamic interrelation as the kaleidoscope turns.

This chapter traces some of the political effects resulting from the creation of predominant public narratives that divide issues from each other, including narratives that promote the sense of issues as singular. The disjunctions created by the assertion that economics, or sex, or race is a singular, coherent, and separable issue have the effect of reinforcing social hierarchies. Kimberlé Crenshaw's initial essay on the concept of intersectionality, for example, showed how the treatment of race and sex as separate and singular issues in the law had the effect of marginalizing Black feminist concerns from the struggles for both feminist *and* antiracist justice.[9] None of these divisions are necessary or necessarily reflective of the parameters of either the issues or the movements that have taken them up, but these divisions do have effects and thus need analytic attention.

Looked at in one way, sexual politics seems like a major point of partisan division in the United States. For example, the "global gag rule," officially known as the Mexico City Policy, was instituted by President Reagan to refuse US funding to any organization that promoted or even mentioned abortion. The policy has been repeatedly rescinded by Democratic presidents (Clinton and Obama) and reinstated by Republican presidents (George W. Bush and Trump).[10] These repeated shifts are often taken as but one instance of fundamental differences between the two major political parties on gender and sexuality. But, as the examples in this chapter will show, there are also longstanding points of consistency between the parties when it comes to sex and gender, a consistency not always recognized. The idea of a clear partisan divide on sexual politics is produced by focusing on gender and sex as if they are singular issues concerned only with reproductive issues, same-sex marriage, or transgender access to public bathrooms—important issues all, and ones that are embedded in dynamic interactions belied by the singular sense of gender or sex. This sense of what makes for sexual politics misses the ways in which gender and sex are part of a broad range of policy issues: economics, immigration, housing, the environment to name a few. Structures of power depend on relations among issues even as they obscure those relations. If it seems as though there are only differences between the Democratic and Republican parties on issues of gender and sexuality, it becomes much harder to follow the effects of sexual politics or to understand the parameters of hegemony.

Because Is Not the Answer

The major examples in this chapter follow the interrelation of different issues of public policy—economic policy, healthcare, and war and peace—as they are imbricated with social relations—race, sex, class, and gender. One of the ways in which the sense of interrelation is lost is through the hope of isolating a primary cause for social issues. The hope embedded in starting any answer to a social question with "because" is a powerful one: finding the cause of social problems promises to tell us how to develop an effective solution. For example, consider the efforts of John Chisholm, a prosecutor in Milwaukee who put this hope into practice. Chisholm worked with the Vera Institute of Justice to do an independent study of the use of prosecutorial discretion in the Milwaukee County district attorney's office.[11] The conclusions of the study showed a racial disparity in cases related to nonviolent crime: "According to the Vera study, prosecutors in Milwaukee declined to prosecute forty-one per cent of whites arrested with possession of drug paraphernalia, compared with twenty-seven per cent of blacks; in cases involving prostitution, black female defendants were likelier to be charged than white defendants; in cases that involved resisting or obstructing an officer, most of the defendants charged were black (seventy-seven per cent), male (seventy-nine per cent) and already in custody (eighty per cent of blacks versus sixty-six per cent of whites)."[12]

Given the results of the Vera Institute study, Chisholm hoped that changes in his office might also shift the disproportion in the number of African Americans sent to prison in Milwaukee County. He instituted an extensive program to change the standard practices, including moving prosecutors' offices into the neighborhoods for which they were responsible. Even though shifts in prosecutorial behavior had been identified as the lead variable in a quantitative analysis of the causes of increased incarceration, and even though Chisholm's program did decrease the number of African Americans prosecuted for crimes like possession of drug paraphernalia, "the change in the makeup of the prison population has been modest."[13] As Chisholm says, "We redesigned our system but we learned that no individual actor can change dynamics of what goes on in a complex larger system like a city."[14]

One possible way to create a more expansive analysis is to move from the search for a single variable as the leading causal factor to a multivariable approach. For example, Theda Skocpol, a historical sociologist, developed a multicausal understanding of the development of the welfare state in relation to multiple axes of social difference, showing the influence of class-based politics and of gender politics, as well as the effects of industrialization, state formation, and the actions of political parties, labor unions, and other activists.[15] And one could certainly add factors to an analysis like Skocpol's: the historian Maureen Fitzgerald demonstrated the relevance of religious difference by showing how Protestant presumptions in government and discrimination against Catholic immigrants in the United States were central to the formation of the welfare state. Its bureaucracy grew in part through ideas about the "welfare" of Catholic children that supported the practice of removing them from their homes and placing them with Protestants.[16] Historian Marisa Chappell has demonstrated how the idea of the "family wage," structured around the responsibilities borne by a man to provide for his family, undergirded arguments on behalf of building the welfare state.[17] Domestic work is also part of this story. As Eileen Boris and Jennifer Klein argue in their recent history of home healthcare in the twentieth-century US, it is productive to "rethink the history of the American welfare state from the perspective of care work."[18] Boris and Klein show in great detail the ways in which state policies, including a "state-subsidized medical sector," have produced an economy in which caring labor both in public institutions and in private homes is a major growth industry. In other words, even when caring labor is marked as "private," that labor is still fundamentally intertwined with state and economic policy.

As you can see, the centrality of racial and sexual politics to the welfare state is a repetitive discovery: Skocpol's book was published in 1992, while Boris and Klein called for a "rethinking" of the history of the welfare state in 2012. Of course! In this example, public policy and private social relations work together to make the welfare state; nonetheless, the centrality of these "private" relations to the welfare state must be reiterated for decades. The reality of interrelation often disappears as public and private are analyzed as separate spheres, effectively removing the consideration of gender, race, and sex from public policy, except when such policy expressly addresses these categories.

Efforts to include all possible variables in a single, coherent vision of "the social" repeatedly prove to be inadequate precisely because the social is created by divisions, such as that between public and private or between religion and secularism. Even a multivariable analysis cannot break through some of the analytical blocks created by the ways in which issues are usually framed.

This problem suggests the need not just for more variables, but also for an approach that can analytically hold together issues like sexual politics *and* issues, like the formation of the welfare state, in which sexual politics is indirectly invoked but nonetheless plays a crucial role. As the example of Clinton's focus on "the economy, stupid" in order to reform "the welfare state" shows, the splits between public and private in this instance have real effects on policy.

The Social Body Multiple

In seeking to analyze these effects, I turn to the method offered by medical ethnographer Annemarie Mol.[19] Mol articulates a feminist and materialist understanding of assemblage.[20] As a medical ethnographer, she focuses on the practices that constitute the body.[21] She details these practices in different sites—doctor's office, lab, and operating room—and shows how these different sites, through different material practices, constitute not only different understandings of embodiment, but different bodies.

Mol also analyzes the habits of thought that produce an understanding of the body as unitary, that is, ways of thinking that suppress potentially disjunctive data so as to reinforce a model of unified knowledge. By providing a critique of these mechanisms, she shows how the diversity and complexity of the world is reduced through habitual ways of thinking. By developing and sustaining a vision of multiplicity, however, one can engage the world in its amplitude.

Mol develops this approach through an ethnography of the disease atherosclerosis, in which plaque builds up inside blood vessels causing blockages that can be quite painful, particularly when walking. By carefully documenting her observations of atherosclerosis in different settings, she shows that the disease itself is different if one is in the clinic listening to descriptions of symptoms; if one is in the operating room creating openings in a patient's veins; or if one is in the lab measuring blockages. These differences create divergent versions of the disease: the symptoms might not be of the relative severity that would be indicated by lab results measuring a patient's blood vessels; or they may be more severe, yet not relieved by surgery; or the surgeon may well be surprised by the diagnostician's conclusion based on the lab work. Mol suggests that an accurate rendering of the disease would acknowledge the multiple realities of illness.[22]

Rather than acknowledge the body multiple, however, the usual approach is to employ various epistemological mechanisms by which these discontinuous versions of the disease are made to line up. A sense of coherence is produced through modes of thinking Mol names "coordination," "distribution," and "inclusion."[23] These mechanisms exclude, obscure, or rearrange certain aspects of reality (in Mol's study, the reality of the diseased body) in order to maintain a coherent sense of the whole. Knowledge can be coordinated by adding elements together or by suppressing some elements and focusing on others so as to produce a single social reality.[24]

Mol writes: "[Atherosclerosis] is *both* pain *and* a clogged up artery but not both in the same site. It is pain in diagnosis and a clogged up artery in treatment. Reality is *distributed*."[25] In the clinic, the physician and the patient deal with a body experiencing pain that may or may not be produced by sclerotic arteries; opened by the scalpel, the veins reveal a different body to the vision of the surgeon and students in the operating theater; as postsurgical tissue samples under the microscope, the body is yet a third, highly magnified reality to the one looking through the lenses. In any single setting the disease appears as one coherent thing because its manifestation in other settings is blocked out. The fact that these different manifestations *might not* cohere when brought together is thereby also obscured by breaking them out into their individual disciplinary and institutional settings.

Yet these different bodies are also actively brought together to create coherence. For instance, different enactments of the disease can be forced into line by focusing on one enactment and suppressing the others. Which of the discordant enactments of the disease comes to dominate has implications for what kind of treatment is involved, the level of invasiveness that accompanies treatment, who provides the treatment (surgeons or physical therapists), how long the treatment takes, and how the success of the treatment is measured.[26]

And as Mol notes, the very idea of the disease "atherosclerosis" that operates as a "coordinating mechanism" among these distributed versions of reality: "[I]t bridges the boundaries between the sites over which the disease is distributed. It thereby helps to prevent distribution from becoming the pluralizing of a disease into separate and unrelated objects. Distribution, instead, sets apart what also, elsewhere, a little further along, or slightly later is linked up again. It multiplies the body and its diseases—which hang together even so."[27]

Most importantly for *The Sex Obsession*, the epistemological mechanisms, like "coordination" and "distribution," that Mol describes are also used in social analysis. Specifically, once gender and sexuality are separated from other issues, sexual politics can be distributed to sites where it can be deemed unimportant—the private concerns of the domestic sphere, for example. Sex can then be linked back to other issues "slightly later" where it can become an incredibly effective driver of all kinds of policies, even as its influence is discredited and ignored because those policies are not the recognized sites of sexual politics. So when gender and sexuality are removed from economics to produce a singular focus like Clinton's on "the economy, stupid," politics is distributed. Sexual and economic politics are separated in Clinton's initial claim to focus only on the economy and then coordinated by being added back together "further down the line" to enact major policies such as "welfare reform."

My interest, then, in reading social relations as constituting a "body multiple" is not based on an analogy between social and physical "bodies," but on the fact that the same epistemological *practices* for producing coherence out of complexity in embodied life are also employed to produce coherence out of the complexity of social relations: "[T]he singularity of objects, so often presupposed, turns out to be an accomplishment."[28] For the social body, this active accomplishment is the production of a singular idea of the "social," despite the complexity, multiplicity, and contradictions of social relations. When understood as a social body multiple, it is possible to study the ways the social does and does not cohere.

Sexual Politics as Public Policy

In the rest of this chapter, I will explore practices in which gender and sexuality are both separate from *and* also integral to political issues like economics, public health, or war. As we have seen, in the usual narrative sex is linked only to religion and morality and is divided from race and economics. As Mol describes, "distribution" and other attendant ways of thinking tend to create a common sense in which different actors who might experience disjunction instead tend to experience coherence across a disjunctive social field. Distribution and coordination create a "productive incoherence."

Looking at examples across the administrations of Bill Clinton, George W. Bush, Barack Obama, and Donald Trump can help us address key questions about "how we got here" and also challenge common narratives about partisan divides as based on a simple division. As always in this book, I am interested in how "liberal" and "secular" policies and politicians often share narratives with "conservative" and "religious" advocates. Although these different presidential administrations represent both Democratic and Republican leadership of the United States, in all of the cases, sexual politics plays a major role in a range of issues, including those rarely associated with sexual politics: economics, healthcare, international relations, war and peace.

Clinton

One might think that an analysis of sexual politics and the Clinton administration would focus on the Defense of Marriage Act, passed in 1996 and overturned in 2013 (see chapter 4), or Clinton's "Don't Ask, Don't Tell" policy with regard to gay people serving in the armed forces, or perhaps his impeachment for lying about his sexual affair with a White House intern, Monica Lewinsky. But, in fact, Clinton's entanglement with sexual politics runs across issues central to his administration. Canvassing the issues not usually associated with "sex" can help us to understand the obscuring effects of distributing issues among categories. Looking at the public policies advanced by the Clinton administration *while keeping sexual politics in mind*—rather than assuming that sex is irrelevant unless directly invoked—is a way to address that complexity.

Clinton advocated for a new welfare system throughout his first term in office, while also resisting Republican measures that seemed to go "too far" for his centrist constituency. He vetoed two early versions of "welfare reform" bills that included cuts to the earned income tax credit; then, in 1996, facing the pressure of his reelection campaign, he signed the Personal Responsibility and Work Opportunity Reconciliation Act (Public Law 104–93), saying that while the bill "has serious flaws . . . [t]his is the best chance we will have for a long time to complete the work of ending welfare as we know it."[29]

The news articles written at the time Clinton signed the Personal Responsibility and Work Opportunity Reconciliation Act hardly mention gender and sexuality, not even the fact that "welfare reform" particularly affects women (studies estimate that approximately 90 percent of welfare recipients are women).[30] But when one turns to expert witnesses testifying before Congress on behalf of the bill, to the *Congressional Record* of debate over the bill, or to Clinton's own statements, including his weekly radio address and his 1995 State of the Union speech, one finds that the focus is rarely on "the economy, stupid" or on the major change to economic policy that "welfare reform" represents. Rather, when it comes to the political process itself, the focus is on "teenage pregnancy."[31]

In the congressional debate, both Democrats and Republicans appealed to rhetoric about illegitimate children and teenage motherhood that followed a long history of connecting policy regarding poverty to a conservative sexual and racial politics.[32] In a set of remarks that shows both the effectiveness and dangers of causal claims in political argument, Democrat Joseph Lieberman argued that a focus on teenage motherhood was one of the central sites of bipartisan support for the bill. Lieberman went on to state directly that "teenage out-of-wedlock pregnancy is a primary cause of long-term welfare dependency,"[33] even though at an earlier point in the debate he had claimed that welfare dependency was a causal factor in the growth of teen pregnancy.[34] Similarly, Republican senator Duncan "Lauch" Faircloth argued "the root cause of welfare dependency is illegitimacy."[35] In Clinton's statement in support of the conference report (which combines the House and

Senate versions of the legislation), the president highlighted "requiring teen mothers to stay in school" as the first relevant policy already accomplished by his administration and reiterated his persistent themes of "work, responsibility, and family."[36]

Democratic Senator Bill Bradley from New Jersey was one of the only voices to point out ways in which the debate repeatedly connected economic policy to the politics of race, gender, and sex: "Welfare reform is a politician's dream [and] a poor person's nightmare. . . . AFDC, $15 billion out of a $1.5 trillion budget, has been a political football in this country for generations; in some cases, a racialized political football, as politician after politician created in the mind of the public the idea that black women had children so that they could collect $64 per month for that third child in New Jersey."[37] He later noted that the entire debate on welfare reform was "built on generations of using this issue as a code word for a lot of other things in American politics,"[38] including race, poverty, unemployment, and violence.

Clinton's appropriation of this longstanding discourse tying together gender, sexuality, race, and economics was in no way unusual.[39] The most famous articulation of this rhetoric has likely been its circulation in the form of the so-called Moynihan Report, produced in the Johnson White House by then Assistant Secretary of Labor Daniel Patrick Moynihan, who later served as an advisor to Richard Nixon and then as a Democratic senator from New York.[40] The basic tenets of the narrative developed in this report were that poverty in the United States, particularly in African American communities, was attributable to a breakdown in family structure, which deviated from the then normative form of the middle-class nuclear family. This narrative restricted the image of appropriate family relations to the supposedly traditional but historically specific (even unusual) postwar American nuclear family and made those domestic arrangements the causal variable with respect to poverty.[41] This narrative has been repeatedly recirculated despite equally repeated interventions on the part of activists, particularly African American women activists, who vigorously contest its logic.[42] And, in fact, this nuclear family and its stability have everything to do with the demobilization of millions of mostly white men from the US military after World War II, and government policies designed specifically to support them. In other words, the type of government support decried by opponents of "welfare" created much of the twentieth-century middle class and its specific familial formation; these programs included the GI Bill, tract housing, and much more. By ignoring this history and instead embedding gender, sexuality, and race in an economic narrative about work ethic and class mobility, politicians and commentators invoke and enact prescriptions for ending poverty through conservative sexual politics and the promotion of marriage.

Religion also had a role to play in the debate over "welfare reform," but it was not as a simple force for sexual regulation. Rather, specifically Christian discourses were invoked on both sides of the debate. As none other than Senator Moynihan noted, some of the strongest opponents of the bill were religious groups. Moynihan opposed the bill because of the seriousness of the change it would make to the structure of the welfare state. And he was joined by many powerful Christian institutions: "[T]here is one unified voice [in opposition to the legislation]: that of every national religious group and faith-based charity. But we seem unable or unwilling to listen. They all oppose ending the entitlement. Catholic Charities USA and the Catholic bishops, especially the National Council of Churches, Bread for the World, have persisted in this matter. Other [nonreligious] organizations are once again silent."[43] This coalition between a mainline Protestant organization (National Council of Churches) a poverty-focused evangelical organization (Bread for the World), and Catholic authorities and organizations stands in striking contrast to the alliance that the Clinton administration and its supporters forged between conservative and evangelical Christians and secular claims about poverty, sex, race, and economics.

In 1995, for example, Clinton made connections among religion, sexual morality, and neoliberal economics in a speech to the Progressive National Baptists.[44] And throughout his advocacy of "welfare reform," Clinton argued that the policy would help to inculcate order and discipline in the American family, invoking a powerful set of assumptions about family structure, ethical values, and the capitalist discipline of the Protestant ethic.[45] When it came to the legislative debate, direct Christian influence proved less powerful than this linkage of conservative Christian rhetoric and a potent neoliberal belief that individuals must be responsible for their own welfare.

One of the most poignant moments in the debate was in Senator Moynihan's statement. He began with a quotation from Hannah Arendt's *The Origins of Totalitarianism* about the moment in which "all hope has died" and went on to the make the point that "something fundamental" was about to happen with the passage of the bill: "What is about to happen is we are going to repeal title IV-A of the Social Security Act, the provision established in 1935 to that act, aid to families with dependent children."[46] Moynihan was one of the few participants in the debate to state directly the gravity of the proposed legislation, which contravened the New Deal emphasis on socializing risk so that no one would be left unprotected and destitute.[47] The disjunction between Moynihan's position on this particular policy and his contribution to the surrounding discourse, specifically to the connection between nonnormative family structure and economic issues, illustrates the ways in which contributions to a broader discourse have power well beyond the intentions or control of those who initially produce them.

When issues are separated through the mechanism of distribution, "cultural issues" or "identity politics" like race, gender, and sexuality are separated from social policy on economics and crime. Then when these issues are relinked "a little further along," powerfully moral understandings of teenage promiscuity and social instability can be articulated with neoliberal language about individual responsibility and productivity. And these issues can be further linked to the importance of getting rid of welfare entitlements that wrongly burden the state. The epistemology of distribution makes such racist, sexist, paternalistic discourse seem sensible. In news articles about "welfare reform" and the new economy, the focus is on politics and policy, with no mention of "teenage pregnancy." In the congressional debate, the focus is on "teenage pregnancy" with little recognition of the magnitude of the change to economic policy. Moynihan's eloquence on the floor of the Senate about the need to secure decent futures for everyone, the very premise of welfare, may be heartfelt, but he alone cannot return the discourse to focus on social security and the magnitude of the change being made.

The final bill set up four major goals for the Temporary Assistance to Needy Families (TANF) program that replaced AFDC, two of which focused on gender and sexuality, including marriage promotion so as to maintain two-parent families and an end to out-of-wedlock births.

A third goal promoted the combination of marriage, job training, and work as the way to "end dependence of needy families on government benefits."[48] In the end, the Personal Responsibility and Work Opportunity Reconciliation Act of 1996 codified racialized sexual politics as the basis for economic policy to fight poverty.[49]

Remarkably, criminal justice legislation enacted during the Clinton presidency also appealed to normative understandings of race, gender, and sexuality in its justifications. In 1994, Congress passed and Clinton signed a major new crime bill, the Violent Crime and Law Enforcement Act, the debate over which had focused on young men of color, rather than young women,[50] although, crucially, the idea of saving women was made part of it as the Violence Against Women Act was folded into the bill.[51] This apex of "criminal justice reform" imposed longer sentences for a number of criminal offenses and expanded funding for both policing and prisons. The bill is now generally acknowledged as a contributing factor in the massive expansion of the prison system in the subsequent decades, making it one of the most economically, socially, politically, and morally consequential acts of Clinton's eight years in the White House.[52]

The Movement for Black Lives has urged the public to take seriously the incalculable moral and material costs of expanded policing and prisons.[53] As Michelle Alexander and a number of other commentators have pointed out, in public statements supporting the bill, Hillary Clinton drew on the same kind of coded language that was found everywhere in the debate over "welfare reform." Only this time the references were to young men of color: "They are not just gangs of kids anymore," she said. "They are often the kinds of kids that are called 'super-predators.'"[54] Senator Bradley understood that when "teenage mothers" are named in a debate, anti-Black racism has already ensured that young Black women are the referent. Similarly, Clinton's comments about specific "kinds of kids" effectively invokes the image of threatening young men of color.

In her 2016 presidential campaign, Clinton expressed regret for her support for the bill and for her statements in articulating that support, but, as with Moynihan's poignant and futile effort to remedy the effects of a discourse he had initially facilitated, the question is not really one of individual comprehension and motivation. Instead we must ask how discourses are institutionally, effectively, and affectively assembled.[55]

Immigration is another point at which politics can be broken down into component parts—"immigration politics" and "sexual politics"—so that those parts can be distributed and then reconnected "a little later." In the Immigration Reform and Immigrant Responsibility Act of 1996, the politics of gender and sexuality disappear into the privatized family at the center of immigration policy.[56] As with the similarly named "welfare reform" bill, "personal responsibility" imagined as a dedication to work and family is central to this immigration policy. As Chandan Reddy points out, the 1996 act built on the 1990 immigration bill, which "capped the number of immigrant visas for so-called unskilled workers at a paltry 10,000 visas each year, while it increased family-based immigrant visas to 480,000 annually beginning in 1995."[57] Such a focus enforces normative understandings of gender, sex, and family and makes immigrants dependent on family members who are often more powerful in terms of both familial status and material resources. With the dismantling of state support through "welfare reform," Reddy notes that "workers brought in through family reunification have increasingly been forced to depend on family ties for access to room and board, employment, and other services, such as healthcare, child care, and what amounts to workplace injury insurance. . . . In sum, the new federal structure has increased immigrants' exposure to and structural dependence on heteronormative and patriarchal relations and regulatory structures."[58] Once again, policy "reform" under the Clinton administration meant immigration law and policy shifted national responsibilities into the private realm of familial support—and the brisk discipline of capital.

As I will explicate further below, Donald Trump's turn of the kaleidoscope kept familialism at the center of the pattern, intensifying the economic pressure on immigrant families while enlarging the central focus on white familialism. The Trump administration's attacks on family reunification policy and his invective against immigrants seems, on the face of it, to be directly opposed to the immigration policies of his predecessors. He rails against all immigration, including legal immigration, and effectively criminalizes all Latinx and Muslim immigrants, including those living in the US legally or waiting for asylum hearings. Yet there is a continuity that links these statements and his policies to those of his predecessors. Specifically, the Trump administration extended the thread of the 1996 bill demanding "personal responsibility" of all immigrants by creating a "public charge" rule that would deny green cards or visas to immigrants, including legal immigrants, who make use of any government services, including food stamps, housing vouchers, or Medicaid.[59] The immigrant family should be made "responsible" for all of its members.

To enforce this privatized "responsibility," immigration policies of the latter part of the twentieth century and the first two decades of the twenty-first have expanded the policing of immigrants and contributed to the militarization of the border. Before Clinton's 1996 "immigration reform," immediate deportation was enforced for crimes carrying penalties of five years or more. The new legislation has made a wide range of crimes, including minor offenses, grounds for deportation, including the deportation of lawful permanent residents of the United States. The Trump administration, with the support of the US Supreme Court, intensified this policy as well, while also increasing restrictions on legal immigration through new policies and changes to asylum law.[60]

In order to shift the popular focus more toward the evocation of family values as embodied in white, Christian, and specifically Protestant, families, Trump picked up the thread of longstanding discourse that focuses on the sexual and reproductive practices of immigrants. He attacked family reunification as "chain migration" and spoke of revoking birthright citizenship, claiming (falsely) that pregnant women are crossing the Mexican border illegally for the sole purpose of giving birth to "anchor babies" who are American citizens.[61] Trump also picked up on the George W. Bush administration's gendered conservatism with regard to Islam, reigniting discourses about Islam and "honor crimes" as a way to raise suspicion about Muslim immigrants.

As we follow the turns of the kaleidoscope from the Clinton administration to the Trump administration, we see that the patterns are not the same, but many of the pieces that make up the patterns are. Trump uses immigration policy to create a nationalist neoliberalism rather than a globalist neoliberalism. This is a significant difference, but it is not the case that Trump changed everything. Instead, he extended policy tracks like personal responsibility and militarized border control that had been laid down decades before while keeping sexual politics at the center of any discussion of immigration.

Public policy is assembled through the relations of moral and material practices. Moral claims make it seem natural that the welfare state should be reformed by promoting marriage and ending "teenage pregnancy," and habits of thought developed in the 1990s—or as far back as the Moynihan Report in the 1960s—continue to constrain what is morally thinkable and materially possible. The alternative to epistemological distribution between moral and material concerns I've traced thus far is to understand issues as dynamically interacting with each other from the start, and to trace their movement in relation to each other. Such an analytical approach does not produce a newly coherent picture of the whole of social life. As Mol points out, analyzing the distribution of issues and its political effects is not meant to recoordinate them so that they all fall into line starting from a single point of equivalence. Rather, addressing the epistemology of distribution can allow disjunctive and incommensurate realities to become knowable in relation to each other.

Bush

In 2005, at the second inauguration of George W. Bush, the president gave a twenty-one-minute inaugural address in which he used the word "freedom" twenty-seven times and mentioned "liberty" fifteen times.[62] Indeed, "freedom" was the major moral claim of his administration and its policies. He emphasized the superiority of free market economics, the freedom enjoyed by citizens of a democracy, and the freedom of women in the United States, who enjoy a liberation supposedly unknown to women living under oppressive regimes.

And sexual politics was central to Bush's politics of freedom, just as it had been central to Clinton's focus on the economy. Returning to an example discussed in the introduction, consider the president and First Lady Laura Bush's sudden concern for saving the women of Afghanistan just before the American invasion in fall 2001.[63] The Bush administration here used gender and sexuality to define the US as the home of freedom and equality, despite the administration's own sexual conservatism on a number of issues.[64]

Freedom was such a catchword for the Bush administration in part because in that single word a number of issues could be tied together. It served as the banner under which the Bush administration pursued war in Iraq, naming the 2003 invasion Operation Iraqi Freedom. And the invocation of "freedom" tied this war together with (1) the "war on terrorism" begun in 2001, (2) global capitalism, (3) the imperative to spread US-style democracy, and (4) a conservative sexual ethic.[65]

The policies enabled by this assembled sense of freedom are exemplified by President Bush's AIDS policy. In his State of the Union address in 2003, Bush announced the formation of the President's Emergency Plan for AIDS Relief (PEPFAR), with significant new levels of funding for AIDS prevention and treatment around the world.[66] It is worth exploring this policy in detail because it is widely regarded as the most progressive—and in some analyses as the most successful—undertaking of the Bush administration. Over the years, however, it became apparent that the enactment of the policy was geared toward promoting sexual conservatism as much as toward disease prevention. The funding structure included requirements that a percentage of the funds go to abstinence-only work with a concomitant reduction in the distribution and use of condoms.[67] The denigration of condoms as a tool for public health was widely reported in the US press, particularly after the Centers for Disease Control in 2002 removed information from its webpage that reported the effectiveness of condoms.[68] What was less frequently remarked upon in the mainstream US press is that this conservative push to remake sexual relations was not confined to the United States, but was, in fact, a global effort.[69]

The evangelist Franklin Graham argued in a 2001 address to Congress that the US should promote fundamental "lifestyle change" in Africa that would bring familial forms into line with Protestant norms; his reasoning was in line with President Bush's ideas as enacted in PEPFAR: "Education is inadequate without the teaching that the only reliable way to avoid contracting AIDS through sexual contact is by maintaining a lifelong monogamous relationship. But just as important, we must recognize that the ability to adopt such dramatic lifestyle changes is almost impossible without the moral conviction that sex outside of a marriage between a man and a woman is contrary to God's law. This crisis will be curbed only when the moral teachings of God's Word permeate African society."[70] This approach centered on "moral teachings" was codified in a policy that the Bush administration called "ABC": abstinence until marriage, being faithful in marriage, and if A and B fail, then (and only then) should condoms be used. Because condoms, not marriage, are the only actual barriers to the spread of HIV, the efforts by both the evangelist and the president to put marriage before condoms signaled a willingness to risk the spread of HIV in an effort to remake sexual values globally.[71] Uganda, for example, which had extensive programs for the distribution of condoms and which had seriously cut rates of HIV infection over the course of the 1990s, curtailed such efforts.[72]

Perhaps most importantly, this policy accounted for neither the economic pressures faced by many poor people, where the intertwining of sexual and economic exchange may be crucial to immediate survival, nor gender hierarchy, where the question of who is faithful to whom and how is not simply one of personal will. But this was not just a failure of ethical accounting; it was also a use of US funds on a large scale to create a discourse, with all of its attendant power of inducement and coercion, of Protestant family values in areas of the world where people may well not have cared about US Protestantism or American ideas about marriage, family, and sexual faithfulness. Nonetheless, the US ramped up the global remaking of the family, an initiative that became a not-inconsiderable part of US foreign policy.

In his annual address to the United Nations in 2005, Bush connected the conservative sexual ethic of his AIDS policy to both winning the "war on terror" and spreading global capitalism. By 2005, the wars in Afghanistan and Iraq that he had begun were looking far from winnable, so he shifted his focus from military victory to winning "the battle of ideas." He professed his conviction that the United States needed to do everything possible to prevent countries anywhere in the world from becoming "havens for terrorists." To win this front in the "war on terrorism," Bush committed the United States to take up the fight against AIDS and malaria, assume leadership in the push to relieve the burden of highly indebted nations, and continue to insist on the importance of eliminating trade barriers and opening free markets worldwide.[73]

Fighting AIDS and malaria are thus intertwined with the US military project and an economic agenda that gestures toward reducing the burden of debt, but that also crucially promotes global trade by lifting "barriers to the free flow of goods and services." Once again, the answer to poverty—including now poverty worldwide—is to connect a conservative sexual ethic (in this case, the "ABC" of Bush's AIDS policy) to the unfettering of capitalism and increasing militarization. "Freedom" for the Bush administration comes to mean markets, militarism, *and* marriage.

Obama

In many ways, the Obama administration could not have been more different than those that preceded it. As the first Black president of the United States, Obama was invested with great hope for change and faced with both extraordinary political opposition and political complications, the effects of which deepened profoundly with the election of his successor. Obama's policies were certainly not those of the socialist that his opponents on the right claimed him to be, nor even those of the left wing of the Democratic party.[74] But he was also in certain ways constrained by the very politics of his historical accomplishment.[75] As a Black man, his commitment to heteronormativity was continually scrutinized. On the first anniversary of his historic election, the *New York Times Magazine* chose to focus not on his policies, but on his marriage as the site for considering the meaning of his election the previous year.[76] Certainly, some of his policy ambivalence on issues of gender and sexuality can be traced to the difficult negotiations he faced as a Black man and thus always already sexually suspect.[77]

One of the ways in which the Obama administration negotiated these political complexities was through relying on, while attempting to recombine, the long-standing tropes of sexual politics in the US. Obama's administration, like its predecessors, was thus committed to weaving together normative sexual politics, economics, and global relations. At its start, the administration reiterated ties among familialism, economics, and national security and located them very close to home in the Office of Faith-Based and Neighborhood Partnerships. As with both Clinton and Bush, the gender and economic relations that Obama was most interested in remaking were those of poor families, and as with the Bush administration, this type of familialism was tied directly to international relations.

This Obama administration office was set up not only to maintain the program that Bush had established as the Office of Faith-Based and Community Initiatives (which was itself an expanded version of the "charitable choice" provision in the Clinton-era "welfare reform" bill), but also to further expand beyond "faith-based" organizations to "neighborhoods" and communities.[78] According to the administration's original vision, published in 2009, the office would no longer simply provide a mechanism for monies to go to community groups, but would also have an advisory role on policy. Moreover, this extension into the administration's development of policy had a broad reach, including both domestic and foreign policy issues:

> The Office's top priority will be making community groups an integral part of our economic recovery and poverty a burden fewer have to bear when recovery is complete.
>
> It will be one voice among several in the administration that will look at how we support women and children, address teenage pregnancy, and reduce the need for abortion.
>
> The Office will strive to support fathers who stand by their families, which involves working to get young men off the streets and into well-paying jobs, encouraging responsible fatherhood.
>
> Finally, beyond American shores this Office will work with the National Security Council to foster interfaith dialogue with leaders and scholars around the world.[79]

This charge is set within an overall mission to support both secular and religious community groups, so as to "work on behalf of Americans committed to improving their communities no matter their religious or political beliefs."[80] The effort begins with the top priority of addressing economic recovery after the crash of 2008 and even directly names poverty as a problem. But this economic agenda is supported by two "key priorities" that are explicitly related to gender and sexuality: support for "women and children," which includes the reappearance of the perennial invocation of "teenage pregnancy" along with abortion reduction, and support for fathers "who stand by their families." In both cases—support for "women and children" and support for (good) "fathers"—we see Obama's frequent approach early in his administration of combining aspects of the policies advocated by what are understood as the two "sides" of American politics into "abortion reduction" and "responsible fatherhood."[81]

While decades after *Roe v. Wade*, Americans cannot agree on the legality of abortion, Obama posits that they should be able to agree that the world would be better if fewer women needed to have abortions. Importantly, unlike the case of "responsible fatherhood," the explicit means of reducing abortion is not mentioned because Obama sees that as a point of conflict across the political spectrum.[82] The key priority of responsible fatherhood, however, names the means of supporting fathers—getting them into well-paying jobs—thus bringing together liberal support for jobs programs with more conservative support for the "traditional" two-parent family.[83]

Despite the sense that each policy brings together liberal and conservative elements, the overall effect of linking the two policies is to create a traditional vision of binary gender roles, family structures, and their implications for policy. We have an explicit gendering in that different policy initiatives are directed toward women and men, and in its explicitness the policy is also traditional: women are tied to children, and while they need to be supported so that abortions are not necessary, they, unlike the fathers, apparently don't need well-paying jobs. Trans, lesbian, gay, or queer people are nowhere named. In this initial charge to the office, the move is relatively swift from a new recognition of the importance of community-based activists—"no matter their political or religious beliefs"—to traditional Christian family values: a two-parent family of complementary genders, with the father working and the mother caring for children (although she may work, there is no mention of government support for mothers working anywhere other than at home).

We also move very rapidly from economic recovery through the Christian family to the somewhat startling naming of the National Security Council in the charge to an office focused on "neighborhood" partnerships. How is it that the domestic (in every sense of the word) gender normativity of the office is tied to what the administration here calls the world "beyond American shores"? The Obama administration's approach is undoubtedly different from that of the Bush administration.[84] The turn globally toward interfaith dialogue instead of a "crusade" for freedom and the directive to take up dialogue with both "leaders" (religious leaders?) and "scholars" (perhaps thought of as secular?) marks the greater openness to the world that many commentators saw in Obama's 2009 agenda-setting speech in Cairo.[85] But, in broad strokes, what Obama offers to the "Muslim world" in his Cairo speech is American religious freedom. Winnifred Sullivan argues that the proffered freedom is "impossible" because it slips so easily into a hierarchical religious tolerance in which the norms and values of institutionalized Christianity form the framework for secular law and democracy.[86] In short, the overall framework upon which Obama draws maintains the Christian hegemony of the neoliberal world order.

Perhaps most disturbingly, the overarching approach of the early Obama administration to national security concerns was articulated a few months later as a "Christian realist" model intertwining secular pragmatism and explicitly Christian values. Obama expounded on this model in his 2009 Nobel Prize acceptance speech.[87] On October 9, 2009, the Nobel Committee announced that Obama was that year's recipient of the Nobel Peace Prize; on December 1, in a speech at the US Military Academy at West Point, he announced a new "surge" of 30,000 US troops into Afghanistan; on December 10, he accepted the prize and gave a speech that put the need for expanding war in the context of peace.[88]

Having committed to extending, rather than ending, the war in Afghanistan, Obama faced a challenge in his Nobel speech. He made his case for war as the path to peace by drawing heavily upon the "Christian realist" framework of twentieth-century Christian ethicist and theologian Reinhold Niebuhr.[89] Obama's dependence upon a Niebuhrian framework was important not only for what it said about the Christian basis for the policies of the secular US government; the response to his speech in the mainstream media was also striking. In the midst of an increasingly fractured media landscape, the speech produced a remarkable moment of consensus, at least among the mainstream, on the value of Obama's use of the Christian realist framework for US policy. Commentators from the conservative Sarah Palin to the conservative centrists David Brooks and Andrew Sullivan to more liberal centrist voices like George Packer in the *New Yorker* specifically praised not just the speech's substance, but also its conceptual framework.[90]

Andrew Sullivan's response to the speech provides the representative strand of Christianity entwined with secularism, of what Ann Pellegrini and I have called "Christian secularism," that strengthens the fabric of this particular common sense.[91] He begins with the move, the slide really, from "Christian" naming a specific religious view to Christianity providing the framework for secular policy: "What strikes me about it most of all—and I do not mean this in any way as a sectarian or non-ecumenical statement—is that it was an address by a deeply serious Christian." And, indeed, Sullivan goes on, "It was not Christianist. . . . It translated a deeply Augustinian grasp of history into a secular and universal language." He then goes through an explication of Christian realism for the current moment, drawing upon long-standing claims (including those made by himself) that violence perpetrated in the name of Islam is different than violence perpetrated in the name of Christianity and concluding: "These are desperately dangerous times. They are dangerous primarily because religion has been abused by those seeking power and control over others—both in the mild version of Christianism at home and the much, much more pernicious and evil Islamism abroad."[92]

With this narrative, secularism not only allows Christian "extremism" to appear less dangerous than Muslim "extremism," but also makes the violence of the secular state into violence in the service of openness, tolerance, freedom, and, yes, peace, rather than in the service of endless war. The violence of the US war on terrorism is, in this analysis, necessary—and necessarily more peaceful—than that directed against the United States. US-sponsored government violence literally becomes less violent (despite the fact that exponentially more people have been killed in the war on terrorism than in the September 11 attacks). These are dangerous times, Sullivan says, but those dangers do not come from the initiation and prosecution of war by the United States. All of the state's violence represents actions that are supposed to be the way out of, not the way into, "desperately dangerous times." In this way, war is supposed to lead to peace.

Of course, the willingness to go to war in the hope of creating peace does not make it so, as the more than a decade of war in Afghanistan that followed Obama's speech makes all too tragically clear. The potential contradiction of this position—that war is the path to peace—is sustained, in part, by links to other sites of morality. The claim that violence enacted by the United States government is essentially peaceful is sustained by the concomitant claim that the US government represents a secular society, one that has a particular religious—i.e., Christian—heritage. This Christian secularism represents an openness and tolerance that are, in turn, supported by a split between public and private: because religion is privatized, the state does not enforce a specific religious practice and is "universally" open (even as religion—specifically, Christianity—is deeply influential on state policy and further institutionalized in secular form).

This relation, in which religion is both privatized and central to the state, is crucially sustained by notions of gender and sexuality. As social ethicist and Niebuhr scholar Gary Dorrien points out, this split is also a way to understand what Niebuhr calls "moral man and immoral society."[93] The split allows a strong emphasis on the importance of morality to the individual human being, which is configured as personal responsibility, while realism also involves a recognition that social interaction will require moral compromise—hence the perennial immorality of society. Because gender and sexuality are supposed to be private, they can be placed under religious authority, while also giving religious voices a particular moral authority when in public. The distribution of gender and sexuality to one side of the public-private divide allows them to provide crucial scaffolding for material issues, in this case the material realities of war.[94] And this gender and sexual normativity is also the sinecure of a moral nation. What many mainstream commentators liked so much about Obama's Nobel speech is that he positioned himself and the United States as *domestically* moral—as humble, diplomatically open to others, and responsible. If in that responsibility we must become entangled in immorality, it is the best that we can do as human beings. Such is reality. If peace becomes war, so be it—as long as we are individually responsible.

The split between moral man and immoral society, between public and private, on which Christian realism depends, can help to explain the oddity of including both "domestic" and "foreign" concerns in the Office of Faith-Based and Neighborhood Partnerships. This split is also an interrelation, and with the approach to war and peace in the Obama administration, we once again see the intertwining of sets of relations—secularism-religion, public-private, foreign-domestic, war-peace—as part of a social fabric throughout which gender and sexuality are woven. The interweaving of religion with the secular state ties together a number of issues that might otherwise seem unrelated, and hence the apparent ease of including familial and international relations in neighborhood concerns. As with the Bush administration before it, the Obama administration took an approach that ties together economics (or at least economic recovery and concern about poverty) with traditionally gendered familialism and national security.

The differences between the Obama and Bush administrations with regard to sexual politics—whether Bush's support of a constitutional amendment to enshrine opposition to same-sex marriage and Obama's eventual support for the institution, or their differences on abortion and transgender rights—are real. *And* the continuities between the Bush and Obama administrations are also real. Similarly, the differences between the Obama and Trump administrations could not be more real. At times, it has seemed that Trump's main policy commitment is to undo the legacy of the Obama administration.[95] And yet the continuities across the administrations are also striking.[96]

Trump

For all of his talk of changing everything, particularly for white working-class people, Trump has held tight to much of the traditional neoliberal playbook, leading some commentators to suggest that his version of nationalism was not so much opposed to neoliberalism as a specifically nationalist brand of neoliberalism.[97] Trump claimed to be on the side of the working class while also promoting policies (both during the campaign and during his administration) that support the interests of corporations and the wealthy elite over those of working people. As we have seen, many commentators see this contradiction as a result of the Democratic Party's focus on "identity politics" or "culture wars" or "sexual politics" to the detriment of economic concerns. *The Sex Obsession* suggests alternatively that one can understand the contradiction as enabled by a politics in which *both* Democrats and Republicans have *actively* intertwined sexual and economic politics with each other and with immigration policy and military endeavors. With this entanglement, both parties have created a mesh substrate of US policy that is extremely resilient, so resilient that that those politicians who were part of its construction—whether Daniel Patrick Moynihan, say, or Bill and

Hillary Clinton—cannot undo the expansive apparatus built upon this substrate.

Trump's turn of the kaleidoscope keeps many of the elements included in the policy patterns of his predecessors as he also shifts toward a nationalist neoliberalism. Even the idea of a "nationalist neoliberalism" is probably too coherent to describe Trump administration policies. As noted in chapter 2, the incoherence of the Trump administration's policy initiatives has been politically productive, allowing the administration to appear "tough" internationally, particularly with regard to Iran, while also promising to pull back from long-contested fronts in the war on terrorism, particularly the war in Afghanistan.[98]

Trump has exhibited a similarly productively incoherent combination of sexual conservatism and an interest in "saving women" as that evinced by the Bush administration. The kaleidoscope did turn; the Trump administration's moves to draw down the war in Afghanistan, for example, showed little concern for the women there, even as media coverage of the efforts often highlighted concerns about women's rights, suggesting that what might be read as a mere pretext for Bush's decision to invade the country was, in fact, a substantive part of the undertaking. Yet with other policies Trump is also concerned with saving women, particularly where Islam is concerned, as exemplified by the invocation of "honor crimes" in his executive order limiting travel from some Muslim-majority countries as necessary for national security.[99] The Trump administration also embraced the well-worn connection between militarism and concern for women's rights by supporting Iranian feminists as part of a strategy to build support for "regime change" in Iran.[100] And with yet another turn, Trump's secretary of state, Mike Pompeo, set up a commission on human rights, in part to question whether women's rights are "unalienable" or merely "ad hoc" human rights.[101]

This incoherence is maintained in part by separation among policy initiatives. When the *New York Times* reported on Trump's apparent abandonment of concern for women in Afghanistan, it did not report on the administration's concern for the women of Iran (or vice versa).[102] The incoherence is also maintained in part by emphasizing the disjunctions between the major American political parties without attending to the interlocking scaffolding that constitutes the infrastructure of US politics.

Rethinking Power and Possibility

How is one to understand the combination of disjunction and continuity that makes for sexual politics in the United States? The usual response to this dual reality is to choose one side as the really real and, as Mol predicts, make the other side coordinate to that reality: make sexual politics the false consciousness of social conservatives that allows them to vote against their real (economic) interests or make sexual politics the site of "culture wars" and simply ignore the involvement of sexual politics in social issues like economics or criminal justice or immigration.

The distribution of sexual politics across issues makes it seem as if all that matters about gender and sex can be removed from certain sites—we can focus on the economy alone—even as this removal allows gender and sex (along with race and religion, among other "cultural" issues) to do all kinds of economic work without appearing to do so (without being mentioned, for example, in press coverage of "welfare reform").

An approach that attends to the social body multiple involves not only attending to the distribution of sexual politics across different issues, but also refusing the coordination that would produce a single site as the "real" site of sexual politics, or of politics *tout court*. Sexual politics is not incidental to the issues canvassed across this chapter, but is rather constitutively active in relation to all of these issues. The sexual politics embedded in war, crime, immigration, and economics really is sexual politics, just as is reproductive justice, the establishment of access to transgender bathrooms, or the institution of pay equity. And sexual politics like questions of access to public space, including bathrooms, are real politics with a materiality of their own—they are not just legitimation for issues that are somehow more material.

We need to attend not only to both division and connection, without subsuming one into the other, but also to the dynamic movements among enactments. As chapter 4 will show, the movement among issues, in which one issue comes to the fore, while others recede, helps to hold the elements together, even as the pattern among them changes. Much seems to have moved and changed, but the power of markets, marriage, and militarism remains firmly in place, and the alliance between corporate and conservative Christian power is ever more tightly bound.

So how is one to respond to the fact that despite their disjunctions and contradictions, various issues are foregrounded together so as to create a tightly woven social fabric, one in which many crucial policies remain intact regardless of the political philosophy or political party of elected officials? The one thing we know in reviewing these multiple issues is that religion is not solely responsible for the shape of sexual politics in the United States. Rather, the Clinton, Bush, Obama, and Trump administrations have pursued sexual politics in conjunction with an extensive and sometimes surprising set of issues, in ways that are simultaneously secular and Christian. Religion, like sex, is entangled with multiple issues.

Social analysis can attend to both the multiplicity and the entanglement.[103] It is possible, for example, to break up the framework that encloses a supposedly coherent whole—whether the frame offered by the overarching concept of "the social" or, as I will consider in the next chapter, that of "progress"—and articulate it in new ways that attend to how issues apparently distant are in fact engaged and how political conflicts apparently far from sexual politics nonetheless articulate with sex. Social analysis can maintain the visibility of disjunctions and hold off preemptively foreclosing the analytical process in favor of coherence. The promise of theoretical promiscuity is that it allows us to hold together potentially contradictory approaches and descriptions so as not to obliterate the complexity of the world.

Maintaining multiple answers simultaneously allows one to move kaleidoscopically among them, opening up previously obscured or invisible avenues for social change. It is true that such politics are more indeterminate, with no single "solution," no absolutely best path of action. But this indeterminacy can be a strength—taking multiple paths at one time may be the best approach to address complex issues.

4

Because Stasis

The usual story of sexual politics, the narrative in which religious conservatism is the reason for the centrality of sexual politics in the US, is part of a larger narrative about religion, secularism, and progress. In the predominant narrative of the United States—and, indeed, of the legacy of European modernity more generally—secularism produces progress toward freedom, and a necessary step in this progress is freedom from the church. In this narrative, secularism is freer than religion, and sexual freedom is an indicator of this secular freedom. Secular freedom provides the framework for the social progress of the nation, in which social injustice is acknowledged to be a part of US history—but the country is in the process of correcting those injustices, thus placing injustice either in the past or the soon to be past.

Democracy expands. Or so the story goes.

In this chapter, relations among Supreme Court cases on different issues provide an example of social relations entangled with each other. By attending to the dynamics of relations among cases, we can begin to see why it is that inequality persists. In other words, why is it that social change seems to be happening all the time and yet very little about social hierarchies seems to actually change? In the end, reading these cases can show how sex is tangled up in injustice and how it might instead become part of building justice.

Mobility for Stasis

How does mobility for stasis work?[1] There are a number of mechanisms for social mobility that, rather than providing the path for progress, reinforce hierarchy in American life.[2] In this chapter, I follow some of them in detail.

One of the most powerful examples of how motion maintains a stable hierarchy in the United States is school segregation by race. In the

1960s and 1970s, white responses to social movements for desegregation in both schooling and housing produced "white flight" as white people moved from urban centers to suburbs in order to avoid sending their children to integrated schools. In later decades, white people moved back to urban centers, yet these movements have not produced desegregated neighborhoods or schools. Instead, "white return" to cities tends to raise the cost of living and create both incentives and financial imperatives for people of color to move to the suburbs once occupied almost exclusively by white people. Despite all of this movement, we find that neighborhoods in US cities and suburbs remain segregated at high rates nearly a half-century after "desegregation," and schools in some areas of the country are increasingly (not decreasingly) segregated.[3] In other words, there has been a great deal of movement with regard to housing and schooling in the US, but the combination of race, housing, and education repeatedly produces segregation and inequality.

Segregation is reproduced despite very real changes over time: social movements in support of integration, court decisions to desegregate public schools, and the passage of legislation to prevent segregation in housing.[4] Some of these initiatives have been blocked or rolled back, but some of them have been incorporated into existing housing segregation and the continuous mobility around housing. Magnet schools, for example, may desegregate some schools while increasing the segregation of others. Law professor Will Stancil argues that, given existing segregation, even the increasing demographic diversity of the US can (counterintuitively) intensify segregation: "The fundamental defect in American schools . . . is that they have long exhibited patterns of racial concentration, mostly due to housing segregation and decades of discriminatory education policy. If schools were already integrated to begin with, you'd expect increasing diversity to raise all boats relatively evenly. Most schools would get less white, but few would find themselves truly segregated. Instead, in a long-segregated system, the effects of increased diversity are inevitably lopsided. Schools already suffering from a relatively high degree of segregation have found themselves completely isolated."[5] If legal issues related to education are understood as about "single issues," one analysis is produced—increased diversity should decrease segregation. If, however, education is connected to housing segregation, an entirely different analysis comes to the fore. Social change in housing policy over the last several decades and social mobility in housing and changes in demographics can all intensify school segregation and its accompanying hierarches: mobility for stasis.

Similarly, if legal cases are read as about single issues, one understanding results, and if they are read as dynamically interrelated, a different understanding becomes possible. This chapter's readings of dynamics among recent cases decided by the US Supreme Court shows how the legal cases that are supposed to connote democratic progress can instead reinforce the existing scaffolding of social relations.

Kaleidoscopic Hierarchies

One of the most important mechanisms of mobility for stasis is the movement of issues in and out of focus that we saw in the preceding chapters when economics was treated as separate from racialized and sexual politics. As the examples throughout *The Sex Obsession* have shown, the import of sexual politics is frequently dismissed and removed from the focus of policy discussion, even as sex can also be brought back into the political fray "a little later" as a dependable part of the policy apparatus.

In this chapter, I consider the ways in which this movement in and out of focus intersects with movement between and among issues, in which public discourse brings sex to the fore as race and class move to the background, then returns to class and/or race as the focus on sex fades. This movement among issues helps to inscribe the idea that the US is progressively addressing past injustices. As one issue comes to the fore and others move to the background, it seems there is always progress on some issue even as there may be retrenchment on others and that retrenchment is kept in the background.

Movement among issues also creates the loosely coherent common sense described by religious studies scholar Catherine Bell in which the coexistence of national narratives about equality and the persistence of inequality can seem perfectly sensible. People and institutions can understand themselves to be not racist or sexist by bringing a single moment to the fore and ignoring contravening actions, relegating them to the background. The idea that the United States is a land moving toward freedom and equality can be the common sense of the nation, even as the US actually offers less social mobility than many other countries.[6]

Is This the End?

In June 2015, the Supreme Court legalized gay marriage at the federal level and in all fifty states with its decision in *Obergefell v. Hodges*, which guaranteed the right to marry as a fundamental freedom in the US, applying equally to "same-sex" and "opposite-sex" couples. This decision was hailed as a principle step forward in the long history of progress toward full equality in the United States. It even led some writers and activists to claim that the (only relevant) civil rights battle over sexual politics is over. Linda Hirshman had already declared "Victory" for the gay rights movement in a *New York Times* bestseller in 2013, and by the end of 2015 New York State's major mainstream gay rights activist group, Empire State Pride Agenda, decided to close its doors on the basis of having fulfilled its "agenda" when Governor Andrew Cuomo announced antidiscrimination protections for transgender people in addition to the *Obergefell* decision.[7]

Many other activists, including other mainstream rights organizations, pointed out, however, that a slew of issues, such as employment and housing discrimination, continued to affect the lives of lesbian, gay, bisexual, transgender, and queer people in the United States. Battles over the rights of transgender people moved to the forefront of political discussion almost as soon as the ink was dry on the marriage decision, with heated debates over state bills to regulate gender division in public restrooms and President Trump's declaration over Twitter of polices to remove trans rights.[8] Of course, political battles over heterosexuality, specifically over contraception and abortion, continued unabated, gaining heat in the same summer as the Supreme Court's marriage decision, with public and political attacks on contraception and on abortion service providers that intensified after the 2016 election.[9] Not surprisingly, same-sex marriage also returned to the center of public debate repeatedly after *Obergefell*, including in a Supreme Court case focused on "religious freedom," *Masterpiece Cakeshop v. Colorado Civil Rights Commission*.

And sexual politics in some form is virtually guaranteed to return again and again. Why would marriage alone end political conflict (just as it ends the plots of nineteenth-century novels or twentieth-century romantic movies)?

The Sex Obsession suggests that, instead of offering an ending, the legal recognition of same-sex marriage at the federal level is one turn in a complex process that makes it seem as though social change is happening, and yet not much is changing. This view of rotating interrelation contrasts with the traditional view of the role of the Supreme Court in US history as the site at which the progress of the nation— from the injustice of racism, sexism, and heterosexism toward freedom and equality—can best be traced. In other words, the progress narrative works as a method of what Annemarie Mol conceptualizes as "coordination" (explored in chapter 3). The progress narrative lines up potentially disjunctive phenomena so that they fit seamlessly into the US national narrative of ever-expanding democracy.

The progress narrative breaks up different issues, taking each as a stepping stone on the path of progress; as each step is laid, it is supposed to become the groundwork for the next step. As exemplified by the *Obergefell* decision on same-sex marriage, the achievement of some aspect of racial justice is often taken as the step that grounds movement forward on sex. Because the fight for the right to marriage by same-sex couples was a struggle to gain civil rights guaranteed by the Constitution to all citizens, both activists and commentators looked back to the civil rights struggle of the twentieth century. They reasoned that the *Obergefell* decision was to the gay rights movement as the 1964 Civil Rights Act and 1965 Voting Rights Act (which aimed to secure the rights laid out in the Fourteenth and Fifteenth Amendments to the Constitution) was to the Civil Rights Movement.

And yet, as indicated by my readings of recent Supreme Court cases, including a set of cases from 2013 that laid the groundwork for *Obergefell*, when the Court brought sexual equality to the center of the visual field, that turn of the kaleidoscope made a victory for gay rights serve as a kind of alibi for a decision of the Court, rendered the same week, that eviscerated the Voting Rights Act. Moreover, in subsequent years, Justice Samuel Alito went on to proclaim the Court's commitment to racial justice as a kind of alibi for finding that claims for gender equality are "vague" while those for racial justice are solid. Mobility for stasis.

Thinking relationally about Supreme Court cases over just a few years allows us to see the complexity of the social field and to understand both the usefulness and the limits of focusing on the law as the site of social change in the United States. What possibilities might become available if we look beyond the law in trying to materialize justice?

Social Change?

To become self-conscious about the turns of the kaleidoscope that bring one issue into focus only to push another to the background—or almost entirely out of sight—we need to look at the decisions leading up to *Obergefell*.[10] In the week of June 24, 2013, the Court released decisions on three issues: affirmative action at public universities, the continuing relevance of the 1965 Voting Rights Act, and same-sex marriage.[11] Reading these decisions in relation to one another, and also to the *Hobby Lobby* case in 2014 and *Obergefell* in 2015, both shows the habits of thought that produce mobility for stasis and facilitates alternative understandings.

Looking one way at this set of decisions—along a single line leading toward same-sex marriage—we see progress, confirming a powerful belief that the United States as a nation moves ever closer to the democratically achieved realization of justice for all. But the bright light pointed in the direction of progress overshadows other legal victories that secure unjust policies, meaning that *Obergefell* can simultaneously be a sign of progressive social change and a screen that obscures profoundly regressive decisions.

In June 2013, the Supreme Court decisions on affirmative action and voting rights were released on Monday and Tuesday, followed by the same-sex-marriage decision on Wednesday. Reading each of the cases in turn, along with the public discourse that surrounded them, one can see their dynamic interrelation. The affirmative action case, for example, invoked a broader discussion of the relation between race and class. The voting rights case has had perhaps the most far-reaching consequences of the three, but it was sandwiched between affirmative action a day before and sexual politics a day after. And it was sexual politics that ended up taking over the public's attention for the week as a whole.

The first of the cases released in that single week of June 2013, *Fisher v. University of Texas, Austin*, concerned affirmative action at the University of Texas. The case focused on the constitutionality of taking race into account as part of the process of determining admission to the university. Fisher, a young white woman who had been denied admission, sued the university, claiming that admissions standards, which took racial diversity into account at specific points in the process, had unfairly denied her access.[12] Through a program often referred to as the "Top 10 Percent," the university automatically admitted students who had graduated in the top portion of their class at any high school in the state (often the top 10 percent of the class, although the exact percentage varied from year to year). For admissions beyond this top percentage, the university considered a variety of factors, including racial and ethnic diversity, in forming the incoming class. Fisher's claim was based on the fact that 47 students had been admitted to the University of Texas at Austin with lower test scores and grades than hers. Of these admitted students, 42 were white. Moreover, 168 students of color with higher test scores than Fisher's were also denied admission.[13]

In deciding the case, the Court did not strike down any and all references to race in admissions policies, but maintained that if such policies are used, they should be subject to a rigorous standard of "strict scrutiny." The decision did not rule out all forms of affirmative action, but it made it more difficult for university affirmative action programs to be legally acceptable. The Supreme Court sent the University of Texas program back to the lower court to be re-reviewed in relation to this stricter standard; it was eventually returned to the Supreme Court, which finally settled the case by upholding the school's program as constitutional.[14]

This final outcome surprised many observers of the Court, in part because Justice Kennedy, who wrote the final majority opinion, had never before voted to uphold affirmative action.[15] Justice Alito opened his dissent (read from the bench as an indicator of deep disagreement) as follows: "Something strange has happened since our prior decision in this case."[16] There is some evidence that a change did occur between the two decisions, specifically in Kennedy's understanding of the relation between race and class.

Continuing policy debates about the relation between race and class amply illustrate how the interaction among issues is crucial to what both law and activism can achieve.[17] Commentators before and after the decision repeatedly argued that only supposedly "race-neutral" means of ensuring fairness in university admissions should address diversity.[18] Some prominent moderates and liberals made the argument that university admissions should focus on addressing class rather than race in-equities. For example, the Century Foundation, which describes itself as a "progressive, non-partisan think tank," advocated "new admissions preferences to low-income and working-class students of all races" as better than those focused on race.[19] Certainly, given the role that higher education plays as a class-sorting institution in the United States, it is important to consider the effects of class in university admissions and higher education as a whole.[20] Yet the focus on class alone may not be as "race-neutral" as proponents claim.

In the Century Foundation's proposal, class mobility will somehow erase all of the effects (or all of the important effects) of racism. But, as Patricia Williams so eloquently wrote in the *New York Times* before the decision was handed down, the effects of race extend beyond class, just as class has effects that extend beyond race:

> The latest attestation to [wealth's] miraculous salutary power is the asser-tion that African-Americans who would but barricade themselves within a wall of middle-classness will be structurally exempted from racial re-sentments. According to this logic, when comfortably situated black peo-ple move into all-white areas, the neighbors will be delighted; property values will rise; police will not stop and frisk their children on their way to school . . . And of course a rich black person who gets good grades and becomes editor of the Harvard Law Review and is elected president of the United States will be regarded as the embodied American Dream. No one will ever say that Harvard isn't what it used to be, or that standards must have been lowered for him to rise so high. . . . Yes, it is true that money can mitigate some of the effects of structural bias; it is a blessing to eat, to have shelter. At the same time, it is as silly to argue that prejudice against African-Americans doesn't exist beyond the wealth gap as it is to say that there is no glass ceiling for women, no backlash against Asians, no resent-ment of Jews, no harmful confusions about Islam. Our careful commit-ment to affirmative action—in law, in politics, in life—must be expanded not contracted. The world is too complex for our remediative aspirations to be limited by the crass metric of priced people.[21]

The focus on class alone produces racially specific effects in part by ignoring the intertwining of social relations. In the case of the Century

BECAUSE STASIS | 137

Foundation proposal, the separation of class- from race-based admissions skips over any sense of the history of profound interrelation between class and race, especially when it comes to African Americans, and especially with regard to access to education. For example, the GI Bill passed after World War II provided support for education, housing, employment, and business opportunities to returning veterans. The effects of this bill created a major shift in class relations in the United States by supporting massive class mobility.[22] Returning soldiers who could not have afforded college without government aid became students by the millions.[23] But this was also a moment of "affirmative action for white people": because the military had been racially segregated, and because admissions at many colleges and universities were still racially restricted, the vast majority of beneficiaries of this policy were white people.[24] In fact, it was a moment in which Americans who had not previously understood themselves to be white—including immigrants like Italian Americans and Irish Americans—became white.[25] This intertwining of class mobility, racial segregation, ethnic identification, and the expansion of "whiteness" is what solidified postwar white supremacy in the United States and made the Civil Rights Movement imperative in the decades that followed. It is in this set of historical relations that affirmative action became a strategy for combating the structural racism that so effectively excluded people of color from benefits that lifted millions into the white middle class.

In the current moment, the continuation of segregation in housing, combined with the widespread policy of funding neighborhood school districts through property taxes, means that schooling also continues to be one of the primary means of perpetuating *both* income inequality and white supremacy. Poor people of all races have difficulty accessing the educational experiences that will prepare them for college. But with continued racial segregation in housing, white people, even if not well-off, are more likely to be able to attend good primary schools and thus to have the credentials for good colleges and universities. They are more likely, for example, to live in highly segregated states in the middle of the country with major public universities. In its initial decision on affirmative action, the Supreme Court not only bypassed the history of legal segregation, but also utterly ignored the fact of continued segregation. In her dissent to the majority opinion, Justice Ruth Bader Ginsburg focused on precisely this issue: "I have said before and reiterate here that only an ostrich could regard the supposedly neutral alternatives as race unconscious. . . . As Justice Souter observed . . . the vaunted alternatives suffer from 'the disadvantage of deliberate obfuscation.' Texas' percentage plan was adopted with racially segregated neighborhoods and schools front and center stage."[26] It seems possible that in the later decision Justice Kennedy was influenced by Ginsburg's argument about this interconnected history, acknowledging that a "race-neutral" admissions policy "that relies exclusively on class rank creates perverse incentives for applicants," including an incentive for parents to keep their children in low-performing schools.[27]

Race and class simply are not the same thing, nor are they interchangeable markers of "privilege."[28] But they are intertwined, and they are intertwined in a dynamic fashion. Instead of analyzing this movement among categories, the Century Foundation report depends on lining up issues in a linear narrative of progress. The introduction to the report acknowledges that racial preferences were needed at one time in the history of US race relations, only to declare that race consciousness should now be replaced by class consciousness.[29]

Justice Sandra Day O'Connor laid out the same logic in writing the majority opinion in a 2003 case upholding affirmative action (*Grutter v. Bollinger*). She declared that progress had been made in the twenty-five years since the Court first approved affirmative action, so she expected such programs to no longer be necessary in another twenty-five years.[30] Thus, the move from race to class consciousness suggested by the Century Foundation can fit into this larger narrative in which it is time to move on from race to other concerns.[31] Because the Supreme Court of the United States has been such an important player in the narrative of historical progress, it can, as O'Connor's position does, use this very narrative of progress to actively undo the defense of racial justice.

The power of the progress narrative was even more evident on Tuesday, June 25, 2013, when the Court handed down its next decision of the week in *Shelby County v. Holder*, which undid significant parts of the Voting Rights Act of 1965. The decision was based on the idea that racism had ended and federal oversight of voting laws was no longer necessary.

The Voting Rights Act was passed in the summer of 1965 in the wake of intense activism that culminated in a march from Selma to Montgomery, Alabama. Civil rights activism had highlighted the ways in which voting laws in various states—laws requiring voter identification, literacy tests, and poll taxes—were used to prevent many people, particularly African Americans, from registering to vote or casting ballots. The Voting Rights Act prohibited states from legally requiring any "voting qualification or prerequisite to voting, or standard, practice, or procedure . . . to deny or abridge the right of any citizen of the United States to vote on account of race or color." Furthermore, the act required states with a history of racial discrimination in voting laws to get federal approval for any change to such laws.[32] It is this federal oversight that was challenged and effectively overturned in 2013's *Shelby County* case. Congress could, of course, choose to renew oversight by passing new legislation reinstating it in ways that would respond to the Court's ruling, but the justices knew perfectly well that having passed fewer pieces of legislation in its first year than any previous congressional session in US history, the Congress sitting in 2013 was unlikely to act on this contested terrain.[33]

The majority decision in *Shelby County* argued that there was no longer any evidence for the continued existence of the type of racism that had led to the need for federal oversight over the preceding five decades. This claim was asserted despite the fact that state legislators in many of the affected states had anticipated the Court's decision and had already prepared legislation to restrict voting in ways that would disproportionately affect African American and Latinx voters. These laws were quickly passed in the days and months following the *Shelby County* decision, and have often had the desired effect of restricting the franchise.[34] Released the day after the affirmative action ruling, this decision took the argument that we should now focus on remedying the inequities of class a step further. It effectively claimed that remedies for racism, previously provided by Congress and the courts, may no longer be necessary at all.

Progress has happened. Racism is ameliorated. Issues can be lined up in linear order, and it is now time to move on.

The Court moved on the very next day, Wednesday, June 26, 2013, when the justices released a decision on same-sex marriage in *U.S. v. Windsor*.[35] In this decision, the Court struck down the federal Defense of Marriage Act (DOMA).[36] Passed in 1996 and signed by President Bill Clinton, DOMA maintained that "the word 'marriage' means only a legal union between one man and one woman as husband and wife, and the word 'spouse' refers only to a person of the opposite sex who is a husband or a wife."[37] In material terms, DOMA meant that the federal government preemptively denied same-sex couples access to any of the federal benefits associated with marriage, such as the ability to receive Social Security benefits as a surviving spouse or to sponsor one's spouse as a citizen through immigration. In striking down DOMA, the *Windsor* case struck down the idea that marriage could *only* be between one man and one woman and recognized same-sex marriages for federal tax purposes. But, it was still up to individual states to decide whether they too would certify same-sex marriages. Thus, *Windsor* effectively set the stage for the *Obergefell* decision two years later.

In writing the majority opinion in *Windsor*, Justice Anthony Kennedy drew upon both the Fifth Amendment right to due process and the Fourteenth Amendment provision of equal protection under the law. He reasoned that "DOMA's principal effect is to identify a subset of state-sanctioned marriages and make them unequal. The principal purpose is to impose inequality, not for other reasons like governmental efficiency. Responsibilities, as well as rights, enhance the dignity and integrity of the person. And DOMA contrives to deprive some couples married under the laws of their State, but not other couples, of both rights and responsibilities."[38] The *New York Times* reported that "Justice Anthony M. Kennedy announced the majority opinion striking down the federal law in a stately tone that indicated he was delivering a civil rights landmark."[39]

Popular discourse supported the idea that gay marriage marks a civil rights landmark by placing it in a progress narrative, in which gay rights is a step along the path laid out by previous struggles for civil rights, despite the fact that the justices had, only the day before, undone key provisions of one of the most important legislative victories of those struggles. For example, in the aftermath of President Obama's election in 2008, the gay magazine *The Advocate* declared "Gay Is the New Black: The Last Great Civil Rights Struggle" on its cover, and young Republican commentator Meghan McCain referred to gay marriage as "my generation's civil rights issue."[40] True, other commentators across a range of political positions questioned stepping-stone metaphors for the relations between sexual and racial movements and issues, and challenged the logic of the analogy between "gay" civil rights and "Black" civil rights, yet such reasoning is still alive in much public discourse about same-sex marriage.[41]

Arguments that conceptualize gay rights as building on previous movements draw upon a well-established habit that has persisted over decades: thinking that every victory for civil rights advances a long and continuing struggle to adhere in practice to the principles of democracy as laid down in the Constitution. Every legislative victory thus builds on previous steps forward. This freezes in time earlier accomplishments that required many years of activism and organizing to achieve, and assumes that social movement is inherently progressive. What's lost are the singular conditions of the past, the simple fact that victories on behalf of justice are never secure, and the necessary understanding of the interrelation among forces in social relations.[42]

We fail to consider the ways in which a turn of the kaleidoscope rearranges parts, but all the parts remain in play. For example, in a previous book, I pursued an analysis of how the 1993 March on Washington for Lesbian, Gay, and Bi Equal Rights and Liberation used frequent analogies to the 1963 March on Washington for Jobs and Freedom, a pivotal moment for the Civil Rights Movement. Videos from the 1993 march produced by the National Gay and Lesbian Taskforce and Human Rights Campaign both use references to the analogy, but neither the march nor the videos make connections to either the content of the 1963 march or to contemporary issues of racial justice. Rather what we see in the videos is a "gay community" *different* from yet putatively *the same as* that depicted in the photos taken of the massed marchers of that earlier national march on Washington, DC. The effect of the analogy is to unite the marchers in the progress narrative of democratic advance so that they are the same. The images tell another story. Most of the marchers pictured in photos from 1963 are Black, with many fewer whites; in the videos from 1993, most marchers are white, with many fewer African Americans.[43]

Reading the *Windsor* decision in relation to *Fisher* and *Shelby County* indicates the Court's participation in precisely this type of linear progress narrative, one in which race-based civil rights can form the stable foundation for other issues, including gay rights, even as those same civil rights are destabilized and face retrenchment. Moreover, reading the cases together shows how the progress narrative creates a sense in which taking steps forward on other issues—whether class or sex—can also reinforce the idea that racism is over. With the country moving forward on gay rights, why would we possibly still need old-fashioned measures like federal protections for voting rights, enacted over fifty years ago, even before the Stonewall rebellion that is supposed to have launched the gay rights movement? Surely, the story seems to imply, we're beyond needing such measures, and we can make similar advances with regard to class if we just give up the archaic focus on race-based affirmative action.

Taken together, this set of decisions, released three days in a row, produces an overarching narrative: despite the possibility of interpreting *Shelby County* as a direct setback to civil rights, with *Fisher* representing the weakening of affirmative action (now subject to the standard of strict scrutiny), we are to imagine that overall progress continues apace and that gay rights are the marker of this progress.

Thus, it is not surprising that on Thursday and Friday of that week in June 2013, all of the major news outlets were talking about the historic victory for gay rights, not historic losses for racial justice—even as several states around the country immediately moved to change their laws in a way that would make voting more difficult for people of color.[44] A LexisNexis search for June 27–30, 2013, produces 1,152 hits for articles on "same-sex marriage," only 281 hits for articles on "voting rights," and 92 for articles on "affirmative action."

In the narrative of the march of progress, "gay rights" are connected to other civil rights but only as separate steps on the path toward full democracy: first the US did away with racism and now it is doing away with discrimination against homosexuality.[45] If we fail to analyze and act on issues together, then the fight for gay rights can be talked about as the "civil rights" issue of a new generation, replacing yesterday's fight against racism, as happened in media coverage of the week's Monday, Tuesday, and Wednesday decisions, one after another, in a linear progression of steps into the future.

When placed in the context of the progress narrative, gay rights are used to enforce the idea that racism is, indeed, over, a thing of the past, not a living, breathing undertaking of the present, an idea that undercuts possible connections between movements for racial and sexual justice. And, in the end, this type of narrative opens the door to the idea that once gay marriage is legal, homophobia can also be declared over.

Anything else that might be associated with gay rights and a liberatory sexual politics is also unnecessary.

The Court offered another turn of the kaleidoscope in the summer of 2014 when it released its decision in *Burwell v. Hobby Lobby*, a case that took up the question of whether Hobby Lobby, a family-owned business with a chain of nearly one hundred stores, could deny insurance coverage of certain forms of contraception in policies for the corporation's employees. The basis for the claim was that "closely held" corporations (those that are not publicly traded) have a right to religious freedom, and this right overrides the regulatory mandate to cover contraception under the Affordable Care Act of 2010. In a decision written by Justice Samuel Alito, the Court ruled 5–4 in favor of Hobby Lobby's right to deny coverage of forms of contraception that the owners believed to be abortifacients and therefore in contravention of their religious commitments.

There are a number of issues raised by this decision. For instance, some commentators focused on the way it significantly extends the idea that corporations are persons, with rights to religious freedom or free speech; other commentators focused on the place held by *Hobby Lobby* in the long line of challenges to the Affordable Care Act, such that the question of insurance coverage for contraception might be the issue taken up in a successful Supreme Court challenge to the Affordable Care Act, where other challenges based on the economics of the bill had previously failed; and others focused on the ways in which the claimants' "sincere beliefs" about how contraceptives work could be the basis of law even if those beliefs were without scientific foundation.[46]

All of these legal and political questions are important, but in relation to the series of decisions released in 2013, Justice Alito's majority opinion once again spins the wheel of mobility among issues so as to reinforce various social hierarchies. Commentators often focused on the case as one in which "women's rights" were opposed to "religious freedom,"[47] thereby erasing religious support for "women's rights," and also erasing the connections between worker's right to contraceptive coverage and sexual practices involving people of different genders. The case was also read as potentially opening the door to discrimination against LGBTQI persons—a possibility raised by many mainstream commentators, including Linda Greenhouse in the *New York Times*.[48] And we can note that the idea that the case is only about gender discrimination erases any connection to sexual rights, including any principle of freedom in sexual practice.

Having (re)established the opposition between religion and liberal or progressive sexual politics, Justice Alito then argues that there is not a compelling government interest in maintaining "gender equality." He dismisses the claim on the part of the US Department of Health and Human Services (HHS) that gender equality is a compelling interest to be protected: "HHS asserts that the contraceptive mandate serves a variety of important interests, but many of these are couched in very broad terms, such as promoting 'public health' and 'gender equality.'"[49] Alito says, however, that the principle of religious freedom on which he dismisses this argument from HHS would never be used to override the state's compelling interest in preventing racism: "The principal dissent [referring to the dissent written by Justice Ginsburg] raises the possibility that discrimination in hiring, for example on the basis of race, might be cloaked as religious practice to escape legal sanction. . . . Our decision today provides no such shield. The Government has a compelling interest in providing an equal opportunity to participate in the workforce without regard to race, and prohibitions on racial discrimination are precisely tailored to achieve that critical goal."[50] Alito here dismisses any concern about racial discrimination and sees the Court's commitment to racial justice to be firmly grounded in a "compelling interest," while ignoring the fact that unplanned pregnancy might undercut "an equal opportunity to participate in the workforce." Instead, Alito highlights the Court's supposed commitment to racial justice so as to shift focus away from the erosion of sexual rights through the invocation of religious freedom in *Hobby Lobby*.

Yet even as he appealed to the solidity of the Court's opposition to racial discrimination, he made the footing quite narrow, basing it on equal opportunity alone. In 2016, when the *Fisher* case on affirmative action was finally decided, his dissent thus advanced the narrow footing he established in *Hobby Lobby* to find the inclusion of race in a university's goals in order to provide "the educational benefits of diversity" to be just as vague—hence failing to reach the standard of a compelling interest—as he found gender equality in 2014.[51]

The only way to bring this ironic reversal into focus is to consider how the pieces of the kaleidoscope have turned. In the *Hobby Lobby* case, the claim that the recognition of the importance of racial politics is secure is used to reinforce the disposable nature of sexual politics, making it seem unimportant to protect the right to contraceptive healthcare and reproductive justice in relation to the more "compelling" issue of religious freedom. And the Court's commitment to racial equality is also clear and firm. Not only is religious freedom more important than gender justice and sexual freedom, but this retrenchment on the ground of gender should in no way be taken as referencing the more important issue of race. Racial politics is here appealed to by Alito to marginalize gender and sex. In the face of firmly established racial equality (so established that voting rights protections could be removed the previous year), those who worry about "civil rights" should not be concerned about the loss of something so supposedly trivial as insurance coverage for contraception.

Turning the kaleidoscope is so effective that even the currently revered constitutional protection of religion can recede from view—if the religion in question is not Christianity. In 2018, challenges to President Trump's executive order banning travel to the US from several Muslim-majority countries reached the Supreme Court in *Trump v. Hawaii*.[52] Chief Justice Roberts wrote the majority opinion. His focus was on national security; religious freedom moved out of the frame. Roberts also took pains to explicitly deny that discrimination was the basis of the travel ban. To demonstrate the ways that claims about national security can be discriminatory, Justice Sonia Sotomayor points in her dissent to the precedent of *Korematsu v. United States*, wherein the Court supported FDR's executive order authorizing the internment of Japanese Americans in World War II. While this decision has never been explicitly overturned, in response to Sotomayor, Roberts denounced *Korematsu* as "objectively unlawful." But he also claimed that it was in no way related to "a facially neutral policy denying certain foreign nationals the privilege of admission."[53] Much like how Alito claimed a commitment to racial justice as a means of downplaying the import of gender equality, Roberts here uses a denunciation of racism in the past to ignore a threat to religious freedom in the present.

Justice Sotomayor read her dissent from the bench so as to make discriminatory basis of the travel ban and the connection to *Korematsu* explicit.[54] She argued that to fail to make this connection the majority had to ignore the facts of the case, a point she made by reading the record of anti-Muslim statements made by Donald Trump as both a candidate and as president, statements that Trump himself connected to the "travel ban."[55] She noted that Trump never disavowed these statements, so they must be taken seriously as the recorded basis of the travel ban. She also cited the majority's opinion in another case, *Masterpiece Cakeshop v. Colorado Civil Rights Commission*. There, "less pervasive" statements on the part of members of the Colorado Civil Rights Commission were taken to be discriminatory against the Christian beliefs of the proprietor of a cake shop who did not want to bake cakes for same-sex weddings.[56] How, then, could the majority ignore President Trump's pervasive attacks on Muslims in his tweets and declarations to the media? How can the president's ban be anything other than anti-Muslim? And what happened to the Court's commitment to religious freedom? How did it disappear? Sotomayor concluded with regard to Justice Roberts's move to denounce the racism of *Korematsu*: "By blindly accepting the Government's misguided invitation to sanction a discriminatory policy motivated by animosity toward a disfavored group, all in the name of a superficial claim of national security, the Court redeploys the same dangerous logic underlying *Korematsu* and merely replaces one 'gravely wrong' decision with another."[57]

To summarize: in the summer of 2013, the Court announced that affirmative action might no longer be necessary and so should be subject to "strict scrutiny" by the judicial system. The next day, the Court acted to deny federal oversight of voting in states with a history of segregation, a key provision of the Voting Rights Act, with the entirely predictable result that many states have acted to undercut voting rights. Both of these decisions were muffled in commentary from journalists, however, because on Wednesday of that week, the Court's decision to strike down the Defense of Marriage Act got all the attention. Moreover, the decision on gay rights was immediately analogized to the Court's midcentury rulings against racial segregation and for civil rights. In the media commonsense narrative, the victory of the Civil Rights Movement laid the mid-twentieth-century groundwork for the struggle for gay civil rights at the beginning of the twenty-first. This analogy was pervasive and effectively obscured the fact that the Court had just (1) undone one of the central achievements of the movement for civil rights, and (2) weakened another way of advancing racial equality, affirmative action in college admissions. The spotlight on gay rights made it hard to see and talk about the history of racial segregation and restrictions on voting or the movements that have challenged these injustices. These actions were analogically celebrated and also consigned to the past.

The kaleidoscope is turned again and again: in the 2014 *Hobby Lobby* decision, the Court ruled in favor of a family corporation whose owners had declared that their religious convictions prevented them from providing their employees with insurance coverage for contraceptives. Justice Alito held that religious freedom allowed this denial of access to medical insurance because gender equality was not a compelling interest of the state. He was quick to reassure Americans, however, that religious freedom could never be used as a blind for *racial* discrimination, though clearly those of all races who need insurance for contraception are injured by the decision. Gender and sexuality are obscured in the Court's decision by this foregrounding of race. In 2015, the kaleidoscope is given another turn in the *Obergefell* decision that federally protected the rights of homosexuals to marry, brightly spotlighting sexuality once again, but drawing attention away from the effects of the Court's earlier attack on African Americans' access to voting in states that once again legislated to keep them from the polls. Finally, in 2018, racism separated Islam from religion and trumped the religious freedom that was so valued in the *Hobby Lobby* case when the Supreme Court supported a ban on travel from some Muslim-majority countries—for the majority of justices, it seems Islam, allows "religion" to fade to the background.[58]

Over five years, this series of Supreme Court decisions demonstrates the entanglement of social relations that make up "mobility for stasis." Different groups move forward and back at different times. The movement forward makes it seem as if democracy is expansive, when, in fact, the Court advances one group only to set another back. The fundamental hierarchies of US society remain relatively stable. The nation appears to be continually making progress toward ever-greater, more inclusive equality, while inequality remains entrenched.

The examples in this chapter show that these relations do not simply run in one direction—sex is not simply a distraction from the politics of class or race; religion is not simply a means of ensuring that sexual politics can effectively serve as such a distraction. Rather, race and class politics are also used to bolster sexual conservatism, just as sexual politics is used to bolster racial and class hierarchies. Most importantly, these dynamics (e.g., sexism bolstering racism; racism bolstering sexism) are also intertwined (e.g., racism and sexism together bolstering class hierarchies). And that entanglement means that effectively dismissing sexual politics as unimportant allows it to be all the more effective in bolstering multiple social hierarchies, including those of race and class.

Religion and the Progress Narrative

The narrative of social progress depends on issues being separated from each other, distributed along a single line that is coordinated through the passage of time. This narrative has such power, in part, because it purports to explain why inequality exists in a society that is supposed to value freedom and equality.

The commonsense power of the narrative of US social progress is subtended by the secularization narrative, which also tells a story about freedom and progress. If secularization is supposed to provide a path to freedom and enlightenment, then the secularization narrative implies that those who resist the moral claims of secularism can be positioned as failures of history, rather than as subjects of injustice.

As the historian and postcolonial critic Dipesh Chakrabarty says, those who refuse to accede to the logic of secularism and its reason are consigned to "the waiting room of history."[59] People whose practices are "not bereft of the agency of gods, spirits and other supernatural beings" are often understood to be "pre-political" or "anachronistic if not reactionary."[60] Secularism is a key component of the narrative method by which entire communities and nations are consigned to the waiting room of history.[61] Chakrabarty connects his critique of secularism to a critique of history and more broadly to a critique of enlightenment-based social analysis. The secularization narrative—in which the European Enlightenment leads to an end of religious dogmatism and an advance in rationalism—is itself a theory of history in which history provides the framework for narrating the unfolding of time in a progressive manner (this happens, then that happens, then a third thing happens). The secularization narrative is also a sociology of religion in which the social has a logic internal to it (an "ology" of the social). For the secularization narrative, this logic involves "development" or "evolution" or some other progressive movement of social change.[62]

This logic assumes the universal, empty time of secularism, which is supposed to draw together every person and every society within a framework of enlightened discussion and the logical resolution of conflict. In this narrative, an end to the post-Reformation "wars of religion" in Europe is possible because the framework provided by secular reason affords the resolution even of severe conflicts like war.[63] This big, open secular framework allows for people of different national affiliations, different ethnic and racial communities, different genders, and even different religions to come together and discuss these differences without violence, provided that they all accept the framework of secular reason within which this discussion will take place.

The proviso—that one must accept secularization as the public framework—is, of course, the key to the narrative as a whole.[64] As long as religion takes place "within the limits of reason alone," it is a welcome and perhaps even helpful aspect of society.[65] Here is the difficulty: although the openness of the secular framework is supposed to be universal, because not everyone accepts secular rationality as the appropriate framework for their lives and societies—because for some religion is itself a framework for living rather than a private system of "belief"—this claim to universal openness also separates "the West" from "the rest," as Stuart Hall famously named the division.[66]

In constituting the boundaries of the imagined space of the "West," the entangled relations of secularism, freedom, progress, reason, and economic development also constitute the conditions of social relations within "Western" spaces. As a result, the progress narrative of history is central to the way in which Americans think of the United States as a unique land of progress, *and* it is central to how inequalities within that land of progress are understood. The sense of American progress is developed, in part, by consigning some people to the "waiting room of history" while others are seen as "moving forward."

Indeed, the progress narrative works in precisely this way with regard to the questions about inequality raised by recent Supreme Court cases.

As the story goes: while some people have been denied basic civil rights, the progress of the nation means that different groups are always moving forward to claim these rights through social movements, landmark legislation, and historic Supreme Court decisions.

The mechanism of consigning some people to wait for their rights allows the popular culture in the United States to maintain a sense of social equality despite the manifest inequality of our social relations. Some people are poor while others are rich, but the poor will catch up—wealth can "trickle down" and people can "move up." Undoubtedly, some are accorded rights that others are not, but any aggrieved parties, whether racial and ethnic minorities, LGBTQ people, and/or women, need to continue fighting for their rights by engaging in the democratic process.

Given that these "other" groups constitute the majority of the population, one might think that the need for so many to fight for their rights would undercut the popular sense of equality in the United States. The claim for democratic pluralism as a form of horizontal equality (rather than hierarchical inequality) seems wobbly at best. Yet the progress narrative repeatedly stabilizes the public response to particular inequalities: it may be that everyone is not now treated equally, but the march of freedom and equality will bring more and more people into the world of democratic pluralism. One just has to wait for progress.

US history is often told as if one group after another does receive rights: African Americans are granted rights with the Emancipation Proclamation in 1863 and the Fifteenth Amendment to the Constitution offering the vote to African American men in 1870, women with the Nineteenth Amendment to the Constitution in 1920—although just which women got to vote is another question. And then African Americans gained their rights (again) with the Civil Rights Act in 1964 and the vote (again) with the Voting Rights Act in 1965, lesbian women (again) and gay men (again) with *their* civil rights in 2015, Latinx people maybe in the 1960s, maybe in a yet to be determined future? For Asian Americans, maybe with the prohibition on employment discrimination in the Civil Rights Act of 1964, or maybe with immigration reform in 1965, or maybe in that same yet to be determined future? How might Native American struggles for sovereignty be accounted for in this narrative about progress toward universal rights? What about poor people's rights, including the exclusion of poor people from voting? The Poor People's

Campaign was part of the Civil Rights Movement in the 1960s and had to be revived (again) in the twenty-first century.[67] And what about religious minorities? Must the Muslims to whom the Trump administration's "travel ban" applies remain forever in the waiting room of history?

Suddenly, instead of facing what looks like a steady march of equality, with one group after another stepping forward to claim their rights, we find ourselves in a much more chaotic world. The waiting room of history is, it seems, a very busy place, not only crowded with the majority of the world's people, but also with people who seem to be constantly moving. They are supposedly moving forward, and yet also seem to need to redo this very movement again and again.

This narrative, one dedicated to change over time, to the march of progress, allows for us to think that people are moving out of the waiting room—were this a hospital waiting room, someone, thank goodness, is finally getting to see the doctor—and yet, this very movement makes it impossible to see that the waiting room remains stubbornly, persistently full. Not to push the metaphor too far, but those who spend a lot of their time in hospital emergency rooms are likely, by the very fact that this room is where they wait to see the doctor, to return again and again. Yet this return is virtually invisible because the progress narrative demands a sense of movement; there is always another group to step forward (as another moves back). In other words, in modernity, the idea that "the more things change the more they stay the same" is not descriptive; it is prescriptive. Mobility for stasis.

Social change can be so repetitive because the very means by which change is supposed to happen also creates the repeated need for "change." Yet understanding the limits of change also opens space for thinking about how it might be possible to produce both social analysis and social change without simply contributing to mobility for stasis.[68] Chakrabarty, for example, suggests the need for "struggling, or even groping, for nonstatist forms of democracy that we cannot yet either understand or envisage completely. This is so because in the mode of being attentive to the 'minority' of subaltern pasts, we stay with heterogeneities without seeking to reduce them to any overarching principle that speaks for an already given whole."[69] Social analysis must resist presuming the coherent social whole that secularism is supposed to provide. This alternative approach to social analysis will not line up different examples to make them fit into a predetermined universal scheme of which they are but particular instances. Instead, it follows multiple lines of analysis as they are knotted together and torn apart.

Possibility

Such analysis and attendant action present a difficult challenge, but not an impossible one. If part of the problem is the universal, empty time of secularism, then one helpful shift is to acknowledge disjunctions both within the universal and at its edges. Secularism is not a universal whole; rather, secularism is many things in different times and places, and this multiplicity does not simply represent different instantiations of "the same" thing. Nor are its edges clearly delineated by an opposition to religion. Rather, secularisms exist in complex relation to each other and to religions.[70]

The liberal polity that is secured by secularism also need not be understood as a coherent whole; rather, it is a social body multiple. The profound impact of the progress narrative in maintaining social hierarchies is all too clear in the work of the United States Supreme Court. As long as change is focused on legal battles, for instance, the categories used by the law will determine the limits of possibility. Mobility for stasis works in part by constraining people within the liberal political imagination, keeping activism focused on the liberal state and legal change. Legal change is clearly very significant and can make a profound impact on people's lives, but it cannot be the only site for action. Though it may be realized for some, the promise of progress simultaneously and repeatedly fails, but such failures are not recorded on a timeline. We need to follow other lines of flight and leave timelines to tell their familiar, and radically incomplete, stories of progress.

Once the field of possibility is opened up, new prospects for action also make sense, such as combining legal reforms with change that exceeds the boundaries of the state (nonstatist solutions) simultaneously. Such a double move can help to resist the forces pushing change for some into stasis for many.

For instance, the National Domestic Workers Alliance (NDWA) has taken up modes of organizing that seek legal change and at the same time challenge the liberal framework of both capitalism and the nation. In 2008, the Barnard Center for Research on Women hosted a national congress of domestic workers' organizations, sponsored by the National Domestic Workers Alliance, founded at the US Social Forum in 2007.[71] NDWA's organizing has been markedly successful, securing a first major legislative victory in 2010 with the passage of the New York State Domestic Workers Bill of Rights. This was the first legislation in the United States to offer basic workplace protections to domestic workers, a victory that has been followed by similar legislation in several other states.[72]

The New York bill's passage was based on NDWA's analysis of domestic workers' status as part of a group of workers excluded from the category of labor. Through histories that deny the personhood of some workers in the United States, those employed in domestic work, farm work, and various forms of piece work that are associated with slavery or immigration have also been excluded from basic labor protections, including the right to time off and basic compensation for severance of employment. In addressing this problem, the bill of rights represents a major victory for domestic workers, as well as a major shift in labor law in the United States. Because of its argument for legislative expansion of the category "protected workers," at one level NDWA's organizing is basic liberal advocacy to expand democracy's protections.

At another level, however, NDWA's organizing expands well beyond this liberal, legal framework. The group's analysis shows that the labor associated with slavery is not as "free" as other forms of work; the effects of the US history of slavery continue. The "free market" is not actually free. It does not allow for the free movement of individuals to sell their labor, but instead uses national boundaries to detain and devalue the labor of immigrants. The political work of NDWA crosses national boundaries. Not only are many of the workers who organize with NDWA themselves migrants, but they critique the "freedoms" of the global labor market, and they work in solidarity with related organizations around the world. The report details both the working conditions experienced by members of the Filipinx migrant workers' organization DAMAYAN and analyzes how the free market and the liberal myth of autonomy enforce global labor migration and exploitation.

Even more profoundly, however, the work undertaken by domestic workers challenges the liberal humanist concept of the autonomous individual who is the subject of modern law, freedom, and wage labor at its core. As we saw in chapter 1, the idea of human beings as autonomous individuals is central to Christian secularism. The title of a DAMAYAN report, "Doing the Work That Makes All Work Possible," insists that people widely recognized as autonomous individuals are not, in fact, autonomous.[73] Rather, those who historically have been able to sell their labor by virtue of protected freedoms have always been and still are dependent on forms of domestic labor provided by others, including family members and paid domestic laborers.

Taking seriously the claims of those who do "the work that makes all work possible" requires more than an expansion of the liberal humanist social contract. The domestic and excluded workers' movements refuse to give up either a deep critique of the conditions of contemporary capitalism or much-needed advocacy focused on legislative change to gain basic legal protections. In maintaining both prongs of action, the fight for workers' rights provides a model for seeking social change that moves beyond the liberal state, while also refusing to leave domestic and other excluded workers vulnerable to the ongoing injustices instituted in the liberal state. This double strategy allows social movements to address both the immediate challenges facing vulnerable people and the need for expansive social change.

Dynamic Change

In the predominant narrative of American sexual politics—"Why sex? Because religion"—the *Obergefell* decision legalizing same-sex marriage would be the end of the story. For some people, this ending is a triumphant victory for progress. Others see it as a loss for religion and a contravention of religious ethics by an ever-encroaching secularism. The intertwined terms of the progress narrative—secularism, gay rights, and progress—can be made to line up over against religion, and some commentators make that move. After all, as noted in chapter 2, before 2012 every presidential candidate, no matter what party, declared that they opposed gay marriage *for religious reasons*. Religious conservatives find it easy to declare that that they must fight back to reverse their historic loss to the secular state, and emphasize that the Constitution mandates not only freedom of religion, but also the free exercise of religious belief.

The *Hobby Lobby* decision demonstrates the power of acting on the idea that religious conviction must prevail over secular law when the two come into direct conflict. But the story doesn't have to be told this way, and it certainly doesn't have to end as did that case.

For example, *Obergefell* can be part of a narrative that challenges the limits of the liberal legal approach and takes up the type of broader critique offered by NDWA's analysis. In the decision, Justice Kennedy described the movement "forward" in a quasi-religious idiom that gives a highly restricted sense of social possibilities: "From their beginning to their most recent page, the annals of human history reveal the *transcendent importance of marriage*. The lifelong union of a man and a woman always has promised nobility and dignity to all persons, without regard to their station in life. Marriage is *sacred* to those who live by their religions and offers *unique fulfillment* to those who find meaning in the secular realm. Its dynamic allows two people to find a life that could not be found alone, for a marriage becomes greater than just the two persons. Rising from the most basic human needs, marriage is essential to our most profound hopes and aspirations [my emphasis throughout]."[74] This trip through the annals of history is not unusual for US Supreme Court decisions on questions of sexuality, and as is common in such opinions, historical diversity in religious commitments and sexual arrangements, including celibacy and diversity in marriage practices, is almost completely invisible.[75]

The idea that marriage between "a man and a woman" is a historically consistent practice regardless of "station in life" ignores historical restrictions on who could marry, including the history of restrictions in US law on the marriage of enslaved persons. Kennedy's decision also suppresses religious diversity in how marriage has been understood, whether the polygamy of the biblical patriarchs or polygamous and polygynous practices in various communities. Historian Henry Abelove has traced a variety of marital practices in eighteenth-century England that did not always involve the state, and historian Nancy Cott has written eloquently about the diversity of marriage practice in the history of the United States. Ominously, Cott's historical work also shows that, despite the diversity of marriage practices, marriage law has been used repeatedly to bolster the structure of the nation-state and to narrow social possibility. Whether it is the militarily backed demand that the

Church of Jesus Christ of Latter-Day Saints give up polygamy and accept US sovereignty or the restriction of political participation by immigrants, marriage has helped to define and solidify the boundaries of the nation.[76]

Justice Kennedy cites Cott's work in his decision, pointing to the history of marriage as one of both "continuity and change."[77] Yet what the New York Times called Justice Kennedy's "paean to marriage" availed itself so freely of the "transcendent" that Michael Cobb, a queer studies scholar, asked whether the effect of the decision would be to make it even *harder* for anyone who was not married to live with the "dignity" afforded to those who are.[78] Cobb points out that single people form a majority of the US population (50.2 percent in 2015), and that "singleness includes *everyone* at some point, even those who are married: love ends; spouses cheat; someone dies first. To be in a marriage, no matter how strong, is always a precarious condition, which means that the dignity you've been given can be taken away at any moment."

Cobb suggests we could have gone elsewhere: "Marriage equality activists could have pursued a different agenda—challenging the need for sexual scrutiny by the state, and the constellation of benefits that belong to marriage—but they didn't." A variety of queer activists and thinkers have, however, been pursuing this "different agenda," and they have found ways in which broadening possibilities for sexual practice might also build connections among movements for social justice. As such, this "different agenda" steps aside from the repetitive exercise of "progress" and "backlash," an exercise enabled by shifting among issues so as to sustain the linear progress narrative as the organizing principle for understanding social change.[79]

As Lisa Duggan and Richard Kim suggest in their preface to the essay collection "A New Queer Agenda," "Most of the essays here examine the issues that have been largely missing from the current 'gay agenda.' They address those 'other' issues that affect the 99 percent—economic justice, housing, healthcare, welfare, immigration, sexual liberation, aging, disability, gender identity and expression, HIV/AIDS, rural and urban community organizing, public space, sex work, drugs, crime, policing and prisons, reproductive rights, racial injustice, and more."[80] Attention to these issues produces an alternative political vision, one organized around "sexual democracy," rather than turning to the state that doles out the crucial benefits through spousal access.[81]

Shifting political imagination in light of a dynamically interrelated analysis adds another angle of approach. Creative proposals like those offered in "A New Queer Agenda" provide a means of building all kinds of relationships that meet both needs and desires. Such creativity also provides a means of building connections across issues, as, for example, when healthcare, economics, and sexuality all come together at the nexus of caring labor and so-called "private life." This is also a point of potential assemblage among social movements that consider alternatives to the privatized family life, which leaves people vulnerable—among, for example, feminist movements, queer movements, workers' rights movements, migrant movements, and antiracist movements. Is it possible, as activist Amber Hollibaugh has asked, to broaden the frame of economic justice, for example, to take account of "queer survival economies"? Hollibaugh emphasizes the significance of creating an agenda that includes all of the ways in which queer people organize their lives to make them sustainable, including working in survival economies that don't even offer the precarious security of minimum wage work.[82]

Clearly articulating the relational basis for social justice can help to build a scaffolding of connection and to resist divisions among those whose interests and values might be actively aligned. Social change need not produce mobility for stasis—it need not be directed toward forward progress. Alternatively, social change can be directed toward relationality, turning activist attention away from the horizon of the future and toward one another.

Conclusion

Melancholy Utopias

Why sex? Because everything.

This answer makes for what I am depicting as a kaleidoscopic movement among issues—sex, gender, race, class, migration, nationalism, capitalism, globalization, healthcare, war, peace—each turn creating a new pattern to be contemplated and acted upon, and then another turn. Each turn generates multiple realizations of sex, and each appears whole unto itself, having its own logical certainties. But with another turn the pattern changes and the pieces relate to each other differently.

The disjunctions between two patterns can be made to seem coherent through various epistemological mechanisms or habits of thought. For example, a slippage between different patterns can make the seeming coherence of one pattern reinforce the idea that other patterns also make sense. The mutual reinforcement among patterns can then be socially productive, creating a common sense that continually shores up already existing patterns of social relation.

In chapter 4, for instance, we saw how this works through movement among issues by considering the treatment of different cases across a relatively short time span by the Supreme Court of the United States. Each time an issue is considered it is fitted into the pattern of the national US narrative of social progress. Perhaps, as with "gay marriage," it is another step along the path of progress; perhaps, as with voting rights, we have moved so far along the path that protections against racist voter suppression are seen by the court as no longer necessary; perhaps that supposed progress in eradicating racism can reassure the nation that ignoring gender equality for the sake of religious freedom is not a major problem, as in the case of refusing to ensure medical coverage for contraception; perhaps, when considering the religious freedom of those from majority-Muslim countries who might want to come to the United States, the Court can claim that the path of progress is so advanced that the US ban on travel from several of those countries couldn't possibly be discriminatory (despite President Trump's statements on Twitter).[1]

The elements of the progress narrative move around in each of these stories—sometimes sexual politics are advanced, sometimes set back; sometimes the Supreme Court is a site for antiracist action and sometimes the very fact that Supreme Court decisions resisted racism once upon a time creates the narrative force for extending racism in the current moment. When brought together so as to follow the movement among the different cases, the stories seem to undercut the idea of the advancement of social progress as an accurate description of the role of the Supreme Court or of US history as a whole. But when each of the stories is told individually they have powerful social force—providing a common sense that runs across much of the political spectrum in the US: democracy expands.

Each story is different, but each story also ultimately says: progress. If it seems for a moment that one story might waver on this point, we can switch to another—voting rights undercut? Let's turn to gay rights. Access to contraception undermined? Let's turn to racial justice. Religious freedom ignored? Let's denounce racism in the past. The stories thus variously buttress each other so that this common sense becomes a relatively immovable social structure as different patterns provide scaffolding and the whole structure has a number of reinforcements that make it difficult to shift or change. The repetition of stories means there is no need to doubt the overall pattern. Mobility for stasis.

Ethnographer Annemarie Mol calls this kind of separation of different stories so as to make them seem coherent "distribution." She argues that, once separated so as to create internal coherence, the stories can then be "coordinated" so as to build a sense of overall coherence—together they create a body multiple. Stories about the body politic told through narrative devices like distribution and coordination produce a social body multiple.

Analysis of the social body multiple—joined by productive incoherence, mobility for stasis, and a willingness to risk theoretical promiscuity—can help to address the complexity of a world in motion, wherein sexual politics are articulated in complex social, cultural, political, and economic relations. Because the social body is multiple, no one set of relations can be promoted to govern all the others, making our world make sense.

Here in the conclusion, I will explore what can be made of the simultaneously precise and promiscuous ways in which sexual politics are a part of the social body multiple. Kaleidoscopic patterns yield productive incoherence that is used to create a sense of change and possibility while keeping the order of things the same. Yet analyzing multiplicity also offers a way not only to refuse the concordance of difference, but to make something else, a sociality incongruent with the forces of domination and exploitation. Another body, another world is possible, but when we develop the analytic tools to understand what we are refusing, we also work toward what, with José Esteban Muñoz, we may call "the then and there of queer futurity"—a melancholy utopia, to be sure, but a future different from the one that has been prepared for us.

Possibilities for Justice

Some of these possibilities can be found in collaborative projects between activists, artists, and academics undertaken by the Barnard Center for Research on Women (BCRW). The Poverty and Public Housing Working Group, led by Pamela Phillips, for example, works with residents of public housing and activists in New York City to change the commonsense narrative about public housing from one of impossibility to one of sustenance and significance. This project connects with long-running work at BCRW with activists committed to prison abolition, including CeCe McDonald, Dean Spade, and Tourmaline.[2] As CeCe McDonald vividly declares, prison abolition is important: "There's not enough Mop-N-Glow to make any prison safe for *anybody*."[3]

The connections between housing and prison abolition were made explicit in the conversation, "Homes for All, Cages for None: Housing Justice in an Age of Abolition," with scholars Christina Heatherton and Craig Willse.[4] Willse argues that homelessness is the "modern incarnation" of the "afterlives of colonialism and slavery that allow the United States to continue to exist." Even as homelessness is the consequence of intertwined racial, economic, and political histories, it is "also specific" to the current moment of neoliberal economics, pivotally effected by the Reagan administration's cuts to government support for housing. Willse's work takes an approach the Argentinian scholar Cecilia Varela calls a "deep form of intersectionality," in which issues that seem separate (access to affordable housing and prison abolition, in this instance) are analyzed through intertwining historical relations, without erasing their specificity.[5] This method of holding together both specificity and interrelation is key to the kaleidoscopic analysis I have pursued in *The Sex Obsession*.

Recognizing disjunction does not do away with the ability to make the connections necessary to address injustice, but it does change how one might go about the work of social change, including the way in which activists might make ethical and political claims. For instance, CeCe Mc-Donald's crucial point that prison cannot be made safe for anybody (not for trans people, not for people of color, not for queer people, not for straight people, not for white people, not for anybody) is effectively a universal claim. And universal claims can be quite powerful. But Mc-Donald's claim is made on a different basis and with a hope for different effects than the results of liberal claims for universal freedom and equality, which produce the progress narrative and its mobility for stasis.[6]

Abolition is a particularly powerful universal claim, as articulated in the No One Is Disposable project through a series of video conversations among CeCe McDonald, Tourmaline, and Dean Spade, produced at BCRW by Hope Dector. As Tourmaline says in the first video: "Abolition means that no one is disposable; no one is expendable. We are not exiling or punishing people in order to solve our problems."[7] Allowing for disjunction—difference, incompleteness, and solidarity, aspiration, grief, and hope—can sustain claims like "*no one* is disposable" without simply reiterating the norms that are usually invoked to turn a disjunctive reality into unity and universalism.

Spade and Tourmaline go on to explain in further conversations that the logic of punishment is both ineffective in solving the problems it claims to address (whether domestic violence or violence on the street) and often dependent on the very same norms of race and gender that create the conditions that spark violent encounters. As the Survived and Punished project organized by Mariame Kaba has shown, if one does not "seem like a victim" (the very words of the police, as discussed in chapter 1), one is likely to end up in jail when police respond to an attack.[8] The state's use of police violence as a primary means to address a range of social issues, from homelessness to addiction to poverty itself, also depends on a flawed logic that divides the world into categories of guilty people and innocent people.[9] This division depends on ignoring some of the most extensive and most threatening forms of violence in which many people generally perceived to be "innocent" participate (such as in consumer economies that depend on sweatshop labor), making it easy to overlook violence by those generally associated with innocence and simultaneously making it likely that policing will focus inordinately on those who are culturally associated with "guilt."[10] The significance of the universal claim, then, is to resist this logic of division between those presumed innocent and those presumed guilty. Only with a universal claim—that all are indisposable—is it possible to "build relationships modeled on a different logic."[11]

Universal claims also allow for a vision of the world that creates possibilities for surviving and even thriving regardless of the prevailing hegemonic logic.[12] McDonald articulates this possibility through the concept of "love." In taking seriously her own acts of self-defense, she had to actively resist the sense that her life was not worth defending. Only with the sense that everyone—including herself, her attackers, and her fellow prisoners—is worthy of love could she find an ethical guide that could sustain her in prison: "You want that person to know that there is love in the world."[13]

Spade has shown how trans and gender-nonconforming lives are thought by the dominant culture to be impossible, and yet trans people have of necessity figured out how to enable survival and thriving. "We demand the impossible; our own survival."[14] Tourmaline has termed this type of trans world-building, "making a way out of no way."[15] This idea of sustaining lives and building worlds for which there is "no way" indexes the utopian, but melancholy, project of universal claims like "no one is disposable." One can be committed to the idea that "no one is disposable" and also know perfectly well that Black people, other people of color, trans people, homeless people, and disabled people are immured in prisons and even killed by the authorities without causing a public stir and understand fully that workers are exploited with no concern for their bodies and minds, their health destroyed for the sake of wages that cannot sustain them.[16]

To claim that no one is disposable is, however, to transpose impossibility into reality. Consider the shift from the Trans Day of Remembrance into the Trans Life and Liberation campaign. The Trans Day of Remembrance is an annual event focused on remembering the lives of trans women and men lost through both legal, state-sponsored violence and extra-legal violence. In 2013, trans writer and activist Janet Mock wrote a widely read essay, "Celebrating Living Trans Women on Transgender Day of Remembrance," about the need to attend to the living as well as the dead, to celebrate trans women who survive: "We can't only celebrate trans women of color in memoriam. We must begin uplifting trans women of color, speaking their names and praises, in their lives."[17] Artist Micah Bazant turned this manifesto into an art series celebrating the lives of trans women and femmes of color. The series provides portraits collaboratively developed "about and *with* living trans people on the frontlines of our liberation movement."[18]

One of the key points to this work is that one cannot simply look away from violence to see life possibilities. Life and liberation together require attending to the violence of impossible lives, mourning their loss, and making communities in which trans people can thrive.

Queering Universalism

The idea that a different type of universalism might be possible comes from a number of different sources, bringing together the religious studies critique of secularism with the queer critique of normativity. If we take seriously historian Ann Braude's idea (discussed in chapter 1) of recognizing "religion" in unexpected places, we do, indeed, find it in very queer sites.[19] Take, for example, the conclusion of José Esteban Muñoz's book *Cruising Utopia: The Then and There of Queer Futurity*, titled "Take Ecstasy with Me," an allusion to the song of the same title.[20] As performed by the indie pop group The Magnetic Fields—whose lead singer, Stephin Merritt, Muñoz describes as "wonderfully languid"—the song offers possibilities that Muñoz names as "pleasures both pharmaceutical and carnal" and evokes utopian possibilities. The song is, however, quite melancholy, invoking both lost childhood pleasures and violence directed against its narrator and a friend or lover for "just holding hands." From this melancholy starting point, Muñoz is able to draw upon a number of sources for the queer world-making embodied in the invitation to "take ecstasy with me": the Christian ascetic ecstasy of St. Teresa of Ávila, the science fiction and life writing of Samuel Delany and Delany's imaginative intertwining with the poetry of Hart Crane, and Muñoz's own reading of poet Elizabeth Bishop. This world is not really religious or secular—it does, however, call upon a carnal ecstasy that is about more than sex. And it is most decidedly queer.

In responding to Muñoz's invitation to take ecstasy, I hear the possibility that queer melancholy could move toward a perverse affirmation of both hardship and political solidarity with others outcast from the normative world. The practice of pursuing melancholic ecstasy so as to produce a perverse solidarity is in its combination of hope and impossibility a utopian undertaking. In the common sense understanding of melancholy, the emotion hardly seems like the feeling that one would like for one's utopia. Utopia is no-place, after all, ours to imagine. So why imagine a queer utopia overcast with melancholy?

But Muñoz's book engages an understanding of utopia that does not represent Elysian fields stretching unproblematically to the horizon. Muñoz reminds us to be critical and think queerly about how utopia might be imagined. One scholar who has done this is Angelika Bammer, who wrote a very persuasive book about feminist utopian literature and how its imagined utopian worlds—in which everything works well and everyone is happy—seemed to always depend on first removing any people who threaten the holistically idealized realm—such as the removal of all men from Charlotte Perkins Gilman's *Herland* (echoed by Gilman's commitment to racial "disappearances," as documented by Tracy Fessenden).[21]

Bammer's critique focuses on the ways in which Gilman's and other feminist utopias create happiness for "everyone" by removing from "everyone" people who might be disruptive or simply different, a line of thought that connects to later queer work, such as Sara Ahmed's questioning of the familial imperative, "I just want you to be happy." Such a wish can be positively oppressive in its assumption that the family already knows what will make one happy. As Simone de Beauvoir observed, "There is no possibility of measuring the happiness of others, and it is always easy to describe as happy the situation in which one wishes to place them." This logic is made vivid by Jeanette Winterson's amazingly titled memoir, *Why Be Happy When You Could Be Normal?*, which is the urgent question her mother asks of her queer daughter as she heads out the door.[22] Both Ahmed and Winterson know that the familial imperative to be happy actually confuses happiness with normalcy, something that queer children have already acted against.

In contrast with a utopian happiness dependent upon disappearances, Muñoz's affectively charged, melancholic cruising of utopia affirms that happiness need not be the most cherished goal of queer world-making. Queer utopias are open to ambivalence and disjunction, are off-kilter, even perverse.[23] Refusing to give up on parts of oneself and one's life in order to join a world, no matter how utopian, in which everyone is "happy" means embracing negative affects that have been the subject of much recent work on public feelings. For instance, David L. Eng and David Kazanjian's important book on grief, *Loss: The Politics of Mourning*, brings together queer scholarship, critical race studies, and postcolonial work. These fields all necessarily engage loss. In none is grief a simply individual event, for individuals are always already part of collectivities that—given the punitive powers of sexism, homophobia, transphobia, racism, and colonialism—have suffered loss.

Grieving therefore requires a "politics of mourning," collective work necessary to address loss and turn toward a sense of fractured possibility.[24] A sense of the future as far from determined, as needing to be created, loosens the hold of a traditional utopian universalism. Utopia is far from assured, and belonging may be quite tentative, which saves utopian possibility from the violence necessary to secure the borders of a holistic world that is also supposed to secure happiness for those who remain inside. An affectively queer utopia is open to crosscutting differences, including those of race, nation, and sex. Not everybody has to be contained within this bounded universal, nor does such a utopia require everybody to share in the same feelings, whether of happiness or of grief. In this sense, norms would no longer be sutured to modern power (as we saw in chapter 1), no longer would the statistically average also represent what everyone *should* do and be. There is no projection of a common course of life progressing from one stage to the next, childhood to adulthood.

Disability studies has an important contribution to make to this disjunctive sense of universal possibility. The queer universalism I imagine is one akin to the concepts of universal access and universal design. Disability is itself so variable that it requires many different approaches to create accessibility—ramps and bathrooms for those with mobility impairments, braille and sign language interpretation, large-type print and environments free from toxins, new ways of conceptualizing mental "health," and a more capacious understanding of healthy "development" that is not already presupposed as progress from one stage to another in a set amount of time. *Universal access* names a fundamental openness to bodily and mental difference from "everybody else" and a recognition that normalcy is achieved only by the willingness to exclude. *Universal design* means rethinking and remaking the world so that it works as best it can for everyone. As with the claim that "no one is disposable," the claim that the world should be designed to be accessible to everyone is both a simple idea and one that is difficult, if not impossible, to enact. This impossibility makes universal design a persistently aspirational undertaking, and thus a necessarily melancholy one.

The usual means of establishing universalism is to make everyone equal to a normative human being. In *Frontiers of Justice*, Martha Nussbaum provides a critique of this approach in her in-depth reading of John Rawls's *A Theory of Justice*.[25] For Rawls, the normative person does not have specific characteristics, but rather is an individual with whom anyone behind a "veil of ignorance" might identify. This "veil of ignorance" allows for a social contract that provides the best possible outcome when individuals do not yet know what their positions in society might be and are therefore loath to create restrictions and assume inequalities.

Nussbaum shows that, despite Rawls's best efforts, his system still requires certain assumptions about what it means to be a citizen who is the subject of justice, including those of nationality as the container of the law, of agency and therefore of ability, and of human reason. She develops a picture of this subject of justice by exploring three factors that challenge the assumptions and boundaries of liberal justice as articulated by Rawls: disability, nationality, and species membership. As Nussbaum lays out in great detail, the presumptions about personhood that are invoked in the forming of the social contract have serious implications for the moral possibilities that will follow. She shows, for example, that Rawls cannot bring disability within the framework of justice as defined by this contract. Rather Rawls hopes that disability will be addressed after the parameters of justice are established. He thus puts people with disabilities in the position of the objects of legislative action like the Americans with Disabilities Act, which affords disabled people basic access to the public sphere. But endowing disabled people with rights that they must struggle to have protected is very different from positioning them as the subjects of justice formation. Rawls effectively makes disabled people petitioners to the normative subjects who actively participate in framing justice, leaving disabled people in the waiting room of history.[26]

Not surprisingly, the progress narrative is part of what stabilizes the liberal claim to offer universal justice despite the limits illuminated by Nussbaum. In the world delineated by progress, the "frontiers of justice" would perpetually expand so that those who can be understood to be somehow equivalent to the normative individual—those nonhuman animals who meet the criteria for human dignity, for example—could be progressively included within its boundaries.[27] As with the progress narrative, this method of expanding equivalence does not actually include everyone (whether all people or all beings). Someone is always waiting to enter the charmed circle.[28]

Significantly, this approach to universalism is not only a liberal one. The practice of equivalences is also the centerpiece of the radical democracy Chantal Mouffe and Ernesto Laclau advance in their now classic *Hegemony and Socialist Strategy*.[29] Laclau and Mouffe tell a story of progressively expanding universalism in which the "rights of man" developed in the French Revolution are expanded as women claim rights equivalent to those of men and colonized people claim rights equivalent to those of citizens of the metropole. With each equivalence a new horizon for democracy is established, and this ever-receding horizon focalizes radical possibility for ever-expanding democracy.

This method of creating universal equality not only shares the challenges of the progress narrative, but also creates the need to constantly assess the criteria for inclusion in the charmed circle and to police its boundaries. These boundaries create the parameters of justice, deciding who eventually seems to be like the normative "us" and should be admitted to full social membership while excluding all others. The method focuses on the normative person, and those within the boundaries created by equivalence to that normative person can part of the coherent—and universal—community.

One of the main analytic benefits of the critique of normativity is to maintain a focus on the differential within any coherent community, whether that coherent community is organized by liberal universalism, radical democratic humanism, traditional communitarianism, or Marxian communism. In short, the demand for coherent community can lead to discipline within a community so as to create a coherent and "authentic" version of that community, and one way to defy this demand is by attending to differences. The queer critique of normativity is definitionally a critique of the norms by which the boundaries of any community might be established. In other words, not only are queers the abject of communities that are defined by nation, gender, religion, race, or class, but also those defined by sexuality. The frequently invoked "gay and lesbian community" is created by normative operations as certainly as is any national or religious community. It is at this point that "queer" parts company with any identity, including the homosexuality that David Halperin has argued tends to "haunt" queer theory.[30] While queer critique is often associated with homosexuality and cannot completely escape this association, neither can it comfortably provide a site for coherent homosexual identity or community.

The melancholy aspect of queer universalism, then, is that it doesn't make life whole again. Everything and everyone does not just fit together without "friction" (as Anna Tsing suggests) or "loss" (as Eng and Kazanjian insist).[31] The world remains disjunctive, open, incomplete. A melancholic approach to universal access or design emphasizes the disjunctions between, for example, those with mobility impairments for whom modern hotels are great places for conferences because full of elevators and long straight hallways, while they are terrible places for those with allergic responses to cleaning products and other chemical substrates of modern commercial venues. The point is not to treat these challenges to moving through the world in "the same" manner or as if they were "equivalent" but to accommodate them both through alternative practices, most immediately through the redesign of the built environment, and more broadly by defending the natural biosphere— truly a melancholic commitment in the face of continued (and legally protected) destruction of the natural world.[32]

It's not enough to hope to include disabled people in an already existing normative world, a world that supposedly includes "everyone" but that both actively and passively excludes most of existence and most of what might be possible. Rather, the hope is to build universal access from the ground up, and to do so by starting from the needs of those who are excluded by the design of the existing world. The argument is that the normative world does not include "everyone," nor, in Rawls's terms, is it even the best that can be imagined for everyone.

Addressing the needs of those who are beyond the frontiers of justice may actually make the social world better for many. Those who suffer from the chemical substrate of the human-made environment would have their concerns addressed, and as a result many living beings would be healthier. "Air fresheners" would be a thing of the past, a small thing, yes, but there would also be fewer dangerous chemical spills that require the evacuation of whole neighborhoods, and fewer carcinogens let loose on the world. Many who suffer from allergies would be relieved, for there would be less particulate matter in the air. More organic food means fewer insecticides and herbicides, so agricultural workers would no longer of necessity be handling poisons. In other words, by looking to shift the blocks to access faced by those who are different, we create a world that works better for nearly everyone. We can find ways to change social spaces, not just so as to include those who have been excluded, but also so as to improve possibilities more broadly, even as gaps and failures will remain.

The difference between the two methods of approaching broader inclusion—that of inclusion within an *existing normative community* and that of *shifting norms* as a basis for universal access—can be seen by comparing curb cuts in New York City and those in downtown New Haven, Connecticut. The curb cuts in the city are special areas cut into the center of each side of any given corner to make it possible to wheel across the street and back up onto the sidewalk (although the actual effectiveness and accessibility of the cuts varies widely). While absolutely crucial for getting around the city in a wheelchair, all curb cuts are not equal. The ones in New York City tend to pool water, which turns to ice in the winter, and then into icy slush right below the cutout section of the curb. On some New Haven streets, by contrast, the entire curb is gently sloped around the corner, so that a wheelchair user and a walking person can traverse at whatever point they wish. There is no specially marked zone of inclusion in a space otherwise made for normative people, and there is also no specially produced pool of water to curse during times of rain and snow.

Rather than thinking of disability as the exception for which special provisions are made, universal access suggests that a universally inclusive built environment is better for all, or at least many more, people. And, in fact, even when the curb cut is a special cutout zone, most walking people walk through the cutout. Why? Because it's actually easier than stepping down off the curb and back up. And anyone wheeling a cart or pushing a stroller uses the curb cut. They would manage, of course, without it, as a wheelchair user could not, but the curb cut makes their lives easier. This ease is one of the main points that disability activists make—our built environment is not particularly easy or healthful for those who understand themselves as able-bodied, which means they often use the special spaces and mechanisms created for people with disabilities, like curb cuts, ramps, and lifts.

Moreover, in a world of universal access the disabling environments against which people living lives of "brilliant imperfection" (in Eli Clare's lovely phrase) must struggle daily are far fewer, making what was once a disabled person into someone who shares in the various struggles of life without being specially marked out. In other words, rather than minute inquiries into the boundaries of categories, universal access takes into account the effortful challenge of living with imperfections, including imperfections experienced by those who understand themselves as able-bodied. These challenges become the stuff of everyday lives even as universal access creates space for those lives to be undertaken in solidarity.[33]

Universal access cannot, of course, be universal, even in its utopian guise. The aspiration leaves a melancholy remainder. That crucial recognition is important in the project of making a queer utopia, because universality, perfect access, and justice, like queer desires, can never be fully satisfied. In *Cruising Utopia*, Muñoz speaks of the "then and there of queer futurity," so it follows that a queer utopia is melancholy in the recognition that irreparable loss cannot be undone, and incompleteness remains inevitable. Queer is not a point of arrival; its temporality refuses such a straight trajectory. And queer is more a verb than a substantive, more a way of doing than a way of being.[34] Justice remains to be done—therein lies the hope.

Kaleidoscopic Action

It is possible to realize some part of this hope by taking up a kaleidoscopic approach not just to social analysis but to action on behalf of social justice. Moving kaleidoscopically allows for the recognition that gender and sex are part of universal social justice, without dissolving the specificity of sexual politics into a more general sense of the social. Correlatively, the promise of practicing theoretical promiscuity by moving kaleidoscopically among approaches is an openness to potentially contradictory approaches and descriptions so as not to overshadow the complexity of the world. This openness also allows for a similar complexity in seeking multiple approaches to social change.

In thinking about how to maintain the power of universal claims without dissolving the specificity of particular lives, for example, I have learned from Eve Sedgwick's critique of the binary pair of universalizing-minoritizing, part of a matrix of other relations including homosexual-heterosexual, natural-unnatural, and so on. Sedgwick is open to *both* a universalizing understanding of sexuality that sees it everywhere *and* a minoritizing realization that attends to the particularities, the singularity, of any specific sexuality. In modernity, *everyone* must have an identifiable sexuality, while simultaneously sex is specifically tied to *minorities*, so that, for example, homosexuals and other sexual perverts are punitively differentiated from heterosexuals, and people of color are punitively set apart from white people by imputed sexual attributes.

This combination produces a dynamic epistemological field in which minoritizing and universalizing views are simultaneously active. In fact, the creation of minorities is part of the process of universalization. Universalism is supposed to include everyone, but that is impossible—no single framework is all-inclusive, so the process of ascribing qualities to the universal leads to the exclusion of certain groups who must be seen as "minorities," separate from the larger, general public, with needs that can be addressed only after the social contract has been framed. Universal access sets this paradigm on its ear, of course, for making the world accessible to nonnormative bodies removes barriers for all. Similarly, the National Domestic Workers Alliance argues that domestic work is not a minor form of labor but rather paradigmatic of contemporary labor more generally: domestic workers are pressured to do more in less time, can be fired with no warning, are paid terribly low wages, and must often travel far to find work. These are the conditions of precarity that the forces of neoliberalism strive to make universal. Disabled lives are both universal and specific; domestic work is both paradigmatic and a distinct form of labor.

Sedgwick argues that challenging the "epistemology of the closet" requires attending to the movement between the claims of the universal and the processes of creating minorities. This dual approach allows for recognition of connections among social issues, without simply dissolving them into one another.[35] Sex is not simply another difference—analogous or homologous to other such differences—that can be pluralistically lined up. Nor can queer methods be generalized as a radical form of analysis that ignores the specifics of genders and sexualities. Maintaining both the universalizing and minoritizing approaches to sex allows for a strategy that leans to universalizing, showing how sex crosses the public-private boundary, for instance—while also recognizing the specificity of sex, which can, sometimes for some people, happily stay behind doors. Sex is central to multiple social formations, so that an adequate social analysis must take it into account; and sex sticks to some bodies more than others and is lived in multitudinous ways.

As Sedgwick notes, the epistemological conditions of modernity make analytic categories come in and out of focus—effectively in and out of the closet—which fundamentally shapes what categories can do in social analysis. To review: we saw this happen in the Supreme Court cases. Justice Alito observes in his *Hobby Lobby* decision that critics say allowing discrimination against women demonstrates that the Court is willing to entertain arguments against racial discrimination, as well. No, he says, the Court is unshakable in its commitment to "racial justice" in contrast to so-called "gender equality," which pushes into the closet the Court's gutting of the Voting Rights Act in 2013. But when it argues before the Court, the Century Foundation opposes race-based affirmative action by declaring we should focus on access to college by *poor students* of all races *rather than* by race, effectively closeting race in favor of class. In the rhetoric of the Court and the parties before it, highly consequential social categories thus come forward in argument or are overshadowed, always in relation to one another. Since the Court routinely decides on questions of constitutionality, the legal consequences of these arguments and the justices' decisions are hard to exaggerate.

Turning the kaleidoscope allows for analytic attention and action in response to both universalized and minoritized instantiations of sex. Sex is central to many issues, despite sometimes being treated as a limited, even trivial, concern. *And* sex is a specific field that does not expansively cover the world. I have repeatedly turned to this metaphor to visualize the ways in which our critical analyses are pushed around, as it were, by biopower, neoliberalism, racial capitalism, patriarchal social reproduction, and more. Yet these very analytic terms name modes of domination and exploitation that radical analysis must account for, leading me to argue for the importance of attending to the kaleidoscopic effects produced by power in the social field. Looking through the kaleidoscope may be mesmerizing, but it also affords us a way to think about and act to undo domination and exploitation.

No single framework can coherently contain everything. That means we need to be ready to entertain multiple analytic possibilities. Hegemonic power works by assembling in a dizzying array binary after binary out of the relations that make up the social categories of race, gender, sex, and class. We need to slow that movement down to follow what moves where, and when, sometimes looking very closely at a particular part of the pattern, sometimes focusing on the social, cultural, political, and economic together, looking at the larger pattern, and sometimes watching the movement among different patterns.

Perverse Possibility for a Melancholy Utopia

Sexual liberation is revolutionary, and sex alone cannot the revolution make. This is the complex reality for those who seek social justice.

The revolutionary aspirations of the movements of the 1960s and 1970s remain inspiring even as they have also become less and less animating for many, as swaths of the feminist movement were captured by corporate interests and gay and lesbian organizing increasingly invested in the right to marriage as a contract with the state along with the right of gay and trans people to serve the state openly in the military. As the ever-expanding frontiers of justice have now apparently encompassed gays and lesbians with access to marriage and perhaps will allow trans people to once again openly join the armed services, what has become of radical practices? Are sex and gender radicals simply left in a bleakly assimilationist America?

The practice of sexual politics remains to be thought anew precisely as a practice that is productive of a remainder in excess of the categories of modern normativity. The animating force of queer desires, for instance, still has something to offer about not just sexual politics, but also capacious political possibility and cacophonous activist practice.[36]

The question of how sex can contribute to a more general project of emancipation has been open for decades.[37] Herbert Marcuse saw in the movements for sexual liberation a real possibility for a revolution in sensibility, a shift in desire that has material effects. In his 1969 *Essay on Liberation*, he writes, "In proclaiming the 'permanent challenge' [*la contestation permanente*] . . . the Great Refusal, they recognized the mark of social repression, even in the most sublime manifestations of traditional culture, even in the most spectacular manifestations of technical progress."[38] To refuse the powerfully regulatory nature of the Protestant ethic and its dedication to work, marriage, and family involves turning way from the "immense collection of commodities that Marx says is the defining image of wealth, which leads people to "sell not only their labor but their leisure time."[39] This appreciation of a refusal of the blandishments of capital and bourgeois culture is further advanced by Antonio Negri's idea that taking back our leisure time can be crucially subversive of capital.[40]

In the end, however, neither the imperative claim of revolt nor the escape from "social repression" was, in truth, revolutionary. For the Protestant ethic derives its power from being both regulatory *and* constitutive of freedom.

Throughout this book I have suggested that gender, sex, and sexual politics work to constitute subjects suited to the prevailing economic system; correlatively, sexual politics can also contribute to the undoing of that system. A perverse sexual politics, in its commitment to difference, can help to create a social world not constructed around the autonomous individual and "his" household (as so powerfully articulated by the Protestant reformer John Calvin). This possibility is particularly important in an era of neoliberal privatization, when the individual household is called upon to carry ever-increasing burdens for the production of social goods.

Perverse sex does not promise a simple disengagement from capitalism. Perversions are themselves produced by the operation of capital.[41] But, as Amy Villarejo points out in a reading of Roderick Ferguson's critique of normativity, normalizing discourses see these perversions as "symptom and nothing more"; if one keeps within the stricture of normativity, one "cannot read perversion as agency."[42] This type of queer theory recognizes capital as an agent of perversion, but also raises the question of whether queer perversity can be an agent of economic justice. In taking this turn, queer theory is following the path laid out by its name, the turning (perversion) of a term of derogation away from its intended effects. In other words, if we do not seek to delineate a pure realm of justice from an impure capitalism, then new spaces open that might admittedly be perverse and that also become sites for building a different kind of justice.[43]

We must understand, however, that even the exuberantly perverse subject is not simply free from norms. Every practice and activity has norms that regulate behavior, *but not all norms are sutured to modern power in the same way.*

The problematic of normativity means that the central question of sexual ethics is not the one that obsesses the American public—whether the ethic is liberatory or regulatory—but how the ethic is sutured to the operation of power. As we saw in chapter 1, sex is a central means by which an individual becomes a recognizable social subject, and a focus on sexual liberation, in which sex is presumed to be the route to freedom, is as much an operation of modern power as is state regulation. A modern ethical life that is organized around normativity disciplines subjects through both state regulation and imperatives to free oneself, whether the Enlightenment imperative to free oneself from religious dogma by embracing secularism or the market imperative to freely choose one's sexual "lifestyle."

Economist David Ruccio argues that if a particular form of human subjectivity is one of the conditions that make for a particular form of economic relations, then "changing the subject" can be a crucial part of changing economic relations. One means of taking up this struggle is to address both the social relations that produce the autonomous individual and alternative formations of subjectivity. If exploitation and domination are mutually constitutive, then the fundamental antagonism of the working class to capital cannot be the only motivation for "fostering [the] communal relations" necessary to socialism.[44]

Ruccio suggests we can think instead of "'decentered communities,' a form of social agency radically different from the individuality that is constituted in a society characterized by commodity exchange."[45] The contribution made by queer theory and politics to this project is the possibility of turning the perversities induced by capitalism toward producing subjectivities that are neither unbearably communal nor impossibly coherent.[46] In the last chapter of *Love the Sin*, Ann Pellegrini and I argue that sex is a site for the production of values.[47] Sex has this productive potential because it is a site for the creation, enactment, and embodiment of different types of relationships that can materialize alternative ethical possibility.

Perverse relations produce ethical values through the cultivation of relational possibilities. While liberal freedom is grounded in the free choice of the individual whose only moral requirements are to respect the freedom of other such autonomous individuals, it is possible to start elsewhere and create relations with differently calibrated norms. Perverse relations have any number of material starting points, in the farm collective or the bathhouse or perhaps a pack of human and nonhuman animals or a school of thought.[48]

This type of relationality can contribute to broader questions of economic and social justice. Let us return for a moment to the question of AIDS policy and global economics considered in chapter 3. Perverse justice might open the door to possibilities that could address economic issues in a different framework. Elizabeth Freeman, for example, has argued that queer relations challenge the neoliberal logic of development, insisting "that various queer social practices, especially those involving enjoyable bodily sensations, produce form(s) of time consciousness, even historical consciousness, that can intervene upon the material damage done in the name of development."[49] Is it possible that a queer approach to the AIDS crisis might also provide for economic justice?

One of the interventions that queer theory suggests is that we look at relational configurations that are in the interstices between and among individual, family, community, nation-state, and the inter- or transnational. How do we think of caring for those children orphaned by AIDS? Do we think of them only in terms of the "family"? In other words, are the choices for these children only adoption by families or institutionalization and care by the state? Are there alternative relational configurations for them and for those who care for them? Nesting the individual in the family, the family in the nation, the nation in the state, and the state in the international makes it difficult to think differently about how our relations with one another make the world. Yet there are a wide range of grassroots organizations taking on the task of caring for children orphaned by AIDS.[50] In addition, organizations like Health Global Access Project (Health GAP) have worked to connect the need for prevention campaigns, including those that distribute condoms, to economic questions like those of providing debt relief and ending budget ceilings imposed by the International Monetary Fund. Such ceilings often do not allow countries who receive IMF loans to adequately fund healthcare.[51] The Treatment Action Campaign in South Africa has connected the distribution of condoms to questions of access to all kinds of education from formal schooling to the development of "life skills."[52]

Gregg Bordowitz, who long worked with ACT UP and various art collectives in the US to fight AIDS, has also worked with the Treatment Action Campaign; he argues that transnational queer AIDS organizing develops precisely the type of alternative subjectivity that could form the basis for new visions of economic justice. He finds helpful the concept of the "multitude" that Michael Hardt and Antonio Negri have proposed as the subject of global movements for justice. The idea of a queer multitude is undoubtedly a perversion of Hardt and Negri's original conception, but Bordowitz argues that transnational AIDS organizing creates the material base of such a multitudinous movement precisely because the fight against AIDS draws together such a wide set of issues. Sexuality, economics, healthcare, and education are each differently, yet crucially, important in thinking through a phenomenon as complex and overburdened with meaning as AIDS.[53] Perhaps most importantly, the persons working together in such a wide-ranging movement do not share a single identity, family, community, or nation. HIV, a virus that does not respect the boundaries of identity, is itself a perverse and powerful adversary, and addressing it requires shifting configurations of both agency and movement.

The demand for relational justice grounded in a perverse multitude is quite different from the AIDS policy of the Bush administration (discussed in chapter 3). That policy and others that have been considered herein are founded in the punitive justifications of the Protestant ethic, as if "faithfulness" in marriage could thwart a virus, or end poverty, or "stop terrorism" in a world of radically unequal power. Religion, sexuality, political economy, war and peace are all entangled. That complex interrelation contributes to biopolitics powered by the disciplinary force of the Protestant ethic.

Yet there is no necessity dictating that reality. There are alternative formations enlivened by queer relationality that perversely, joyfully refuse that ethic in order instead to enliven possibility.

Justice from the Ground Up

Throughout this book, I have been making connections between the process of thinking differently and the project of acting differently on behalf of a more inclusive and less unjust world. Developing new ways of being in the world requires new ways of thinking about and understanding that world. I am animated by the hopefulness of a perversely utopian justice that does not secure its borders, while I understand that universal inclusiveness can never be achieved. The question for activists is how to stick with enabling paradoxes like this one.

As we saw in chapter 2, the incoherence of complex social relations can be taken up in ways that are unfortunately productive for both exploitation and domination. Fortunately, activists and thinkers have also developed methods to grasp the incoherence of the world and make it productive for justice. In *Methodology of the Oppressed*, Chela Sandoval develops an approach she terms "differential consciousness" that does not claim one side of a binary opposition over the other, a refusal that addresses the double binds created by such binaries embedded in complex, hegemonic social formations.[54] She is writing about the modern idea of logical coherence based on the choice between "A" and "Not-A" (the cat is *either* on *or* off the mat, not both at once). She argues that such coherence creates a double bind of sameness/difference in which those who are different from dominant norms must either claim sameness to the norm (in an "equal rights" framework) or claim their difference—only to have that difference become wholly definitive of their social subjectivity. If one is categorized as a religious minority in the majority/minority binary, one will then be required to exhibit proper authenticity to demonstrate *how one is different* from the majority.[55] The same logic drives the gender binary, M/F, in which the two sides of the binary constrain all possibility and the feminine is defined by its negativity—that which is feminine is *not* masculine and the binary allows no other possibilities. Instead of being bound to this either/or logic, Sandoval urges "weaving 'between and among' oppositional categories."[56]

Sandoval identifies different modes of activism for social justice, and she suggests that it is possible to move among these different modes of action. Instead of being *either* revolutionary *or* reformist, social movement may be both at the same time.[57] Dean Spade has adopted Sandoval's method of "differential consciousness" specifically in the context of "trans resistance," pointing out that differential consciousness provides a means of addressing the paradoxical world created by the administrative state.[58] Spade shows how no single strategy vis-à-vis the state will automatically meet the needs of those oppressed by the state.

Differential consciousness allows for the type of state and nonstate action deployed by the National Domestic Workers Alliance (discussed in chapter 4). Such complex activism can register the simultaneous, if disjunctive, value of legal reform, organizing beyond the limits of the state, and action directly opposed to the state. The choice to oppose the state, for example, offers the same revolutionary hope as that invoked by liberationists who refuse the demands of capital. But such action alone can also leave many people who are directly affected by state policy without recourse.[59] Take efforts to legally reform marijuana laws: some people can expect never to have to engage with the police over their possession and use of marijuana, whereas for others, primarily people of color in neighborhoods highly surveilled by the police, the possession of even small amounts of marijuana can lead to imprisonment. Legal reform of various kinds—such as reform of drug laws—can be a crucial part of improving life chances for those people regularly targeted by the police.[60] In responding to these realities, activist Tarso Ramos, executive director of Political Research Associates, recommends a three-part strategy—work with the state; work against the state; work separately from the state to build alternative spaces, institutions, relationships, and possibilities.[61]

The practices of such a multiplicitous strategy are often most effective when articulated together, but not necessarily to recreate a liberal whole (which may never have existed). Rather, they can be connected in networks that are perhaps looser than those of liberal politics, but also less rigid in their demand for coherence, and thus less likely to create inescapable double binds. Holding in mind a both/and of political possibility rather than the either/or of common sense enables work that actively invites intersection with multiple movements seeking justice. In other words, when differential consciousness is adopted in conceptualizing an approach to political action it may result in more promiscuous practices than are usually associated with political strategy.

Spade takes as his measure of any approach the effects on those most directly affected by a particular action. Trans resistance would consider the effects of policies on those who must in Tourmaline's terms "make a way out of no way." This approach is akin to the liberation theology version of the Catholic "preferential option for the poor," and also intersects with the work of universal design and universal access—both concepts developed to address the specific needs of different, and sometimes radically disadvantaged, disabled people that have wider application. Any universal preferential option for the poor would include the multitude of people with AIDS around the world about whom Bordowitz is concerned, for instance. This starting point means that justice will be built not by moving toward an ever-receding horizon but by starting from the material grounding that enables impossible lives and building from there.

As we have seen, one of the major contributions made by disability studies is to encourage thinking about universal design and access as invoking a complex universal. This complexity means that there is no single site of those who are most affected, but instead multiple sites, each of which is crisscrossed by overlapping and entangled social relations. Disabled people need different and even contradictory changes to end social disablement and access the world. Addressing the needs of those most affected requires doing different—and potentially contradictory—things.

Differential consciousness allows for weaving between and among the entanglements among, for example, poverty, gender, race, sex, and disability. Working with such multiplicity implies the need for the active pursuit of solidarity. Writing in 1991, Sandoval bases her efforts in the coalitional formation in the United States of the collective social project "U.S. Third World feminism." This collectivity is by no means unified in sameness—but rather in difference: "U.S. Third World feminism arose out of the matrix of the very discourses denying, permitting, and producing difference."[62] This contradictory multiplicity calls for active awareness of difference within unity, the need to work on multiple fronts, and "the ability to read the current situation of power" and respond with "grace, flexibility, and strength" to its complexities.[63]

Universal access suggests that moving toward justice requires much more than inclusion, as the tangle of relations created by categorization involves not only the lines drawn to create categories but also the simultaneous interactions among subjects cut off from each other when placed within categories. And differences may multiply: we may move beyond the early feminist troika of gender, race, and class to consider nation, religion, and disability or beyond the mid-twentieth-century religious consensus of Protestant, Catholic, and Jew to recognize that there are Muslims, Hindus, and "nones" in the US public sphere or add letters to LGBQTI, or, or, or. These expansions are vital, but what adding up these differences does not do is disturb the lineup—by, say, indicating that transgender and intersex are not just "other" versions of gender or sexual identity, or that not all ethnic groups can be represented during particular months of the year, or that not all religions can be called "faiths." The critique of this pluralist lineup is not so unusual, but it indicates that expanding the horizon while keeping the picture plane flat will continue to exclude those whose differences disrupt the lineup—whose lives exceed the boundaries of any particular category, thus disturbing the equivalence between and among the categories themselves.[64] The universal does not already exist, somewhere out there beyond the horizon (or even over the rainbow).

Building a universal from the ground up means that the universal needs to be actively produced. Such a universal is built by putting together pieces that do not necessarily fit together but that are rather tied together through complex connections, such that the pieces are sometimes imbricated with one another and sometimes leave open gaps. Such a project holds out greater hope for justice than does the politics of inclusion (or diversity or pluralism or multiculturalism) that is frequently offered as a response to categorization and exclusion, but it is not simply a given.[65] The pieces of such a complex coalition must be connected through action and are likely to fit together oddly.

I am thus interested in how different practices for social change can be actively articulated. Alison Kafer, in her groundbreaking book *Feminist, Queer, Crip*, advocates "accessible futures" for social movements, and she identifies the ways in which both disabled and trans people have an interest in universally accessible bathrooms. Indeed, there is some deep intertwining (and confusion) between gender and disability, both in bathroom signs—in which "wheelchair" stands next to or perhaps outside of gender—and in the broader world in which, as Christina Crosby says about her experience when out in public: "I don't have a gender, I have a wheelchair." Kafer describes the embodiment of this potential alliance through a description of direct action by the wittily named group PISSAR, People in Search of Safe and Accessible Restrooms.[66]

Building on this articulated approach to accessible futures, I suggest drawing upon the idea of queer world-making described by Muñoz to develop a practice of *making*, rather than simply identifying, such mutuality. Specifically, such articulations must often be made at the point where movements have historically been divided. For example, disabled people and domestic workers who care for them have historically been placed on different sides of legislation meant to help either workers or disabled people—but rarely both at once. It is not necessary, however, to divide the needs of these two groups; indeed, Grace Chang has argued that they are at a fundamental level aligned.[67] And NDWA has formed a partnership with Hand in Hand, a network of employers of domestic workers, so that the two groups can work together for change, a partnership that is now affiliated with a larger advocacy network, Caring Across Generations.[68]

In a world of social policy organized by the economics of scarcity, in which any gain for domestic workers is made to be a loss for the disabled people who need their care (and vice versa), the activism of these groups—especially when addressing policy questions—has often been at odds. And the relations between disabled workers and those for whom they care are indeed quite complex. One reason for "revaluing domestic work" as a way of both protecting and supporting those in need of care and those who provide it is to shift the focus to the act of caring labor. By shifting the focus of value from "groups" or "identities" to an interrelation, like the act of caring, it is possible to rethink both ethical possibility and political economy.

Elizabeth Freeman suggests, for example, that it is possible to make something queer of the materials that are produced in the interstices of capitalism, although she is somewhat skeptical of the demands even of the term "queer." Her hopes are for queer modes of living that are not held to the ascetic standards of the perfectly, perpetually oppositional queer:

> I find myself emotionally compelled by the not-quite-queer-enough longing for [literary, cultural] form that turns us backward to prior moments, forward to embarrassing utopias, sideways to forms of being and belonging that seem, on the face of it, completely banal. This is the essence of what I think Sedgwick means by reparative criticism: that because we can't know in advance, but only retrospectively if even then, what is queer and what is not, we gather and combine eclectically, dragging a bunch of cultural debris around us and stacking it in idiosyncratic piles *"not necessarily like any preexisting whole,"* though composed of what preexists. For queer scholars and activists, this cultural debris includes our incomplete, partial, or otherwise failed transformations of the social field.[69]

Freeman organizes her work around what she terms "revolutions in the 1960s and 1970s—political programs not only as yet incompletely realized but impossible to realize in their original mode—that nevertheless provide pleasure as well as pain."[70] She turns to artistic practices that draw on the material from these social movements and also develop projects "aslant" to both these projects and the dominant culture that they engaged and critiqued.[71] Freeman and other thinkers, like Muñoz, Sandoval, Spade, Ramos, Kafer, Tourmaline, and McDonald, provide an approach to social change that encourages both critique and openness, and that recognizes the realities of pain and social injustice while keeping in mind an equally real sense of pleasure and possibility.

Let us return for a moment to the series of projects at the Barnard Center for Research on Women that have appeared at various moments in this book: Changing the Narrative on Public Housing with Pamela Phillips and No One Is Disposable, with Tourmaline, Dean Spade, and CeCe McDonald (in this conclusion); Responding to Violence, Promoting Justice, led by Tiloma Jayasinghe, the former executive director of Sakhi for South Asian Women (in chapter 1); Revaluing Domestic Work, with the National Domestic Workers Alliance, and Queer Survival Economies, led by Amber Hollibaugh (both in chapter 4). These projects use various differential approaches, ones aslant of traditional organizing along the well-worn pathways of single issues. In doing so, they refuse the usual binaries and separations among issues. They make universal claims from the nonnormative margins as they claim public housing as a public good that might support raising a family, even if that family is not of the supposedly traditional nuclear variety, or as they make a way for trans lives out of no way (No One Is Disposable); as they connect sex and economics (Queer Survival Economies); as they make demands of the nation-state while organizing well outside of the state in the era of global capitalism (Revaluing Domestic Work); and as they refuse both patriarchal religiosity and secular state policing so as to promote justice (Responding to Violence, Restoring Justice).

In one way, the refusal to separate the religious from the secular lies at the heart of *The Sex Obsession*. The answer to the question that initiates the book's investigations—"Why sex?"—is definitively not religion. Nor is secular freedom the answer to norms and policies driven by religious conservatism. Instead, in chapter 1 I considered approaches that are neither precisely religious nor precisely secular, or perhaps both religious and secular. In other words, refusing to choose either religion or secularism as the hero or villain of the story may open possibilities, as may taking gender and sex seriously as politics. If, for example, one imagines relational possibilities that are not confined by the split between religion and secularism, public and private, nor normative genders, then perhaps sex will become a space of openness, rather than moral collateral for the nation.

So perhaps the question is not "Why?" but "How?": How to articulate the politics of gender and sex into relations that sustain alternative possibilities, assemblages that connect and create different worlds, values that contribute differently to economic value? How to make sexual politics and social justice?

One could imagine a freedom alternative to the freedoms granted to the supposedly autonomous individual, a freedom of racial and sexual liberation, a freedom at once religious and secular, a freedom tied to justice, including economic justice. This relational freedom strengthens rather than dissolves the bonds of care even as it strengthens the connections between caring and justice.[72] One could imagine a justice different than the imperative to discipline and punish, a justice that embraces perversity in all of its promise and possibility, a justice that consorts with caring and does so queerly.

Conditions that require care often involve incapacity and loss, and possibility may be overshadowed by melancholy. Yet the work of care can animate the long and hopeful project of making justice from the ground up.

And, importantly, this project can begin with local, even intimate, relations and/or with translocal possibilities. Taking care work seriously is about justice in the home. It is also about a new basis for the economy, one that centers caring labor rather than extractive production of commodities. The work of care opens an aperture to envision and enact new affiliations as part of making a universally accessible world, one in which queer and trans people of color, disabled people, survivors of violence and the memories of those lost to violence, those in need of care and those who do the work of care can all thrive.

Building justice from the ground up does not restrict possibility to the bounded framework of community and is not oriented to a previously calculated horizon of meaning. Openness to possibility allows for promiscuous practice and productive incoherence, for fundamentally recalculating value, and for sustaining melancholy while seeking utopia. Building justice from the ground up offers the perverse pleasure of imagining the world in fundamentally different terms, and organizing to make it so.

Why not?

ACKNOWLEDGMENTS

The Sex Obsession is, in part, a book about how one's life is dynamically intertwined with and truly dependent upon the efforts of others. I learned this lesson reading feminist theory in graduate school and ended up writing a dissertation on the moral labor that makes the good life possible. The lesson of an interdependent life was brought home to me in a new way after my beloved Christina Crosby was injured and paralyzed in a bicycle accident. To detail everything that people did for us, and specifically for me, during and in the many years since Christina's recovery from that accident would take another book (and so, I refer the reader to Christina's lovingly written *A Body, Undone: Living On after Great Pain*). The multitude who helped me to live on, to do so with Christina, and to (re)build a life that includes writing books is somewhat astonishing, creating a gratitude that cannot be fully represented. And so, by way of acknowledgement, I simply offer the names of many, many people and dogs (thanks to Laura Levitt for showing the way) and cats (your fault, Ann Pellegrini) who have kept me going and in so doing made this book possible. It is necessarily a partial list. My gratitude goes back to gifts that were given many years ago for which I remain grateful. And I did not even know some of the people who made food and left it on the back porch when Christina was in the hospital or who have done other, innumerable life-sustaining activities since then, including contributing to the intellectual project of this book. But even with an incomplete account, I am happy for the opportunity to say "thank you" in writing.

I hope that in this list and in the chapters of *The Sex Obsession* the value of queer consanguinity and making connections is evident: Henry Abelove, Katherine Acey, Ana Amuchástegui, Rebecca Alpert, Carol Anderson, Ulrike Auga, Sally Bachner, Paola Bacchetta, Kate Bedford, Lee Bell, Jonathan Beller, Lauren Berlant, Elizabeth Bernstein, Laura Berry, Elizabeth Bobrick, Abbie Boggs, Liz Boylan, Nella van den Brandt, Laura Briggs, Liz Budnitz, Tina Campt, Elizabeth Castelli, Sealing Cheng, Yvette Christiansë, Rebecca Chopp, Laura Ciolkowski, Pam Cobrin, Lisa Cohen, Donna Collier, Sally Cooper, Crosbys and those who love them (Jeff, Beth, Kirsten, Matt Blose, Colin, Andrea Molina), Avi Cummings, Ann Cvetkovich, Flora Davidson, Casey Davis, Tayo Davis, Hope Dector, Mercer Dector, Pamela Dickey-Young, Carolyn Dinshaw, Babe the Dog, Moxie Doxie, Ann duCille, Lisa Duggan, David Eng, Katherine Franke, Jenna Freedman, Susan Adler Funk, Allen Funk, Abosede George, Faye Ginsburg, E. Grace Glenny, Kaiama Glover, Che Gossett, Lori Gruen, Gisela Fosado, Kim F. Hall, Amber Hollibaugh, David Hopson, Maja Horn, Gertrude Hughes, Christine Jacobsen, Jakobsens and those who love them (Jane, Tom, Nickie, Emily, Ryan Flynn, Craig, Pooja Louis), Tiloma Jayasingha, Anne Jonas, Maisey Cooper Jordan-Young, Rebecca Jordan-Young, Miranda Joseph, Tally Kampen, Kapya Kaoma, Jennie Kassanoff, J. Kehaulani Kauanui, Laura Kay, Kerwin Kaye, Hamid Khan, Surina Khan, Elizabeth Lapovsky Kennedy, David Kyuman Kim, Dorothy Ko, Natasha Korda, Julie Kubala, Zoe Kubala, Shoshana Lautner, Maria Elena Letona, Laura Levitt, Walden Levitt, Eng-Beng Lim, Katie Lofton, Marget Long, Liza McAlister, Sean McCann, Kate McCullough. Molly McGarry, Moses, Louisa Merchant, Monica Miller, Minoo Moallem, Brenna Moore, Manijeh Moradian, Jill Morawski, Sydnie L. Mosely, José Esteban Muñoz, Premilla Nadasen, Afsaneh Najmabadi, Tami Navarro, Celia Naylor, Maggie Nelson, Miriam Neptune, Ellen Nerenberg, Ren Ellis Neyra, Tavia Nyong'o, Richard Ohmann, Shannon O'Neill, Mark Padilla, Mario Pecheny, Gayle Pemberton, Gretchen Phillips, Pamela Phillips, Ann Pellegrini, Orlando, Zanzibar, Spartacus, Tiberia Pellegrini, Alex Pittman, Victoria Pitts-Taylor, Sine Plambech, Jasbir Puar, Dania Rajendra, Tarso Ramos, Jen Rhee, Alex Roe, Ali Rosa-Salas, Jordy Rosenberg, Mary-Jane Rubenstein, Teemu Ruskola, Avgi Saketopoulou, Samuel AKA Sam, Ranu Samantrai, Catherine Sameh, Claudia Schippert, Linda Schlossberg, Laurel Schneider, Beverly Seckinger, Svati Shah, Ann-Lou Shapiro, Michael Shapiro, Susan Shapiro, Anu Sharma, Herb Sloan, Ebonie Smith, Dean Spade, Kathryn Bond Stockton, Bill Stowe, Andy Szegedy-Maszak, Timea Szell, Neferti Tadiar, Martha Tenney, Jennifer Terry, Theo, Milo Thiesen, Lisa Tiersten, Tourmaline, Emilie M. Townes, Karin Trainor, Lucy Trainor, Betsy Traube, Tracey

Trothen, Jennifer Tucker, Gina Ulysse, Shannon Upshur, Anthony Vale-rio, Walden, Erin Ward, David Harrington Watt, Margot Weiss, Shelly White, Robyn Wiegman, Melissa Wilcox, Nancy Worman, Nicci Yin, Angela Zito. I do owe special thanks to everyone who read this book (all or in part) and made it better: Elizabeth Bernstein, Mary Pat Brady, Joshua Chambers-Letson, Christina Crosby (her words do sometimes appear in the text), Hope Dector, Lisa Duggan, Dave Eng, Julie Kubala, Laura Levitt, Vincent Lloyd, Tavia Nyong'o, Ann Pellegrini, Anthony Petro, Mayra Rivera, Erin Runions, Roberto D. Sirvent, David Harrington Watt, and Eric Zinner. And particular gratitude for some opportunities to workshop parts of the book in its later stages: at the American Philo-sophical Association—Pacific Division, organized by Roberto Sirvent; at the University of Pennsylvania's Gender, Sexuality and Women's Studies Program, organized by Kathleen Brown and Deborah Thomas; at Vanderbilt University's LGBT Policy Lab and Vanderbilt Divinity School, organized by Kitt Carpenter, Emilie M. Townes, and Ellen Ar-mour; and at Chinese University of Hong Kong, organized by Sealing Cheng. Thank you.

If living is a collaborative project, thinking most certainly is, and my thinking has been fashioned and forged by a particularly generous group of collaborators and a particularly capacious set of collabora-tions: Laura Levitt and Julie Kubala (my first collaborators), Ann Pel-legrini (*Love the Sin*, *Secularisms*, and everything), Elizabeth Bernstein (walking and talking and Gender Justice), Elizabeth Castelli (*Interven-tions* and much more), Rebecca Alpert (all things American Academy of Religion), Elizabeth Lapovsky Kennedy (Sex and Freedom), Kate Bedford (Sexual and Economic Justice), Amber Hollibaugh and Su-rina Khan (Desiring Change), Rebecca Jordan-Young and Lucy Trainor (Reproductive Justice in Action), Tiloma Jaysinghe (Responding to Violence, Restoring Justice), Pamela Phillipa (Changing the Narrative: A Public Housing Project), Anne-Marie Korte (Religion and Gender: Post-Colonial, Post-Secular and Queer Perspectives), and Lila Abu-Lughod (Religion and the Global Framing of Gender Violence). Some of these projects and, hence, parts of the thinking for this book were developed with grants from the Ford Foundation, Mellon Foundation, Overbrook Foundation, Luce Foundation, and the New York Women's

Foundation. None of this thinking would have been possible without the fifteen extraordinary years I spent as the director of the Barnard Center for Research on Women. This book is my homage to the staff, faculty, advisory board, and activist and artistic partners who continue to inspire me through their fierce and fabulous engagements with the world. You make both justice and joy.

Thank you to Christina Crosby for living on.

NOTES

INTRODUCTION

1 I use the term "sexual politics" as a means of maintaining the connection between the politics of gender and those of sexuality. I will argue that the movement among issues in US public discourse, including movement back and forth between sex and gender, is a form of mobility for stasis that maintains predominant power relations. Mary Anne Case makes a strong argument for the intertwining of sex and gender in Catholic thinking and in US law: "Seeing the Sex and Justice Landscape through the Vatican's Eyes: The War on Gender and the Seamless Garment of Sexual Rights," in *The War on Sex*, ed. David Halperin and Trevor Hoppe (Durham, NC: Duke University Press, 2017), 211–25. For an earlier feminist conceptualization, see Kate Millett, *Sexual Politics* (New York: Doubleday, 1970).

2 The literature on "culture wars" is now vast. A few key texts are James Davison Hunter, *Culture Wars: The Struggle to Control Family, Art, Education, Law and Politics in the United States* (New York: Basic Books, 1992); Robin D. G. Kelley, *Yo' Mama's Disfunktional!: Fighting the Culture Wars in Urban America* (Boston: Beacon Press, 1998); and Andrew Hartman, *A War for the Soul of America: A History of the Culture Wars* (Chicago: University of Chicago Press, 2016).

3 Alex Ross, "Love on the March," *New Yorker*, November 12, 2012, www.newyorker.com.

4 Linda Burnham, "The Absence of a Gender Justice Framework in Social Justice Organizing," Center for the Education of Women, University of Michigan, July 2008. For a few of the major texts in these schools of thought, see Kimberlé Crenshaw, "Demarginalizing the Intersection of Race and Sex: A Black Feminist Critique of Antidiscrimination Doctrine, Feminist Theory and Antiracist Politics," *University of Chicago Legal Forum* (1989), https://chicagounbound.uchicago.edu; Cathy Cohen, "Punks, Bulldaggers, and Welfare Queens: The Radical Potential of Queer Politics?," in *Black Queer Studies: A Critical Anthology*, ed. E. Patrick Johnson and Mae Henderson (Durham, NC: Duke University Press, 2005), 21–51; Arnaldo Cruz-Malavé and Martin Manalansan, eds., *Queer Globalizations: Citizenship and the Afterlife of Colonialism* (New York: New York University Press, 2002); Gayatri Gopinath, *Impossible Desires: Queer Diasporas and South Asian Public Cultures* (Durham, NC: Duke University Press, 2005); Dean Spade, *Normal Life: Administrative Violence, Critical Trans Politics, and the Limits of Life* (Durham, NC: Duke University Press, 2015).

5 Rebecca Alpert, "Religious Liberty, Same-Sex Marriage, and the Case of Reconstructionist Judaism," in *God Forbid: Religion and Sex in American Public Life*, ed. Kathleen M. Sands (New York: Oxford University Press, 2000), 124–34.

6 For an analysis of the 2016 and 2020 electoral dynamics that simply conflates evangelicals with sexual conservatism, see Julie Zauzmer, "'He Gets It': Evangelicals Aren't Turned Off by Trump's First Term," *Washington Post*, August 13, 2019, www.washingtonpost.com.

7 Max Strassfeld, "Transing Religious Studies," *Journal of Feminist Studies in Religion* 34.1 (Spring 2018): 37–53. Strassfeld shows how the presumption that trans lives are opposed to religious commitment is both inaccurate and contributes to conservative legislation that is damaging to trans people.

8 Gillian Frank, Bethany Moreton, and Heather R. White, *Devotions and Desires: Histories of Sexuality in the Twentieth-Century United States* (Chapel Hill: University of North Carolina Press, 2018).

9 On common sense, see Stuart Hall et al., *Policing the Crisis: Mugging the State and Law and Order* (London: Macmillan, 1978), and Stuart Hall, "Gramsci and Us," in *The Hard Road to Renewal: Thatcherism and the Crisis of the Left* (London: Verso, 1988).

10 There is now a great deal published in both academic and memoir form on "purity culture" and its development in the late twentieth century among young Christians, particularly on how adolescent girls are encouraged to display their Christian identities. See Bearman and Hannah Brückner, "Promising the Future: Virginity Pledges and First Intercourse," *American Journal of Sociology* 106.4 (January 2001): 859–912; Linda Kay Klein, *Pure: Inside the Evangelical Movement That Shamed a Generation of Young Women and How I Broke Free* (New York: Touchstone, 2018); and Rebecca Lemke, *The Scarlet Virgins: When Sex Replaces Salvation* (Norman, OK: Anatole Publishing, 2017).

11 Kate Zernike and John M. Broder, "War? Jobs? No, Character Counted Most to Voters," *New York Times*, November 4, 2004, P1.

12 Although there was subsequent criticism of the *Times'* conclusion that voters in 2004 were more concerned with "values" than were voters in previous elections, there was little to no criticism of the presumption that "values" was a synonym for sexual conservatism. Frank Rich reported that 22 percent of voters said that "moral values" were their primary concern in 2004, down from 2000 (35 percent) and 1996 (40 percent). While Rich provided this criticism of the numbers, he made no comment on the limitation of values to those of sexual conservatism. See Frank Rich, "The Great Indecency Hoax," *New York Times*, November 28, 2004, www.nytimes.com.

13 Consider Bill Clinton's response to his impeachment over lying about his sexual relationship with Monica Lewinsky. Clinton was only the second president in history to be impeached, an indicator of some kind of public concern about sex (although what kind this book will continue to explore in its pages), but Clinton claimed that this matter was really between him, his family, and his God.

See Gary Scott Smith, *Religion in the Oval Office: The Religious Life of American Presidents* (New York: Oxford University Press, 2015). And the same can be said for his detractors—if you read the statements of Clinton's congressional opponents, including Newt Gingrich, you will find plenty of references to God. Steven M. Gillon, *The Pact: Bill Clinton, Newt Gingrich, and the Rivalry That Defined a Generation* (New York: Oxford University Press, 2008).

14 Robert Byrd, *Congressional Record—Senate,* vol. 142, no. 123, Tuesday, September 10, 1996.

15 FRC Action, the lobbying arm of the Family Research Council, sponsored the original Values Voters Summit in 2006 to promote an assemblage that ties together sexual politics and religion while further knotting them to small-government conservatism. As their website states: "Values Voter Summit was created in 2006 to provide a forum to help inform and mobilize citizens across America to preserve the bedrock values of traditional marriage, religious liberty, sanctity of life and limited government that make our nation strong." Values Voter Summit, www.valuesvotersummit.org.

16 Louis Althusser, "Ideology and Ideological State Apparatuses (Notes towards an Investigation)," in *Lenin and Philosophy and Other Essays* (New York: Monthly Review Press, 1972), 117.

17 Nick Corasaniti, "Donald Trump Quotes Scripture, Sort of, at Liberty University Speech," *New York Times,* January 18, 2016, www.nytimes.com.

18 As I discuss in chapter 4, the Trump administration's executive order banning travel mainly from Muslim-majority countries and the eventual Supreme Court decision declaring its legality undermine the possibility that Muslims might be accorded any serious sense of religious freedom in the United States at present. Trump, President of the United States v. Hawaii et al., Certiorari to the United States Court of Appeals for the Ninth Circuit, No. 17–965, argued April 25, 2018, decided June 26, 2018. Justice Sotomayor writes of President Trump's statements and tweets about the ban: "The full record paints a far more harrowing picture, from which a reasonable observer would readily conclude that the Proclamation was motivated by hostility and animus toward the Muslim faith" (4). And she goes on to list instances in which the president expressly stated that the "travel ban" was directed toward Muslims (4–10).

19 David Chidester, *Savage Systems: Colonialism and Comparative Religion in Southern Africa* (Charlottesville: University of Virginia Press, 1996); Richard King, *Orientalism and Religion: Postcolonial Theory, India, and the "Mystic East"* (London: Routledge, 1999); Tisa Wenger, *We Have a Religion: The 1920s Pueblo Indian Dance Controversy and American Religious Freedom* (Chapel Hill: University of North Carolina Press, 2009); Tomoko Masuzawa, *The Invention of World Religions: Or, How European Universalism Was Preserved in the Language of Religious Pluralism* (Chicago: University of Chicago Press, 2005).

20 Henry Abelove demonstrates the ways in which religion can become a self-evident explanation for anything in his prescient study of the development of

Methodism, *The Evangelist of Desire: John Wesley and the Methodists*. Why did the evangelist John Wesley have followers? Abelove opens the book with this question and goes on to show that the historiography of the field provides an apparently straightforward answer: Wesley attracted followers because he was religious. Yet there were other charismatic religious revivalists in Wesley's day who could not attract and maintain the faithful following he did. Religion can thus provide the explanation for Wesley's success only if it serves as a self-evident cause such that no further investigation is necessary. Henry Abelove, *The Evangelist of Desire: John Wesley and the Methodists* (Stanford, CA: Stanford University Press, 1990).

21 Because "sex" is often similarly positioned as an irrational counterpart to "reason," it too can serve as that which explains everything—or nothing—and, as Paul Morrison points out, "is explained by x or y (or by everything)." Movement between these possibilities is one of the things that makes sex so powerful. Paul Morrison, *The Explanation for Everything: Essays on Sexual Subjectivity* (New York: New York University Press, 2001).

22 John D'Emilio and Estelle B. Freedman, *Intimate Matters: A History of Sexuality in America* (New York: Harper & Row, 1988). D'Emilio and Freedman write, "Even among the Puritans and their Yankee descendants sexuality exhibited more complexity than modern assumptions about their repressiveness suggest" (15).

The narrative of "America" and its Puritan origins remains culturally powerful even as it has been widely contested. There is, for example, a lively Internet debate on whether the "founding fathers" were Christian, including entries from a state Supreme Court judge in Missouri and significant proof texts of famous quotations. See Robert Ulrich, "Were the Founding Fathers Christian?," www.shalomjerusalem.com, and the rebuttal by Jon Rowe, "One of the Worst Christian Nation Articles Yet," May 2006, http://jonrowe.blogspot.com.

For scholarly debates, see Tracy Fessenden, Nicholas F. Radel, and Magdalena A. Zaborowska, eds., *The Puritan Origins of American Sex: Religion, Sexuality and National Identity in American Literature* (New York: Routledge, 2000), Jon Butler, *Awash in a Sea of Faith: Christianizing the American People* (Cambridge, MA: Harvard University Press, 1990). Edwin Gaustad and Leigh Schmidt begin their book, *The Religious History of America: The Heart of the American Story from Colonial Times to the Present*, revised edition (New York: Harper Collins, 2002): "Throughout the nineteenth century and into the twentieth century, much of the magical power of [Plymouth] rock came from the desire for many Americans to identify themselves closely with these Pilgrims and Puritans, to cherish them in all their piety and courage as the forefathers of the nation. . . . But, what happens when now in the twenty-first century when so many have grown weary of Pilgrims and Puritans, when so many find Anglo-American relations with Indians to be thievish and worse, when so few in this polyglot and multiracial nation identify with them as fathers, let alone as mothers? Where should a religious history of America begin when the old New England stories of origin now seem so contrived, so narrow, so political?" (3).

23 Daniel K. Williams, *Defenders of the Unborn: The Pro-Life Movement before Roe v. Wade* (New York: Oxford University Press, 2016). Mary Anne Case has similarly argued that the Catholic focus on gender complementarity as the basis for "theological anthropology" has not been a timeless commitment. Mary Anne Case, "Anathematization of Gender," *Religion and Gender*, March 29, 2016, www.religionandgender.org. Moreover, Case notes that more recent "strategic alliances [pursued by the Vatican] have resulted in an almost centripetal increase in conservatism with respect to gender issues among participating religious denominations as, for example, American evangelical Protestants over time moved closer to the Catholic position in opposition to abortion and birth control while the Vatican gave center stage at the Humanum Conference to Southern Baptists, Orthodox Jews and Mormons, whose views on male headship in marriage would be a step backward for the Catholic Church" ("Seeing the Sex," 212–13).

24 And, of course, in addition to Trump, the only other president who had divorced and remarried was Ronald Reagan, who also strongly identified with the Christian right, who also rarely went to church. Elizabeth Bruenig notes that some evangelicals she interviewed recognize the ways in which Reagan provides the political precursor for the split between character and policy that has been of so much remark with regard to Trump. Elizabeth Bruenig, "Why Evangelicals Will Stand by Trump in 2020," *Washington Post*, August 14, 2012, www.washingtonpost.com. Those commentators who appear baffled by the acceptance by conservative Christians of Trump as a leader because of Trump's lack of "family values" miss both the history of accepting such "flawed" leaders and the overlap between Trump and some conservative Christians in their patriarchalism and dedication to a white Christian nation marked by policies of gender and sexual regulation (regardless of what any individual does). Sarah Jones, "How Trump Stole the Soul of the Values Voters Summit," *New Republic*, October 17, 2017, www.newrepublic.com.

25 Harriet Sherwood, "Evangelical Christians 'Uncritical' in Support for Trump, UK Bishop Says," *Guardian*, December 28, 2017, www.theguardian.com.

26 In his response to Buttigieg's candidacy, Wehner similarly ignores Obama's open declaration of his faith (as, it seems, does Buttigieg). He quotes Buttigieg as saying, "I think it's unfortunate [the Democratic Party] has lost touch with a religious tradition that I think can help explain and relate our values." Peter Wehner, "Pete Buttigieg's Very Public Faith Is Challenging Assumptions," *Atlantic*, April 10, 2019, www.theatlantic.com.

27 Michael Cobb traces this back and forth across the political spectrum in *God Hates Fags: The Rhetorics of Religious Violence* (New York: New York University Press, 2006).

Recently, there has been some public discussion objecting to the use of "queer" as a positive term for sexual politics. The term was reappropriated in the 1990s from its earlier, derogatory use and has been employed by activists and academics alike to signal a radical, critical politics. In 1993, a discussion of the politics associated with the term, featuring Eve Kosofsky Sedgwick and Judith Butler, was published in the inaugural issue of *GLQ: A Journal of Lesbian and Gay Studies*. See Eve Kosofsky Sedgwick, "Queer Performativity: Henry James's *The Art of the Novel*," *GLQ: A Journal of Lesbian and Gay Studies* 1.1 (November 1993): 1–16; also Judith Butler, "Critically Queer," *GLQ: A Journal of Lesbian and Gay Studies* 1.1 (November 1993): 17–32.

28 Studies addressing the relation between sexual politics and the Christian right include Cynthia Burack, *Sin, Sex, and Democracy: Antigay Rhetoric and the Christian Right* (Albany: SUNY Press, 2008); Seth Dowland, *Family Values and the Rise of the Christian Right* (Philadelphia: University of Pennsylvania Press, 2015); Doris Buss and Didi Herman, *Globalizing Family Values: The Christian Right in International Politics* (Minneapolis: University of Minnesota Press, 2013); and Daniel Bennett, *Defending the Faith: The Politics of the Conservative Christian Legal Movement* (Lawrence: University of Kansas Press, 2017). There has also been much excellent activist work on this topic, including Jean Hardisty, "Pushed to the Altar: The Right-Wing Roots of Marriage Promotion," Political Research Associates and Women of Color Resource Center, 2008, www.politicalresearch.org; and Kapya John Kaoma, "Colonizing African Values: How the U.S. Christian Right Is Transforming Sexual Politics in Africa," Political Research Associates, 2012, www.politicalresearch.org.

29 Elizabeth Bernstein has, for example, documented the ways in which liberal investments in preventing "sex trafficking" have contributed both to conservative sexual politics and to the expansion of the carceral state over the past several decades. Elizabeth Bernstein, *Brokered Subjects: Sex, Trafficking and the Politics of Freedom* (Chicago: University of Chicago Press, 2018).

30 A Gramscian tradition of political thought understands common sense to be part of the cultural apparatus that helps to hold hegemonic social formations in place. See Antonio Gramsci, *Selections from the Prison Notebooks*, trans. and ed. Quintin Hoare and Geoffrey Nowell-Smith (London: Lawrence & Wishart, 1971), 323. Gramsci's main point about hegemony is that it requires cultural consent as well as the force of government, and this consent is produced in part through common sense, through those ideas that are held in common across conflict and division. So even those on different sides of major political conflict often share certain assumptions and these assumptions are common sense. On this understanding, hegemony is not just one thing—it is not the dominance of a single idea over all others—but is rather a social fabric that is woven together with various strands running in different (and potentially contradictory) directions but nevertheless bound together so as to be both strong and flexible. In particular, *The Sex Obsession* explores sexual politics in relation to persistent habits of thought and action that tend to reinforce hegemonic social relations through the logic of the argument itself—regardless of which "side" one takes up. The very idea that two "sides" of debate should be assumed in major policy discussions is just one of these habitual ways of organizing social analysis so as to constrain possibilities for

social change. Ann Pellegrini and I analyzed this habitual structure of argument with regard to sexual politics in *Love the Sin*, where the idea that fairness requires hearing from "two sides" creates a sense that gay people are just the "other side" of the coin from those who hate them. Janet R. Jakobsen and Ann Pellegrini, *Love the Sin: Sexual Regulation and the Limits of Religious Tolerance* (New York: New York University Press, 2003), chapter 2.

31 Thomas Frank, *What's the Matter with Kansas?: How Conservatives Won the Heart of America* (New York: Henry Holt/Metropolitan Books, 2004). For the persistence of this argument, see, on the 2016 election, Thomas Frank, *Listen, Liberal, or What Ever Happened to the Party of the People?* (New York: Metropolitan Books, 2016) (analyzed in chapter 2); Thomas B. Edsall, "Can Hillary Clinton Manage Her Unruly Coalition?," *New York Times*, August 18, 2016, www.nytimes.com; and the repeated back and forth about whether Trump's election was the result of economics *or* culture, e.g., Isabel V. Sawhill, "Donald Trump's Election: Was it Economics or Culture?," Brookings Institution, December 6, 2016, www.brookings.com.

For an argument that ties an idea of "cultural permissiveness," like Frank's, to the claim that progressives should not focus on racial justice for fear of alienating the white working-class, see Thomas B. Edsall, "The Deepening 'Racialization' of American Politics," *New York Times*, February 27, 2019, www.nytimes.com. William Spriggs points out that the theme of dividing "economic" from "cultural" issues stretches back decades. Spriggs puts a fine point on Edsall's longstanding commitment to reading the "racialization" of American politics as a necessary divide between the "culturally permissive" and "pro-Black" on one side and the white working-class on another. He summarizes Edsall's work since the 1980s (including that with his wife, Mary): "Thomas Edsall and Mary Edsall similarly warned in the pages of *The Atlantic* that the South was key, and it was lost because the liberal orthodoxy was too tied to race, and out of touch with white working-class voters. . . . And much of the theme remains the same as in 1989—that there is a noble white worker who has been betrayed." William E. Spriggs, "Why the White Worker Theme Is Harmful," *American Prospect*, June 21, 2017, http://prospect.org.

32 See, for example, Mark Lilla, *The Once and Future Liberal: After Identity Politics* (New York: Harper, 2017). At the end of this widely criticized paean to political unity as the solution to the problems that led to Trump's election in 2016, Lilla invokes a union hall at which he sees people of apparently different genders and races joined together in common cause. How did this unity that Lilla values so highly come into being? Through historical struggle, much of which was organized around the "identity politics" of which he is so critical. For critiques of Lilla, see Katherine Franke, "Making White Supremacy Respectable Again," *Los Angeles Review of Books*, November 21, 2016, http://blog.lareviewofbooks.org; Ta-Nehisi Coates, "The First White President," *Atlantic*, October 2017, www.theatlantic.com.

33 Lisa Duggan, *The Twilight of Equality: Neoliberalism, Cultural Politics and the Attack on Democracy* (Boston: Beacon Press, 2003).

34 Sasha Breger Bush, "Trump and National Neoliberalism," *Dollars & Sense*, January/February 2017, and "Trump and National Neoliberalism, Revisited," *Dollars & Sense*, January/February 2018, www.dollarsandsense.org.

35 As Roger N. Lancaster has argued, for example, "the techniques used for marking, shaming, and controlling sex offenders have come to serve as models for laws and practices in other domains." Roger N. Lancaster, "The New Pariahs: Sex, Crime and Punishment in America," in *The War on Sex*, ed. David Halperin and Trevor Hoppe (Durham, NC: Duke University Press, 2017), 65–125.

In a comparative study of religious conservatism in the US and Iran, Martin Riesebrodt shows that commitments to patriarchal versions of Christianity and Islam are not the result of some other—more material—concern but are, in fact, sustained even when such commitments undermine other values and interests. Martin Riesebrodt, *Pious Passion: The Emergence of Modern Fundamentalism in the United States and Iran*, trans. Donald Reneau (Berkeley: University of California Press, 1993).

36 In a typical back and forth between those who would take sex—and sexual violence—seriously as a political issue and those who would dismiss it, Newt Gingrich accused the media, in an interview with Megyn Kelly, of being obsessed with sex for focusing on the story about Donald Trump and sexual assault. Of course, Gingrich was also Speaker of the House during the impeachment of President Clinton in relation to his affair with Monica Lewinsky. Anna North, "Newt Gingrich's Strange Fascination with Sex," *New York Times*, October 26, 2016, www.nytimes.com.

37 Thomas Friedman, interview by Katie Couric, *Today Show*, September 11, 2002. For a reading of this material that plays out its implications for the development of the "war on terror," the 2003 invasion of Iraq, and the sexualized torture of prisoners at Abu Ghraib, see Janet R. Jakobsen, "Sex, Secularism, and the 'War on Terror': The Role of Sexuality in Multi-issue Organizing," in *A Companion to Lesbian, Gay, Bisexual, Transgender, and Queer Studies*, ed. George E. Haggerty and Molly McGarry (New York: Blackwell, 2007), 17–37.

38 In 2016, two television series were dedicated to the Simpson case, a season of the true crime series *American Crime Story* on the FX network, "The People vs. O.J. Simpson: An American Crime Story," www.fxnetworks.com, based on Jeffrey Toobin's book, *The Run of His Life: The People vs. OJ* (New York: Touchstone Books, 1997); and a five-part documentary on ESPN, *OJ: Made in America*, http://espn.go.com.

39 The National Organization for Women, reporting Bureau of Justice statistics. "Violence against Women in the United States: Statistics," National Organization for Women, https://now.org.

40 In the run-up to the US invasion of Afghanistan in fall 2001, First Lady Laura Bush took over the president's weekly radio address to focus on women's "plight" under the Taliban government. For the full text of her address, see www.whitehouse.gov. The *New York Times* reported that this was the first time that a first lady delivered the weekly White House radio address, and that the unusual

speech was "the beginning of an international campaign to call attention to the oppression of women and children under the Taliban." David Stout, "A Nation Challenged: The First Lady; Mrs. Bush Cites Women's Plight Under Taliban," *New York Times*, November 18, 2001, www.nytimes.com. For a discussion of the larger context, see Lila Abu-Lughod, *Do Muslim Women Need Saving?* (Cambridge, MA: Harvard University Press, 2013).

Sexualized violence was a disturbing part of the "war on terror" that followed, as the pictures of US soldiers torturing prisoners in Abu Ghraib so terribly revealed. On Abu Ghraib, see Seymour M. Hersh, "Torture at Abu Ghraib," *New Yorker*, May 10, 2004, www.newyorker.com. See also Janet R. Jakobsen, "Sex, Secularism, and the 'War on Terror.'"

41 Alessandra Stanley, "Scandals to Warm To," *New York Times*, December 20, 2008, www.nytimes.com.

42 For examples of the way in which movement among issues holds conservative politics together, see Sarah Posner, "The Secret History of Bathroom Bills," *Type Investigations*, January 1, 2018, www.typeinvestigations.org; the Southern Baptist Convention resolution on Trans Rights, Southern Baptist Convention, "On Transgender Identity," 2014, www.sbc.net; and the National Organization for Marriage's anti–trans rights moves after *Obergefell*: Caitlin Dickson, "The Man behind NOM's New War on Transgender Students," *Daily Beast*, July 11, 2017, www. thedailybeast.com.

43 Dan Levin, "North Carolina Reaches Settlement on 'Bathroom Bill,'" *New York Times*, July 23, 2019, www.nytimes.com.

44 Lawrence Wright, "America's Future Is Texas," *New Yorker*, July 10–17, 2017, 51–52.

45 Lauren Berlant and Lisa Duggan, eds., *Our Monica, Ourselves: The Clinton Affair and the National Interest* (New York: New York University Press, 2001), 5.

46 For an example of this suspicion of sexual politics on the left, see David Harvey, *A Brief History of Neoliberalism* (New York: Oxford, 2007). For a liberal example, see Thomas B. Edsall, "Our Broken Social Contract" (the web link runs with the subtitle: "At Their Core, Are America's Problems Primarily Economic or Moral?"), *New York Times*, June 19, 2013, www.nytimes.com.

47 Barbara Goldsmith, *Other Powers: The Age of Suffrage, Spiritualism, and the Scandalous Victoria Woodhull* (New York: Harper Perennial, 1999); Debby Applegate, *The Most Famous Man in America: A Biography of Henry Ward Beecher* (New York: Three Leaves Press, 2006).

48 The activist group Queers for Economic Justice produced a 2011–12 themed issue of the web journal *Scholar & Feminist Online* (http://sfonline.barnard.edu/a-new-queer-agenda) on this topic; in 2008, the Barnard Center for Research on Women (henceforth BCRW) produced a report on the relations between economic and sexual justice (http://bcrw.barnard.edu/wp-content/nfs/reports/NFS4-Sexual_Economic_Justice.pdf).

49 One notable example here is the FBI's investigation of Martin Luther King Jr.'s sexual practices as part of the government's attempt to discredit the Civil Rights

Movement. See David Garrow, *The FBI and Martin Luther King, Jr.* (New York: W.W. Norton, 1981).

50 Nate Cohn, "How Trump's Campaign Could Redraw Voter Allegiances," *New York Times*, June 28, 2016, www.nytimes.com. Cohn's analysis depends on the removal of sexual politics as the basis for the redrawing of voter allegiances: "Along with his departures on immigration and the welfare state, Mr. Trump is moving away from the labor fights and culture wars that defined 20th-century politics, and toward the new divide over globalization and multiculturalism that might define 21st-century politics." One need not be a student (or journalist) of the culture wars to remember that they included battles over "multiculturalism" on college campuses in the 1980s and 1990s. (See, for example, Joan Scott, "Multicultural-ism and the Politics of Identity," *October* 61 [Summer 1993]: 12–19; Henry Giroux, *Living Dangerously: Multiculturalism and the Politics of Culture* [New York: Peter Lang, 1993]; Amy Gutmann, ed., *Multiculturalism and the Politics of Recognition* [Princeton, NJ: Princeton University Press, 1994].) The central claim of the article is that Trump's appeal to white working-class voters is somehow importantly different from previous Republican Party strategies deploying racism to woo white voters and white working-class voters in particular, despite the fact that Trump explicitly drew upon earlier Republican strategies. In the midst of the 2016 election season, for example, Rachel Maddow tracked the various themes from Richard Nixon's 1968 campaign that were explicitly adopted by the Trump campaign, including appeals to a "silent majority," the idea of a "secret plan" to end the war in Vietnam (or, in Trump's case, to defeat ISIS), and the claim that he is the law-and-order candidate. Rachel Maddow, "Trump Resurrects Fearful Nixon Themes to Advocate Law and Order," MSNBC, July 11, 2016, www.msnbc.com.

51 T. A. Frank, "What Democrats Can Learn from Trump's Culture War," *The Hive*, October 13, 2017, www.vanityfair.com.

52 Patrick Joseph Buchanan, "Culture War Speech: Address to the Republican National Convention," *Voices of Democracy: The U.S. Oratory Project*, August 17, 1992, http://voicesofdemocracy.umd.edu.

53 Matthew N. Lyons, *Ctrl-Alt-Delete: The Origins and Ideology of the Alternative Right* (Somerville, MA: Political Research Associates, 2017).

54 Frank's writing throughout the 2016 campaign and the early years of Trump's presidency demonstrates great sympathy for Trump's populism and a desire for Democrats to take up aspects of his white nationalist agenda, even as he also hopes to distinguish his version of Trumpian populism from the most directly racist aspects of the Trump administration. See, for example, T. A. Frank, "The Democratic Case for Restricting Immigration," *Vanity Fair*, August 9, 2017; "Can Trump Afford to Divorce His Deplorables?" *Vanity Fair*, April 12, 2017; "How Trump Became the GOP's Ideological Prisoner," *Vanity Fair*, June 30, 2017; "Decoding Stephen Miller's Nationalist Mind," *Vanity Fair*, February 6, 2017, www.vanityfair.com.

55 For in-depth analyses of some of these issues, see Janet R. Jakobsen, "Family Values and Working Alliances: The Question of Hate and Public Policy," in *Welfare Policy: Feminist Critiques*, ed. Elizabeth Bounds, Pamela Brubaker, and Mary Hobgood (New York: Pilgrim Press, 1999), 109–32, and "Economic Justice after Legal Equality: The Case for Caring Queerly," in *After Legal Equality: Family, Sex, Kinship*, ed. Robert Leckey (New York: Routledge, 2015), 77–96.

56 Class mobility, for example, is less likely in the United States than throughout the rest of the industrialized world. Markus Jäntti, "Mobility in the United States in Comparative Perspective," *Focus* 26.2 (Fall 2009): 38–42.

57 For example, Randall Balmer's history of the role of opposition to school integration in the formation of the Christian right in the 1970s is often read as implying that sexual politics is merely a "cover" for racism. Randall Balmer, *Evangelicalism in America* (Waco, TX: Baylor University Press, 2016). See, especially, chapter 8, "Re-Create the Nation: The Religious Right and the Abortion Myth." Journalist Margery Eagan glosses Blamer's work in a *Boston Globe* column as raising "unsettling questions" like "How much of antiabortion rhetoric is really about the unborn, and how much is a convenient and even cynical cover for white evangelicals to support, as they did, a white supremacist like Roy Moore, in Alabama, or Trump himself, leader of the American birther movement and defender of neo-Nazis in Charlottesville, Va.?" Margery Eagan, "Race, Not Abortion, Was the Founding Issue of the Religious Right," *Boston Globe*, February 5, 2018, www.bostonglobe.com. My analysis instead traces the interaction among these issues both in the 1970s and in the contemporary moment.

58 Sachs is the director of the Center for Sustainable Development of the Earth Institute at Columbia University. In 2017, he published an essay taking a more liberal tack: Jeffrey D. Sachs, "GOP Tax Cut Is Daylight Robbery," *Boston Globe*, November 14, 2017, www.bostonglobe.com.

59 Take, for example, a related analysis before the 2016 election by George Packer that also depends on the movement of the elements of the argument into a specific—but not necessary—set of connections and divisions. George Packer, "Hillary Clinton and the Populist Revolt," *New Yorker*, October 31, 2016, www.newyorker.com. Packer is a reporter for the *New Yorker* and, like Sachs, a recognized voice in liberal circles. He hopes for a conjoint analysis of race and class, even as such conjunction seems virtually unimaginable to him. Nonetheless, Packer's essay demonstrates the ways in which an analysis can embed racism, sexism, and xenophobia into both interests and values without seeming to do so— while instead seeming to be quite liberal and actively advocating for liberalism: "'Americanism, not globalism, will be our credo,' Trump declared in his convention speech. In his hands, nationalism is a loaded gun, aimed not just at foreigners but also at Americans who don't make the cut. But people are not wrong to want to live in cohesive communities, to ask new arrivals to become part of the melting pot, and to crave a degree of stability in a moral order based on values other than

just diversity and efficiency. A world of heirloom tomatoes and self-driving cars isn't the true and only Heaven." In an amazing but nonetheless persistent move in this type of analysis, addressing racism becomes an "elite" concern: "But Democrats can no longer really claim to be the party of working people—not white ones, anyway." Movement among issues makes this argument seem reasonable: some issues that might be separated are tied together (the supposed interests of migrants and elites) and others that might be tied together are separated, as if elites, including the corporate elites that supported Trump, have no commitments to nationalism. Note the effect of the last sentence in the quotation above—the (petty and self-indulgent) concerns of the *most privileged* white people serve as a synecdoche for all those who think that freedom, equality, and economic, racial, and gender justice are central American values that extend well beyond diversity and efficiency. In other words, "cohesive communities," the "melting pot," and "stability" are not the only alternative values to those of "diversity and efficiency." And with the alternatives of freedom, equality, and justice, one might easily perceive an alignment among the interests of immigrants, people of color, and working-class people (categories that can easily overlap), including white working-class people.

60 Jeffrey D. Sachs, "Brexit Is a Symptom of Globalization's Deeper Ills," *Boston Globe*, June 27, 2016, www.bostonglobe.com.

61 There has been a great deal of work addressing how public feelings importantly contribute to setting the parameters of public discussion and political possibilities. *The Sex Obsession* is interested in connecting the well-established work on public feelings to the moral values that are invoked by making claims about facts and feelings, even when morality is not named. Eve Kosofsky Sedgwick, *Touching Feeling: Affect, Pedagogy, Performativity* (Durham, NC: Duke University Press, 2003); Ann Cvetkovich, *An Archive of Feelings: Trauma, Sexuality and Lesbian Public Cultures* (Durham, NC: Duke University Press, 2003); José Esteban Muñoz, *Cruising Utopia: The Then and There of Queer Futurity* (New York: New York University Press, 2009); Sara Ahmed, *The Promise of Happiness* (Durham, NC: Duke University Press, 2010); Lauren Berlant, *Cruel Optimism* (Durham, NC: Duke University Press, 2011); Melissa Gregg and Gregory Seigworth, eds., *The Affect Theory Reader* (Durham, NC: Duke University Press, 2011).

62 Even the conservative Cato Institute argues that immigration is not at an all-time high; in other words, contra Sachs, the "facts on the ground" do not necessarily support the "feeling" of having lost control of US borders. David Bier, "Why Unemployment is Lower When Immigration Is Higher," Cato Institute, July 26, 2016, www.cato.org. Increased immigration in the UK was also the result of a policy decision on open borders within the European Union. In the US, immigration has risen in relation to a specific change in US policy in 1965.

And, as Mae Ngai notes in her important history of immigration, even the "liberalization" represented by the 1965 legislation was accompanied by the codification of efforts to count and control immigration, such that *control* of

US borders has actually continued to increase. Ngai writes: "The Hart-Celler Act furthered the trend begun in the 1920s that placed questions of territoriality, border control, and abstract categories at the center of immigration law. That shift in the law's center of gravity naturalized the construction of 'illegal aliens' and, increasingly, of 'illegal aliens' as 'Mexican.' Narrating Western Hemispheric restriction as an expression of the liberal principle of fairness reinforced the notion that illegal immigration was a problem that could be blamed on the Mexican migrant (or on Mexico) and, moreover, one that could be solved with enforcement. . . . Certainly, patterns of immigration changed dramatically in the period after 1965, as the abolition of quotas based on national origin opened the way for increased immigration from the third world. Yet Hart-Celler's continued commitment to numerical restriction, especially its imposition of quotas on Western Hemisphere countries, ensured that illegal immigration would continue and, in fact, increase." Mae M. Ngai, *Impossible Subjects: Illegal Aliens and the Making of Modern America* (Princeton, NJ: Princeton University Press, 2005), 264–65. Immigration policy was reformed legislatively in 1996 (as I discuss in chapter 3), even before the draconian administrative reforms of the Trump era.

63 The number of unregulated border crossings dropped during the Obama administration even as the number of deportations increased. Larry Buchanan, Haeyoun Park, and Adam Pearce, "You Draw It: What Got Better or Worse in Obama's Presidency," *New York Times*, January 15, 2017, www.nytimes.com.

64 The status of the plaque on the Statue of Liberty that includes this poem became a matter for debate in 2017 after the Trump administration proposed limits on legal immigration and advisor Stephen Miller argued in a press conference that the poem did not represent core public values. Nolan D. McCaskill, "White House Aide Blasts CNN Reporter for 'Cosmopolitan Bias,'" *Politico*, August 8, 2017, www.politico.com. In 2019, the acting director of US citizenship and immigration services, Ken Cuccinelli, claimed the poem only applied to potential immigrants who could "stand on their own two feet." Sasha Ingber and Rachel Martin, "Immigration Chief: 'Give Me Your Tired, Your Poor Who Can Stand on Their Own 2 Feet,'" NPR, August 13, 2019, www.npr.org.

On July 4, 2018, the Statue of Liberty became a major site for protest against the Trump administration's policy of separating children from parents who crossed the southern US border seeking asylum. Joanna Walters, "'I Must Continue': Statue of Liberty Climber Still Protesting despite Facing Arrest," *Guardian*, December 13, 2018, www.theguardian.com.

65 The mistaken conflation of globalization with other aspects of neoliberalism (such as financialization, austerity, and debt restructuring) has far reaching consequences. If "globalization" is the problem, then "nationalism" must be part of the answer. When liberals put forward this narrative about globalization, they slice out one group—those who most identify with the nation—from all those who have paid the price of the consolidation of wealth over the last few decades. If, however,

one names the problem as inequality, austerity or neoliberalism, then economic justice (rather than nationalism) can come into view as an answer to the problem. Renaming the problem in this way, one can take seriously the harm that redistribution upward has done to many people in the United States, including white people in the Rust Belt, and perhaps most importantly, one can do so without blaming people who have also been harmed by these policies, including immigrants.

66 This is the kind of work brought together in Paula Chakravartty and Denise Ferreira da Silva, eds., "Race, Empire, and the Crisis of the Subprime," special issue, *American Quarterly* 64.3 (September 2012).

67 Scholars like Lauren Berlant, Mary Pat Brady, Cathy Cohen, Lisa Duggan, Roderick Ferguson, Gayle Rubin, Nayan Shah, and Christine Stansell have tracked the recurrent obsession with sex in US public life, showing how sex has repeatedly been deployed in political conflicts over not just sexual activity, but also the social relations that define the borders of the United States, along with relations of race and class within the country. Cohen ("Punks, Bulldaggers, and Welfare Queens") has argued persuasively that gender and sex are always imbricated with race and class, and that understanding so is potentially radicalizing. Both Duggan and Ferguson have shown how the violence of race relations is maintained—given both emotional charge and legitimacy—through a discourse of sexuality. Nayan Shah has shown how the legal apparatus of sodomy prosecutions could be deployed to manage immigrant communities, establishing both racial boundaries and the boundaries of citizenship, while Mary Pat Brady has traced the ways in which the "War on Drugs" has been organized by sexualized images and fantasies. Lisa Duggan, *Sapphic Slashers: Sex, Violence, and American Modernity* (Durham, NC: Duke University Press, 2001); Roderick A. Ferguson, *Aberrations in Black: Toward a Queer of Color Critique* (Minneapolis: University of Minnesota Press, 2003); Nayan Shah, "Policing Privacy, Migrants, and the Limits of Freedom," *Social Text* 23.3–4 (Fall–Winter 2005): 275–84; Mary Pat Brady, "Quotidian Warfare," *Signs: Journal of Women in Culture and Society* 28.1 (Fall 2002): 446–47, doi: 10.1086/340885; Mary Pat Brady, *Extinct Lands, Temporal Geographies: Chicana Literature and the Urgency of Space* (Durham, NC: Duke University Press, 2002). Berlant takes up questions of nationalism throughout her work. See, especially, Lauren Berlant, *The Queen of America Goes to Washington City: Essays on Sex and Citizenship* (Durham, NC: Duke University Press, 1997). On questions of global migration, see Brad Epps, Keja Valens, and Bill Johnson González, eds., *Passing Lines: Sexuality and Immigration* (New York: David Rockefeller Center for Latin American Studies, 2005), and Eithne Luibhéid and Lionel Cantú Jr., eds., *Queer Migrations: Sexuality, U.S. Citizenship, and Border Crossings* (Minneapolis: University of Minnesota Press, 2005). Whether it is the deeply sexualized violence of lynching or the coldly analytic discourse of sociological studies that picture African Americans as sexually deviant, race and sex are inextricably intertwined in US society. Moreover, these ideas extend to immigration enforcement and the

"war on terror" of the early twenty-first century. Christine Stansell's foundational study of class and sex in the eighteenth and nineteenth centuries demonstrates that class relations are maintained by a discourse of appropriate gender roles and sexual respectability. When sexual activity troubles those roles, economic degradation is taken to be a moral failing, rather than a problem of class relations. Christine Stansell, *City of Women: Sex and Class in New York, 1789–1860* (Champaign: University of Illinois Press, 1987). See also Maimie Pinzer, *The Maimie Papers: Letters from an Ex-Prostitute*, ed. Ruth Rosen and Susan Davidson (New York: Feminist Press, 1977). For a related study of sex and class in Britain, see Judith Walkowitz, *Prostitution and Victorian Society: Women, Class and the State* (New York: Cambridge University Press, 1982); also Judith Walkowitz, *City of Dreadful Delights: Narratives of Sexual Danger in Late Victorian London* (Chicago: University of Chicago Press, 1992).

68 Crenshaw, "Demarginalizing the Intersection."

69 For my initial exposition of mobility for stasis, see Janet R. Jakobsen, "Different Differences: Theory and the Practice of Women's Studies," in *Women's Studies for the Future: Foundations, Interrogations, Politics*, ed. Elizabeth Lapovsky Kennedy and Agatha Beins (New Brunswick, NJ: Rutgers University Press, 2005), 125–42.

For an example of one mechanism by which mobility creates stasis, consider the narrative of individual class mobility through education in the United States. While mobility through education can be incredibly important to individual students, this mobility can also be used to reinforce the system of class stratification as a whole because changes in individuals' lives come to stand in for social change. Despite the fact that education provides mobility for individuals, the system as a whole continues to serve as a central mechanism for class sorting. When some individuals can significantly change their lives, continuing stratification becomes justified, and the role of the educational system in reinforcing that stratification is elided.

Another mechanism is what critical legal scholars call "preservation for transformation." Rather than centering on individuals whose mobility masks stable hierarchies at the level of social groups, "preservation for transformation" focuses contained change on a single social issue so as to maintain the status quo of social hierarchy. In Reva Siegel's explanation of "preservation for transformation," for example, civil rights law can lead those defending social hierarchies to translate hierarchical relations "into a more contemporary, and less controversial, social idiom. I call this kind of change in the rules and rhetoric of a status regime 'preservation through transformation,' and illustrate this modernization dynamic in a case study of domestic assault law as it evolved in rule structure and rationale from a law of marital prerogative to a law of marital privacy." Reva B. Siegel, "'The Rule of Love': Wife Beating as Prerogative and Privacy," *Yale Law Journal* 105 (1996): 2119.

Mobility for stasis takes seriously the ways in which attempts to reinforce hierarchies can incorporate transformation, but expands the concept beyond a retranslation of existing hierarchies to the multiple mechanisms that can recuperate efforts at social change, moving the analysis beyond shifts in a single issue to focus on the mobile relations among issues, so as to maintain what Catherine Bell terms the "loosely coherent whole" of hegemony. Catherine Bell, *Ritual Theory, Ritual Practice* (New York: Oxford University Press, 1992).

70 Recent histories of Christianity in the United States have added important background to this story of the 1970s; see, for example, R. Marie Griffith, *Moral Combat: How Sex Divided American Christians and Fractured American Politics* (New York: Basic Books, 2017).

71 See Elizabeth Bernstein and Janet R. Jakobsen, eds., "Gender, Justice, and Neoliberal Transformations," themed issue, *Scholar & Feminist Online* 11.1–2 (Fall 2012–Spring 2013), http://sfonline.barnard.edu; Harvey, *Brief History of Neoliberalism*; and Lisa Duggan, *Mean Girl: Ayn Rand and the Culture of Greed* (Berkeley: University of California Press, 2019).

72 These relations are refracted in a number of directions. For example, the shifting period from colonialism to neoliberal austerity overlaps with the Cold War, often understood as a bilateral conflict between the US and the Soviet Union, but which can instead by understood as a global Cold War that shifted relations between and among multiple areas of the world. Odd Arne Westad, *The Global Cold War: Third World Interventions and the Making of Our Times* (Cambridge: Cambridge University Press, 2005). Petrus Liu argues, for instance, that contemporary Chinese queer cultures should not be read as responses to neoliberalism but in relation to the Cold War division of China in 1949 into the People's Republic of China (PRC) and the Republic of China in Taiwan. Liu, *Queer Marxism in Two Chinas*, 4. This shift in perspective focuses on concerns that include "the incomplete decolonization in Asia, the achievements and failures of socialist democracy, the contradictory process of capitalist modernization, the uneven exchange of capital and goods" (7).

   Paul Amar also raises questions about whether neoliberalism is the appropriate framework for analyzing social formations throughout the world and traces the development of a "security archipelago" with nodes in Egypt and Brazil in the 1990s and early twenty-first century as a means of articulating "intercontinental flows of security practices and protective discourses" imbricated with both morality and materialism, sexual and religious politics. Paul Amar, *The Security Archipelago: Human-Security States, Sexuality Politics, and the End of Neoliberalism* (Durham, NC: Duke University Press, 2013), 7.

73 Leela Fernandes makes the important point that transnational forces and flows do not simply dissipate or dissolve the power of the nation-state. Leela Fernandes, "Toward a Feminist Analytic of the Post-Liberalization State," in *Feminists Rethink the Neoliberal State: Inequality, Exclusion, and Change,* ed. Leela Fernandes (New York: New York University Press, 2018), 225. Ann Pellegrini and I take up this both/and approach in *Secularisms,* developing an analysis that considers both the global genealogies of secularism and the specific formations of secularism in

different religious and national sites. Janet R. Jakobsen and Ann Pellegrini, eds., *Secularisms* (Durham, NC: Duke University Press, 2008).

74 For a description of this project, see "Gender, Justice, and Neoliberal Transformations," http://bcrw.barnard.edu/transnational/?portfolio=gender-justice-neoliberal-transformations.

I have also been deeply influenced by work with Elizabeth Bernstein on Religion, Politics and Gender Equality for the United Nations Research Institute for Social Development (Janet R. Jakobsen and Elizabeth Bernstein, "Religion, Politics, and Gender Equality: USA Country Report," United Nations Research Institute for Social Development (2009), www.unrisd.org) and by our subsequent transnational collaboration on

75 On racial capitalism see, for example, Cedric Robinson, *Black Marxism: The Making of a Radical Tradition* (Chapel Hill, NC: University of North Carolina Press, 1983); Ruth Wilson Gilmore, *Golden Gulag: Prisons, Surplus, Crisis and Opposition in Globalizing California* (Berkeley: University of California Press, 2007); Chandan Reddy, *Freedom with Violence: Race, Sex, and the U.S. State* (Durham, NC: Duke University Press, 2011); Jodi Melamed, *Represent and Destroy: Rationalizing Violence in the New Racial Capitalism* (Minneapolis: University of Minnesota Press, 2011); and Walter Johnson and Robin D. G. Kelley, eds., *Race, Capitalism, Justice* (Boston: Boston Review Forum 1, 2017). On queer materialism, see, for example, Liu, *Queer Marxism in Two Chinas*; Jordy Rosenberg and Amy Villarejo, eds., "Queer Studies and the Crises of Capitalism," special issue, *GLQ: Journal of Gay and Lesbian Studies* 18.1 (2012); Miranda Joseph, *Against the Romance of Community* (Minnesota: University of Minnesota Press, 2002); Kevin Floyd, *The Reification of Desire* (Minneapolis: University of Minnesota Press, 2009); and David L. Eng and Jasbir Puar, "Left of Queer?," *Social Text* (forthcoming). The focus on paradoxes of neoliberalism comes from Sealing Cheng's contribution to the Gender Justice group. See BCRW, "Paradoxes of Neoliberalism" (video), in "Gender Justice and Neoliberalism Transformations," ed. Bernstein and Jakobsen, http://sfonline.barnard.edu. On social reproduction theory, also see Tithi Bhattacharya, ed., *Social Reproduction Theory: Remapping Class, Recentering Oppression* (London: Pluto Press, 2017), and Silvia Federici, *Revolution at Point Zero: Housework, Reproduction, and Feminist Struggle* (Oakland, CA: PM Press, 2012). The development of these different approaches as separate fields raises questions about their relation. My analysis maintains the specificity of categories of social difference—they are not all the same type of axis of oppression intersecting at various points—without the need to find a way to unify these different categories in their difference. Sustaining a focus on interrelations, particularly *dynamic* interrelations, allows for a recognition of persistent multiplicity as constitutive of the social body multiple.

76 Kamala Kempadoo, "Sex, Migration, and Neoliberalism in the Global South," in "Sex Migration, and New World (Dis)Order," panel discussion, Danish Institute for International Studies Conference, June 1, 2017.

77 As Ann Pellegrini and I have argued, both of these narratives—that the US is exceptionally religious and that the US is an exemplar of secularism—can be part of the same narrative, one in which "good" religion and secularism work together to produce a healthy "nation," while bad religion represents a fundamental threat. Jakobsen and Pellegrini, *Secularisms*.

On American exceptionalism, see Amy Kaplan, *The Anarchy of Empire in the Making of U.S. Culture* (Cambridge, MA: Harvard University Press, 2005), and Donald Pease, *The New American Exceptionalism* (Minneapolis: University of Minnesota Press, 2009).

78 Allan J. Lichtman, *White Protestant Nation: The Rise of the American Conservative Movement* (New York: Atlantic Monthly Press, 2008). Robert P. Jones has argued at length that 2016 marked the end of "white Christian America," and yet he has also argued that conservative Protestants played a major role in the rise of Donald Trump's presidential candidacy, despite Trump's lack of standard Christian credentials. Jones notes that the anxieties expressed by evangelicals about demographic and cultural change are not just about sexual politics (though he highlights gay marriage as a leading edge), but also include anxieties about a loss of white supremacy, such as the anxiety over immigration tapped by Donald Trump's 2016 campaign for president and repeated in his administration. Jones argues that Senator Ted Cruz, Trump's major opponent in the 2016 Republican primaries, "assured evangelicals that he'd secure them exemptions from the new realities, while Mr. Trump promised to reinstate their central place in the country. Mr. Cruz offered to negotiate a respectable retreat strategy, while Mr. Trump vowed to turn back the clock." Indeed, "Mr. Trump's ascendancy has turned the 2016 election into a referendum on the death of white Christian America, with the candidate appealing strongly to those who are most grieving this loss." Robert P. Jones, *The End of White Christian America* (New York: Simon & Schuster, 2016).

79 See, for example, Frank Rich, "It Was the Porn That Made Them Do It," *New York Times*, May 30, 2004, Arts and Leisure, 1.

80 As Liu summarizes, "global dialogue is necessarily impure in its methodology, entangled in its historical trajectory, and varied in modes of dissemination" (*Queer Marxism in Two Chinas*, 15).

81 Intersectionality and assemblage have sometimes been placed in opposition to each other, and Jennifer Nash's careful readings of both the multiple substantive meanings of intersectionality and of this debate provide an important method for attending to the effects of "intersectionality wars" (*Black Feminism Reimagined*, 26) while also opening ethical and conceptual possibilities. Nash is specifically reimagining Black feminism, while also hoping to "put pressure on women's studies to recognize the utopian world-making of our still unfolding political dreaming, which *includes* but also *exceeds* intersectionality" (138). For example, Nash is interested in both specific readings of intersectionality that recognize its Black feminist genealogy and an inclusive intersectionality that argues for the relevance of intersectional method to all social analysis. Nash provides a particu-

larly insightful and incisive reading of the ways in which Jasbir Puar's advocacy of methods employing the Deleuzian concept of assemblages is positioned as a criticism of intersectionality (50–56). Nash reads Puar as ambivalent in her different readings of assemblage and also shows how Puar's thinking develops from *Terrorist Assemblages* to the essay "I'd Rather Be a Cyborg than a Goddess." Jasbir Puar, "I'd Rather Be a Cyborg than a Goddess: Intersectionality, Assemblage, and Affective Politics," *European Institute for Progressive Cultural Politics Journal* (2011), http://eipcp.net. I find particularly important the point in this later essay where Puar argues that "an intersectional approach is needed along with assemblage." For Puar, the combination of intersectionality and assemblage allows for a shifting emphasis in reading between the solidity and instability of social categories.

82 Puar writes that the category "queer" can be both helpful and in need of displacement: "displacing queerness as an identity or modality that is visibly, audibly, legibly, or tangibly evident, assemblages allow us to attune to intensities, emotions, energies, affectivities, textures as they inhabit events, spatiality and corporealities." This displacement can allow for "both the temporality of being and the temporality of becoming" by bringing out the queerness that is already in any subject (*Terrorist Assemblages*, 127). Insofar as any identity is built on the projection of that which is different—queer—within the subject outward beyond the boundary of self, onto "others," queerness is part of the subject. This queerness is already within the subject—it is part of being—and it also represents the queer that anyone can become. This reading scrambles the lines between being and becoming, between what is and what could be, in ways that open to new possibilities. And yet, Puar also recognizes that identities are part of what we have become. This blurring between what is and what might be militates for an ethics and politics focused on possibility, one grounded in a strong analysis of contemporary conditions without seeing those conditions as determining what might be.

83 For a description of Interdisciplinary Innovations in the Study of Religion and Gender: Postcolonial, Post-secular, and Queer Perspectives, see http://annemariekorte.org/?page_id=18. And for one of the publications resulting from these conversations, see Elizabeth A. Castelli, ed., "Queer/Religion," themed issue, *Scholar & Feminist Online* 14.2 (2017), http://sfonline.barnard.edu. Religion and the Global Framing of Gender Violence has deepened my understanding of Islam in the context of global relations, as well as sharpening my thinking about the category of "religion" and US military interventions. For a description, see http://socialdifference.columbia.edu/religion-and-the-framing-of-global-violence.

84 Kadji Amin suggests that this multiplicitous approach is a necessary part of queer theoretical work, even while highlighting the need for attention to disjunctions, as well as affinities: "A genealogical approach demonstrates that queer theory has always been a promiscuous borrowing, reworking, and interested claiming of disparate theoretical traditions. As such, scholars might rework queer theory by rerooting it in its own forgotten genealogies as well as in alternate theoretical traditions. To say this is not, however, to claim that queer theory is infinitely

mobile and open to redefinition. I have argued elsewhere that queer theory bears the trace of its discursive travels and of the intellectual genealogies that have most repetitively defined it. These genealogies cannot simply be cast off, for they have come to shape some of the key sensibilities, methodological moves, and scholarly orientations of queer theory. If Queer Studies is to become a genuinely inter-disciplinary field, it is critical to multiply its theoretical genealogies. However, this process of multiplication will inevitably give rise to both dissonances and resonances with the habits of thought and feeling that had previously shaped the field. Investigating the source of these dissonances and amplifying the resonances should be part of the work of claiming alternate theoretical genealogies for queer scholarship." Kadji Amin, "Genealogies of Queer Theory," in *The Cambridge Companion to Queer Studies*, ed. Siobhan Sommerville (New York: Cambridge University Press, forthcoming).

85 The term "theoretical promiscuity" entered my vocabulary from Christina Crosby, who has long used it as a way to engage her students in the feminist critique of disciplines. Feminist studies has on this reading been an interdisciplinary pursuit on the grounds of both an epistemological critique of the disciplines as organized by masculinist bias and by the need to develop a field that can encompass the complexity of intersecting feminist issues. Crosby argues similarly that any singu-lar theoretical perspective is unlikely to be able to overcome all epistemological limitations and comprehensively articulate the complexity of social relations. The idea of such promiscuity has also been advocated by other scholars who think seriously about how to address the limitations of academic thought and what philosopher José Medina has termed "epistemic injustice." In addition to Amin, "Genealogies of Queer Theory," see José Medina, *The Epistemology of Resistance: Gender and Racial Oppression, Epistemic Injustice, and Resistant Imaginations* (New York: Oxford University Press, 2013). Medina argues that drawing on "feminist theory, queer theory, and critical race theory" produces a "polyphonic contextualism" that is "methodologically promiscuous." Melissa Wilcox has also suggested that "methodological promiscuity" is the best approach for scholars working at the intersections of queerness and religion, both of which are inter-disciplinary fields of study. See Melissa Wilcox, "Methodological Promiscuity and Undisciplined Intellectual Orgies," in "Queer/Religion," ed. Castelli, www.sfon-line.barnard.edu. Wilcox here draws upon the work of queer scholars like Lynne Huffer, *Mad for Foucault: Rethinking the Foundations of Queer Theory* (New York: Columbia University Press, 2009), and Jack Halberstam, *The Queer Art of Failure* (Durham, NC: Duke University Press, 2011).

86 Many different approaches have been developed to articulate this complexity, including intersectionality, assemblage (both Deleuzian and actor-network-theory genealogies), new materialisms, and object-oriented ontologies. On intersection-ality, in addition to Crenshaw, "Demarginalizing the Intersection," see Crenshaw's "Mapping the Margins: Intersectionality, Identity Politics, and Violence against Women of Color," *Stanford Law Review* 43.6 (July 1991): 1241–99, and *On Inter-*

sectionality: Essential Writings (New York: New Press, 2020). See also Patricia Hill Collins and Sirma Bilge, *Intersectionality: Key Concepts* (New York: Polity Press, 2016), Patricia Hill Collins, *Intersectionality as Social Theory* (Durham, NC: Duke University Press, 2019); and Jennifer C. Nash, *Black Feminism Reimagined: After Intersectionality* (Durham, NC: Duke University Press, 2019); on assemblage: Jasbir Puar, *Terrorist Assemblages: Homonationalism in Queer Times* (Durham, NC: Duke University Press, 2007), Alexander Weheliye, *Habeus Viscus: Racializing Assemblages, Biopolitics, and Black Feminist Theories of the Human* (Durham, NC: Duke University Press, 2014), Mayra Rivera, *Poetics of the Flesh* (Durham, NC: Duke University Press, 2015), and Aisha M. Beliso-De Jesús, *Electric Santería: Racial and Sexual Assemblages of Transnational Religion* (New York: Columbia University Press, 2015); on actor-network theory: Bruno Latour, *Reassembling the Social: An Introduction to Actor-Network Theory* (New York: Oxford University Press, 2007), and Annemarie Mol, *The Body Multiple: Ontology in Medical Practice* (Durham, NC: Duke University Press, 2003); on new materialisms: Karen Barad, *Meeting the Universe Halfway: Quantum Physics and the Entanglement of Matter* (Durham, NC: Duke University Press, 2007), and Jane Bennett, *Vibrant Matter: A Political Ecology of Things* (Durham, NC: Duke University Press, 2010); on object-oriented ontologies: Katherine Behar, *Object-Oriented Feminism* (Minneapolis: University of Minnesota Press, 2016); and on decolonial theory: Walter Mignolo, *The Darker Side of Western Modernity: Global Futures, Decolonial Options* (Durham, NC: Duke University Press, 2011). I not only take a promiscuous approach to these methods but also put them in relation to a broad range of approaches, such as Marxism, poststructuralism, and deconstruction, as well as feminist, queer, postcolonial, and critical race theories.

87 Douglas Crimp made promiscuity foundational to queer theory in his salutary commitment to the value of sexual practice in response to the AIDS crisis. Douglas Crimp, "How to Have Promiscuity in an Epidemic," *October* 43 (Winter 1987): 237–71.

88 Charles Taylor, *A Secular Age* (Cambridge, MA: Belknap Press, 2007).

89 This critique builds on a large body of work, including Bruno Latour's *An Inquiry into Modes of Existence: An Anthropology of the Moderns* (Cambridge, MA: Harvard University Press, 2013), which takes up the challenge of relativizing the claims of secularism. This book is largely a step away from the actor-network theory Latour developed in *Reassembling the Social*. Latour takes secular reasoning, particularly scientific reasoning, seriously and so wants to maintain its significance. But he also recognizes the ways in which epistemological claims, including those of science, depend on authority structures and traditions of knowledge. He tried to fully ground epistemological claims outside of these traditions through the development of actor-network theory, an approach that followed the most minute details of any empirical situation while refusing to abstract from those details. This method was intended to ensure that all aspects of a claim about reality were actually empirical. But Latour ultimately adduced this approach as

limited. One difficulty with actor-network theory, as Latour sees it, is that the theory can make it seems as though, "everything can be associated with everything without any way to know what [of these associations] may succeed and what may fail" (*Inquiry into Modes of Existence*, 64). In response, Latour turns to rethinking the institutions on which claims to "truth" reside in a postsecular age. His hope is that in acknowledging, for example, that "evolution" is only a theory, the response need not be to give up on evolution, but rather to refuse to claim more than the scientific method can sustain. It is not that secular reason doesn't provide a meaningful way to grasp the world; it is that secular reason is not the only such meaningful approach. Secular reason is thus relativized along with different religious traditions, requiring the investigator to code-switch among ways of knowing, so as to produce the fullest understanding possible. By not claiming any single approach as comprehensive and recognizing the limits of any and all views, one can actually build a broader and more accurate view of reality.

90 Sandra Soto, for example, suggests that social and cultural analysis needs not to find the perfect concept-metaphor, but rather to engage more concepts and more metaphors. Soto declares that "race, sexuality and gender are much too complex, unsettled and porous . . . mutually constitutive, unpredictable, incommensurable, and dynamic, certainly too spatially and temporally contingent, *ever* (even if I only use that word for an instant) to travel independently of one another." And she concludes, "I do not want to offer a better metaphor. . . . What I want to suggest is that we be *wordy*." Sandra K. Soto, *Reading Chicano Like a Queer: The De-mastery of Desire* (Austin: University of Texas Press, 2010), 6.

91 Ludger Viefhues-Bailey, personal communication. Viefhues-Bailey's translation of Wittgenstein: "We find that what connects all the cases of comparing is a vast number of overlapping similarities, and as soon as we see this, we feel no longer compelled to say that there must be some one feature common to them all. What ties the ship to the wharf is a rope, and the rope consists of fibres, but it does not get its strength from any fibre which runs through it from one end to the other, but from the fact that there is a vast number of fibres overlapping." The German version reads: "Wir finden, daß das, was die Fälle des Vergleichens verbindet, eine große Anzahl einander übergreifender Ähnlichkeiten ist; und wenn wir dies sehen, so fühlen wir uns nicht mehr gezwungen zu sagen, es müsse allen diesen Fällen eines gemeinsam sein. Sie sind durch ein Tau mit einander verbunden; und dieses Tau verbindet sie nicht daduch, daß irgeneine Faser in ihm von enem Ende zum anderen läuft, sondern dadurch, daß eine Unzahl von Fasern einander übergreifen." *Eine Philosophische Betrachtug. Das sogennannte Braune Buch.* Werkausgabe Band 5 (Frankfurt am Main: Suhrkamp, 1984), 127ff., www.wittgensteinsource.org.

92 Amber Hollibaugh, "Queer Survival Economies," http://queersurvivaleconomies.com, and "Immigrants and Refugees Are Welcome Here: A Resource Guide for Service Providers Working with Immigrants Who Are LGBTQ, Sex Workers, and/or HIV-Positive," *New Feminist Solutions* 11 (November 2018), http://bcrw.

barnard.edu; Tiloma Jayasinghe and Erin Ward, "Responding to Violence, Restoring Justice," *New Feminist Solutions* 10 (September 1, 2018), http://bcrw.barnard. edu; Rebecca Jordan-Young, Lucy Trainor, and Janet R. Jakobsen, "Reproductive Justice in Action," *New Feminist Solutions* 6 (April 2011), http://bcrw.barnard.edu; Premilla Nadasen and Tiffany Williams, "Valuing Domestic Work," *New Feminist Solutions* 5 (January 2011), http://bcrw.barnard.edu; Dean Spade, Tourmaline, and Hope Dector, "No One Is Disposable: Everyday Practices of Prison Abolition" (video), BCRW, February 7, 2014, http://bcrw.barnard.edu; CeCe McDonald, Tourmaline, and Dean Spade, "I Use My Love to Guide Me" (video), BCRW, March–April 2014, http://bcrw.barnard.edu.

For more detailed descriptions of the process of developing some of these collaborative projects, see Janet R. Jakobsen, "Collaborations," *American Quarterly* 64.4 (December 2012), and "Expanding Feminism: Collaborations for Social Justice" (video), in "Activism and the Academy," ed. Janet R. Jakobsen and Catherine Sameh, themed issue, *Scholar & Feminist Online* 12.1–2 (Fall 2013–Spring 2014), http://sfonline.barnard.edu.

93 For an initial argument on sexual relations as a site for the production of values, see Jakobsen and Pellegrini, *Love the Sin*, chapter 5.

CHAPTER 1. BECAUSE RELIGION

1 Wendy D. Manning et. al., "Healthy Marriage Initiative Spending and U.S. Marriage and Divorce Rates, A State-Level Analysis," National Center for Family and Marriage Research, Bowling Green State University, 2014, www.bgsu.edu. For a reading of earlier iterations of federal marriage promotion as anti-poverty programs, see Stephanie Coontz and Nancy Folbre, "Marriage, Poverty, and Public Policy: A Discussion Paper from the Council on Contemporary Families," Fifth Annual CCF Conference, April 26–28, 2002, https://files.eric.ed.gov.

2 M. V. Lee Badgett, Laura E. Durso, and Alyssa Schneebaum, "New Patterns of Poverty in the Lesbian, Gay, and Bisexual Community," Williams Institute, June 2013, https://williamsinstitute.law.ucla.edu; Jillian Edwards, "Transgender People are Facing Incredibly High Rates of Poverty," National Women's Law Center, December 9, 2016, https://nwlc.org.

3 Kristi Williams, "Promoting Marriage among Single Mothers: An Ineffective Weapon in the War on Poverty?" Council on Contemporary Families, January 6, 2014, https://contemporaryfamilies.org; Jennifer Randles and Orit Avishai, "Saving Marriage Culture 'One Marriage at a Time': Relationship Education and the Reinstitutionalization of Marriage in an Era of Individualism," *Qualitative Sociology* 41 (2018): 21–40.

4 As I discuss in more detail in chapter 3, marriage promotion was instituted as a major part of the "charitable choice" provisions, which allowed "faith-based" organizations to receive federal funding, of the "welfare reform" bill in 1996. Thus, marriage promotion and religious social service are intertwined at the level of policy, as well as public discourse. Teresa Kominos, "What Do Marriage and

Welfare Reform Really Have in Common?," *St. John's Journal of Legal Commentary* 21.3 (2007): 915–49.

5 See, for example, Masterpiece Cakeshop, Ltd., et al. v. Colorado Civil Rights Commission et al. Certiorari to the Court of Appeals of Colorado, No. 16–111, argued December 5, 2017, decided June 4, 2018.

6 Joel Siegel, "Hil Nixes Same-Sex Marriage," *New York Daily News*, January 11, 2000, www.dailynews.com.

7 Jakobsen and Pellegrini, *Love the Sin*, xiii.

8 Pellegrini and I document some of this discourse in *Love the Sin*. For example, in 2000, when Vermont governor Howard Dean threatened to veto a bill that allowed same-sex marriage but accepted one for civil unions, he described the difference as turning on the religious nature of marriage (xiv).

9 In his memoir *The Audacity of Hope*, Obama attributed both his statement against same-sex marriage and his openness to changing his position to his Christian faith. Becky Bowers, "President Obama's Shifting Stance on Same-Sex Marriage," *PolitiFact*, May 11, 2012, www.politifact.com.

10 Liam Stack, "Trump's Election Alarms Gay and Transgender Groups," *New York Times*, November 10, 2016, www.nytimes.com; Jeremy Diamond, "Donald Trump to LGBT Community: I'm a Real Friend," CNN, June 13, 2016, www.cnn.com; Frank Bruni, "The Gay Truth about Trump," *New York Times*, June 22, 2019, www.nytimes.com.

11 Ian Kullgren, "Trump Rule to Protect Contractors Who Discriminate against LGBT Workers," *Politico*, August 14, 2019, www.politico.com.

12 David Wayne Machacek and Melissa Wilcox, eds., *Sexual Ethics and the World's Religions* (Santa Barbara, CA: ABC-CLIO, 2003); Rebecca T. Alpert, *Like Bread on a Seder Plate* (New York: Columbia University Press, 1991); Kecia Ali, *Sexual Ethics and Islam: Feminist Reflections on Qur'an, Hadith, and Jurisprudence* (London: Oneworld, 2006); and Mark D. Jordan, *The Ethics of Sex* (Oxford: Blackwell, 2002), 3.

13 As with Robert Byrd's speech on the Senate floor referenced in the introduction, the focus on marriage as synonymous with monogamy, despite the long history of polygamy in many religious traditions, including the very biblical text that Byrd brought with him to the Senate floor, shows that when a politician like Clinton speaks of the "content" of marriage that goes back to the "beginning of time," she actually means an historically specific idea, which Ann Pellegrini and I argue is associated with Christian secularism. Janet R. Jakobsen and Ann Pellegrini, "Bodies-Politics: Christian Secularism and the Gendering of U.S. Policy," in *Religion, the Secular, and the Politics of Sexual Difference*, ed. Linell E. Cady and Tracy Fessenden (New York: Columbia University Press, 2013), 139–74. On the history of the relationship between the practice of polygamy across much of the world and the presumption of Christian monogamy in the United States, see Nancy F. Cott, *Public Vows: A History of Marriage and the Nation* (Cambridge, MA: Harvard

University Press, 2000), chapter 1, and Sarah Barringer Gordon, *The Mormon Question: Polygamy and Constitutional Conflict in Nineteenth Century America* (Chapel Hill: University of North Carolina Press, 2003).

14 Pope Francis, *Praise Be to You—Laudato Si': On Care for Our Common Home* (San Francisco: Ignatius Press, 2015); Jim Yardley and Laurie Goodstein, "Pope Francis, in Sweeping Encyclical, Calls for Swift Action on Climate Change," *New York Times*, June 18, 2015, www.nytimes.com; Bart Jones, "Pope Francis Draws Criticism from Some Conservative Catholics over Stances on Economy, Environment, Social Issues," *Newsday*, August 24, 2015, www.newsday.com.

15 For example, there was an outcry when the Attorney General, Jeff Sessions, invoked the Bible to justify the Trump administration's policy of separating children from their parents when asylum seekers were detained at the US-Mexico border. Some of the outcry centered on the fact that Sessions invoked Romans 13, a verse repeatedly used to justify slavery. Jessica Durham and Sean Billings, "Jesuit Priest Responds to Jeff Sessions's Use of Bible to Defend Separating Immigrant Families: 'Read All the Verses,'" *Newsweek*, June 20, 2018, www.newsweek.com. Even the conservative website *The Federalist* posted an opinion piece arguing that Session's biblical appeal was inappropriate, given that the US is "not a religious nation" and "The Constitution . . . is an entirely secular document." Donna Carol Voss, "Quit Saying the Bible Supports Your Immigration Preferences," *Federalist*, June 20, 2018, https://thefederalist.com. There are no such articles with regard to gender and sexuality on the site. Instead, it includes offerings such as Holly Scheer, "Planned Parenthood Tried to Cloak Itself in Religion and Christians are Having None of It," *Federalist*, December 12, 2017, https://thefederalist.com.

16 Eliza Griswold, "The Renegade Nuns Who Took on a Pipeline," *New Yorker*, April 19, 2019, www.newyorker.com.

17 *Burwell v. Hobby Lobby Stores, Inc.*, Supreme Court of the United States, No. 13-354, decided June 30, 2014; *Masterpiece Cakeshop, Ltd. v. Colorado Civil Rights Comm'n*, 584 U. S. ___, ___ (2018) (slip op., at 18)."

18 *Zubik v. Burwell*, 578 Supreme Court of the United States, No. 14-1418, decided May 16, 2016, 3, www.supremecourt.gov/opinions/15pdf/14-1418_8758.pdf.

19 Jakobsen and Pellegrini, *Secularisms*.

20 In *Love the Sin*, Pellegrini and I provide readings of US Supreme Court cases in which Christian symbols and Christian holidays are treated as so prevalent in US culture and society that they are essentially secularism. In other words, the dominant secularism of the United States is so deeply infused with Christian assumptions that specifically Christian symbols are representative of a general secular public (Jakobsen and Pellegrini, *Love the Sin*, chapter 2). This reasoning was reiterated in a 2019 case about a large Christian cross that is part of a memorial to World War I on public land in Maryland, in which the fact that the cross "originated as a Christian symbol" is legally contained by the fact that it "took on an added secular meaning" as part of a war memorial and thus did not violate the

establishment clause of the First Amendment to the Constitution. Adam Liptak, "Supreme Court Allows 40-Foot Cross on State Property," *New York Times*, June 20, 2019, www.nytimes.com.

21 Tracy Fessenden, *Culture and Redemption: Religion, the Secular, and American Literature* (Princeton, NJ: Princeton University Press, 2007), 33.

22 Mayanthi Fernando with Christine M. Jacobsen and Janet Jakobsen, "Gender, Sex, and Religious Freedom in the Context of Secular Law," *Feminist Review* 113 (2016): 93–102. Fernando notes with regard to secularism in France, "The way in which one needs to approach secularism not so much as a site of emptiness or a kind of space-clearing neutrality, but rather a formation that has a series of norms and protocols around sex and gender. . . . Methodologically and analytically I think there is a lot to gain from approaching the secular and secularity as itself full of sensibilities, affect and embodied practices."

23 Jakobsen and Pellegrini, *Secularisms*, 4.

24 Laurie Goodstein, "After the Attacks, Finding Fault: Falwell's Finger-Pointing Inappropriate Bush Says," *New York Times*, September 15, 2001, www.nytimes. com; "O'Reilly: Left 'Delirious with Joy' Because Gay Marriage Has 'Anti-Church Ramifications'" (video), Real Clear Politics, July 2, 2015, www.realclearpolitics. com.

25 Heather Shipley, "Challenging Identity Constructs: The Debate over the Sex Education Curriculum in in Ontario," in *Religion and Sexuality: Diversity and the Limits of Tolerance* (Vancouver: University of British Columbia Press, 2015), 97–118.

26 For example, see UN Women, Expert Group Meeting, "Envisioning Women's Rights in the Post-2015 Context," New York, New York, November 3–5, 2014.

27 Anver Emon, *Religious Pluralism and Islamic Law:* Dhimmis *and Others in the Empire of Law* (Oxford: Oxford University Press, 2012). See also Anver Emon, "Pluralizing Religion: Islamic Law and the Anxiety of Reasoned Deliberation," in *After Religious Pluralism: Reimagining Religious Engagement*, ed. Courtney Bender and Pamela Klassen (New York: Columbia University Press, 2010), 59–81.

28 On the three-way split between secularism, reasonable religion, and unreasonable religion, see Arvind-Pal S. Mandair and Markus Dressler, *Secularism and Religion-Making* (New York: Oxford University Press, 2011).

29 On the history of the category "fundamentalism" and the political effects of its deployment in the US context, see David Harrington Watt, *Antifundamentalism in Modern America* (Ithaca, NY: Cornell University Press, 2017).

30 Since the boundary between "good" religion and "bad" religion can be blurry, nonnormative religious practitioners and traditions may shore up their standing as adherents of "good" religion by sustaining normative sexual politics against less normative commitments. David Harrington Watt's ethnographic study in *Bible-Carrying Christians* (New York: Oxford University Press, 2002), for example, shows how congregations that are in certain respects nonnormative and might be considered Habermasian "counterpublics," such as Mennonite congregations that

oppose both capitalism and the engagement with the state, especially with state militarism, may nonetheless be highly committed to normative sexual politics as crucial to ethical identity.

31 Samuel P. Huntington, *Who Are We?: Challenges to America's National Identity* (New York: Simon & Schuster, 2005).

32 See, for example, the Social Science Research Institute at Duke University study "The Racial Marriage Gap and Student Achievement: A New Look at an Old Conundrum," https://scholars.duke.edu/display/gra226465. See also K. S. Kendler et. al., "The Role of Marriage in Criminal Recidivism: A Longitudinal and Co-Relative Analysis," a study sponsored by the National Center for Biotechnology Information of the National Institutes of Health, www.ncbi.nlm.nih.gov/pubmed/28095932, and published in *Epidemiology and Psychiatry Sciences* 6 (December 26, 2017): 655–63.

33 Lauren Berlant and Michael Warner's essay "Sex in Public," *Critical Inquiry* 24.2 (Winter 1998): 547–66, provides a brilliant description of "heteronormativity."

Since the publication of Berlant and Warner's essay, some aspects of normative sexuality have opened up to gay and lesbian people (in some places) who are willing and able to participate in normative practices—to form social units recognizable as families, for example, or to get married and have children, or participate in the self-help and wedding industries. This shift has prompted scholars such as Lisa Duggan to speak of "homonormativity," while Jasbir Puar (*Terrorist Assemblages*) articulated the concept of "homonationalism" to index how these practices constitute national, as well as sexual, boundaries. Lisa Duggan, "Queering the State," *Social Text* 39 (Summer 1994): 1–14.

For additional discussion of the place of normativity in queer theory, see Robyn Wiegman and Elizabeth A. Wilson, eds., "Queer Theory without Antinormativity," special issue, *differences: A Journal of Feminist Cultural Studies* 26.1 (May 2015), and, in response, Lisa Duggan, "Queer Complacency without Empire," September 22, 2015, https://bullybloggers.wordpress.com; J. Jack Halberstam, "Straight Eye for the Queer Theorist—Review of 'Queer Theory without Antinormativity,'" September 12, 2015, https://bullybloggers.wordpress.com.

I argue that all practices involve norms and that the critique of normativity drawn from Foucault involves a critique of the ways in which particular norms are imbricated in power relations. Modern normativity is thus part of the institutional practice of biopolitics. See Janet R. Jakobsen, "Ethics after Pluralism," in *After Pluralism*, ed. Courtney Bender and Pamela Klassen (New York: Columbia University Press, 2010), 31–58, and Janet R. Jakobsen, "Queer Is? Queer Does?: Normativity and Resistance," *GLQ: A Journal of Lesbian and Gay Studies* 4.4 (1998): 511–36.

34 Roderick A. Ferguson, "Of Our Normative Strivings: African American Studies and the Histories of Sexuality," in "What's Queer about Queer Studies Now?," ed. David L. Eng, Judith Halberstam, and José Esteban Muñoz, special issue, *Social*

Text 84–85 (Fall/Winter 2005): 85–100; Amy Villarejo, "Tarrying with the Normative: Queer Theory and *Black History*," in "What's Queer about Queer Studies Now?," 69–84.

35 On relative autonomy, see Cornel West, "Marxist Theory and the Specificity of Afro-American Oppression," in *Marxism and the Interpretation of Culture*, ed. Cary Nelson and Lawrence Grossberg (Chicago: University of Chicago Press, 1983), 17–33.

36 Berlant, *Cruel Optimism*, 184–85.

37 This focus on normativity has been deeply influenced by the work of Michel Foucault, most prominently *The History of Sexuality, Vol. 1*, but also the writings that have been collected in Michel Foucault, *Ethics: Subjectivity and Truth (Essential Works of Foucault, 1954–1984, Vol.1)*, ed. Paul Rabinow (New York: New Press, 1998). It is significant that at the time this collection of the "essential" works began to be published, "ethics" was the first volume.

38 Alison Kafer, *Feminist, Queer, Crip* (Bloomington: Indiana University Press, 2013).

39 Audre Lorde, "Age, Race, Class, and Sex: Women Redefining Difference," in *Sister Outsider: Essays and Speeches* (Freedom, CA: Crossing Press, 1984), 116.

40 For a more extensive definition of norms and an explanation of the relationship between norms and values, see Janet R. Jakobsen, *Working Alliances: Feminist Ethics and the Politics of Difference* (Bloomington: Indiana University Press, 1998), and "Ethics after Pluralism."

41 Mary Poovey, "Sex in America," *Critical Inquiry* 24.2 (Winter 1998): 366–92.

42 Michael Cobb, *Single: An Argument for the Uncoupled* (New York: New York University Press, 2012).

43 Susan M. Schweik, *The Ugly Laws: Disability in Public* (New York: New York University Press, 2010). On the connections between sequestering nonnormative persons and the development of eugenic practices in the United States, see Eli Clare, *Brilliant Imperfection: Grappling with Cure* (Durham, NC: Duke University Press, 2017).

44 Jac Gares, "Free CeCe," Jac Gares Media, 2016.

45 BCRW, "Ky Peterson: Survived and Punished" (video), August 9, 2017, https://vimeo.com/228965945.

46 See the "Survived and Punished" campaign website: www.survivedandpunished.org.

47 Jakobsen, "Queer Is? Queer Does?," 511–36.

48 One of Foucault's central questions in the second and third volumes of *The History of Sexuality* is whether norms and their practices could ever be disengaged from normalization and from dominant or hegemonic regimes of power. Michel Foucault, *The History of Sexuality, Vol. 2: The Use of Pleasure*, trans. and ed. Robert Hurley (New York: Vintage Books, 1985), and *The History of Sexuality, Vol. 3: The Care of the Self*, trans. and ed. Robert Hurley (New York: Vintage Books, 1986). Foucault argues that the ancient Greek practice of "care of the self" is materialized through particular norms, norms that are tied to the prevailing power

relations of the time but that are not those of normalization. The norms for "care of the self" are those of stylizing freedom to attain mastery over the self and others, rather than those of producing the self to fit a sense of being normal. These norms are those of ideal Greek citizenship, and they are saturated with patriarchy and power just as are those of modernity, but the power relations are organized in a different way, as are the relations between morality and power. Thus, "care of the self" does not represent a practice free from power, but Foucault's genealogy does demonstrate that power and one's relation to power could be different. Foucault concludes that three axes of what he calls "experience" can be differently configured at different historical moments. For him, "experience" is a technical term, and it is comprised of: (1) a domain of knowledge, (2) a type of normativity; and (3) a mode of relation to oneself. Michel Foucault, "On the Genealogy of Ethics," *Ethics: Subjectivity and Truth*, ed. Paul Rabinow, trans. Robert Hurley (New York: New Press, 1997), 351.

49 As Nick Mitchell says in describing possible connections between queer antinormativity and abolitionist politics: "Regarding the use of the concept of antinormativity, the question for me has to do with whether, and how, antinormativity can found a politics that lives beyond oppositionality. Perhaps it also has to do with the fact that oppositionality, that is, the taking of a stand against the norm, may not exhaust all the political possibilities that become available to us when we are asking about how not only to oppose directly but also to *inhabit* normativity in a way that is corrosive to it." Liat Ben-Moshe, Che Gossett, Nick Mitchell, and Eric A. Stanley, "Critical Theory, Queer Resistance, and the Ends of Capture," in *Death and Other Penalties: Philosophy in a Time of Mass Incarceration*, ed. Geoffrey Adelsberg, Lisa Guenther, and Scott Zeman (New York: Fordham University Press, 2015), 271.

50 Reading histories of different Christian communities and different periods in relation to one another, one finds a complex array of overlapping ethical trajectories. See Elaine Pagels, *The Gnostic Gospels* (New York: Random House, 1979); Peter Brown, *The Body and Society: Men, Women, and Sexual Renunciation in Early Christianity* (New York: Columbia University Press, 1988); and Shannon McSheffrey, *Marriage, Sex, and Civic Culture in Late Medieval London* (Philadelphia: University of Pennsylvania Press, 2006).

51 Caroline Walker Bynum, *Holy Feast, Holy Fast: The Religious Significance of Food to Medieval Women* (Berkeley: University of California Press, 1987); Rudolph M. Bell, *Holy Anorexia* (Chicago: University of Chicago Press, 1985).

52 The critique of liberal autonomy has been pursued in a number of other traditions as well, including feminist and womanist critiques such as Katie G. Cannon, *Black Womanist Ethics* (Atlanta: Scholars Press, 1988); Carole Pateman, *The Sexual Contract* (Stanford, CA: Stanford University Press, 1988); Nancy Armstrong, *Desire and Domestic Fiction: A Political History of the Novel* (New York: Oxford University Press 1990); and Rey Chow, *The Protestant Ethnic and the Spirit of Capitalism* (New York: Columbia University Press, 2002). Nonetheless, the presumption

that moral agency depends on autonomy—that agency can only be moral if acts are undertaken without coercion—remains at the center of many fields of study. See, for example, Walter Johnson's critique of social history and its efforts to "give slaves back their humanity" by attributing to slaves some form of autonomous agency. Walter Johnson, "On Agency," *Journal of Social History* 37.1 (Fall 2003): 113–24.

53 In *Terrorist Assemblages*, Puar invokes the example of "assemblages of 'militarized bodies'" by which American citizens are encouraged through various forms of exhortation to participate actively in security measures that differentially affect populations. On the intertwining of control and hegemonic individualized freedom as the organization of neoliberal societies, see Marcus Taylor, *From Pinochet to the Third Way: Neoliberalism and Social Transformation in Chile* (London: Pluto Press, 2006).

54 Puar, *Terrorist Assemblages*.

55 For an example of this kind of debate in which the problem of sex in US public life is configured as either a regulatory Christian conservatism that produces state policy or a popular culture that promotes licentiousness, see Hanna Rosin's review of Dagmar Herzog's book on conservative Christian sexual culture, in which Rosin concludes that Herzog misses the point because the "problem is not" Christian conservatism but the licentiousness of teen sexual culture. Hanna Rosin, "In Bed with the Christian Right," *New York Times*, August 31, 2008, BK 16.

56 Dorothy Roberts, *Killing the Black Body: Race, Reproduction and the Meaning of Liberty* (New York: Vintage Books, 1998); Loretta Ross, *Reproductive Justice: An Introduction* (Berkeley: University of California Press, 2017).

57 See Rush Limbaugh's attack on Georgetown student Sandra Fluke for her testimony in Congress about the need for health insurance to cover contraception. Jenna Johnson, "Sandra Fluke Says She Expected Criticism, Not Personal Attacks, over Contraception Issue," *Washington Post*, March 3, 2012, www.washingtonpost.com.

58 Loretta Ross and Lynn Roberts, *Radical Reproductive Justice: Foundation, Theory, Practice, Critique* (New York: Feminist Press, 2017).

59 Margot Sanger-Katz, "Set It and Forget It: How Better Contraception Could be a Key to Reducing Poverty," *New York Times*, December 18, 2018, www.nytimes.com. Further articles in the *Times* pointed out the eugenic history of government support for and enforcement of long-term contraceptives for young, poor women of color, including forced sterilization. Christine Dehlendorf and Kelsey Holt, "The Dangerous Rise of the IUD as Poverty Cure," *New York Times*, January 2, 2019; Robert Pear, "Trump Proposes a New Way around Birth Control Mandate," *New York Times*, November 17, 2018, www.nytimes.com. A biopolitical analysis allows this history of the eugenic control of some women's reproduction to be placed in relation to eugenic incitement of other women's responsibility to reproduce.

60 Senator Marco Rubio, "Reclaiming the Land of Opportunity: Conservative Reforms for Combatting Poverty," January 8, 2014, www.rubio.senate.gov.

61 Andrew L. Yarrow, "Marriage, Poverty, and the Political Divide," *New York Times*, January 24, 2016, www.nytimes.com.

62 See, for example, Wendy D. Manning et. al., "Healthy Marriage Initiative Spending and U.S. Marriage & Divorces Rates: A State Level Analysis," National Center for Family and Marriage Research at Bowling Green State University, 2014, www.bgsu.edu/content/dam/BGSU/college-of-arts-and-sciences/NCFMR/documents/FP/FP-14-02_HMIInitiative.pdf.

63 Although Kant is widely understood as a secular thinker, philosopher J. B. Schneewind has extensively documented that he was deeply influenced by German Protestantism. J. B. Schneewind, *The Invention of Autonomy: A History of Modern Moral Philosophy* (Cambridge, MA: Cambridge University Press, 1998). For a straight history of the broader traditions, see John Witte Jr., *From Sacrament to Contract: Marriage, Religion, and Law in the Western Tradition* (Louisville, KY: Westminster/John Knox Press, 1997).

64 For an earlier reading of this genealogy, see Jakobsen, "Sex + Freedom + Regulation: Why?," *Social Text* 84–85 (Fall/Winter 2005): 285–308.

65 Martin Luther, *Martin Luther: Selections from His Writings*, ed. John Dillenberger (New York: Anchor Books, 1961), 30.

66 Luther can be read here as offering a precursor to Kant's "good will."

67 Luther, *Martin Luther: Selections*, 30.

68 Biblical scholarship has shown that the canonical letters written under the name "Paul" were not all written by a single individual. See Elizabeth A. Castelli, *Imitating Paul: A Discourse of Power* (Louisville, KY: Westminster/John Knox, 1991).

69 Luther, *Martin Luther: Selections*, 30.

70 See, for example, Merry Wiesner's account of how strictly the Reformers enforced the idea that marriage represents women's calling. While some women voluntarily left their convents to become Protestants and marry, others in areas controlled by Reformers fought to keep their religious communities together even when cut off from the Catholic Church. Wiesner also documents the ways in which the Counter-Reformation Church moved to restrict some of the freedoms that women in religious orders had experienced, thus further narrowing women's possibilities. Merry Wiesner, "Nuns, Wives, and Mothers," in *Women in Reformation and Counter-Reformation Europe*, ed. Sherrin Marshall (Bloomington: University of Indiana Press, 1989), 8–28.

71 See Henry Abelove, *Deep Gossip* (Minneapolis: University of Minnesota Press, 2003), particularly the chapter "New York City Gay Liberation and the Queer Commuters." Abelove traces the influence of anticolonial movements on American writers of homophile movements and on gay liberationists, leading to the formation of the Gay Liberation Front as a movement that understood sexual liberation to be part of worldwide liberation struggles,

including anticolonial struggles around the world and opposition to the US war in Vietnam.

72 Calvin elaborates a morality that runs counter to both the specific vows of the Catholic religious life and the process of taking vows itself. For him, the interior intention of the individual is the crucial indicator of morality, rather than vows taken before the community: "For, because the Lord looks upon the heart, not the outward appearance, the same thing (as the purpose in mind changes) may sometimes please and be acceptable to him, sometimes strongly displease him." John Calvin, *The Institutes of the Christian Religion*, ed. John T. McNeill, trans. Ford Lewis Battles, 2 vols. (Philadelphia: Westminster, 1960), 1258, 4.12.4.

73 Ibid.

74 Ibid., 1274, 4.13.19.

75 My claim is not that the secular Protestant dominance of US politics is uniquely patriarchal, but that patriarchy has developed a particular form within Protestantism, one that emphasizes the autonomous individual in relation to an economic calling and the family. This emphasis on individualism—as opposed, for example, to Catholic communalism—develops from the earliest influences of the Protestant Reformation and takes on renewed intensity in relation to neoliberalism's focus on the individual and the population as the aggregation of individuals.

76 Martha Fineman, *The Autonomy Myth: A Theory of Dependency* (New York: New Press, 2005).

77 For documentation of Calvin's views on marriage and sexuality, see John Witte Jr. and Robert M. Kingdon, *Sex, Marriage, and Family in John Calvin's Geneva*, 3 vols. (Grand Rapids, MI: William B. Eerdmans, 2005–forthcoming). As Witte and Kingdon state in their introduction, "Building on a generation of Protestant reforms, Calvin constructed a comprehensive new theology and jurisprudence that made marital formation and dissolution, children's nurture and welfare, family cohesion and support, and sexual sin and crimes essential concerns for both church *and* state. . . . [I]t stands today as one of the most enduring models of marriage and family life in the Protestant world and well beyond" (1–2, emphasis mine).

The foundational role of the Puritans in American culture establishes the place of the Calvinist heritage in mainstream American cultural and political life, although more recent histories, like Jon Butler's *Awash in a Sea of Faith*, have contested the focus on Calvinism as an overemphasis on the role of the "familiar" theme of "New England Calvinism" (1). For a basic background among the extensive number of sources on this legacy, as well as an introduction to some of the complexities of religion in America, see Jon Butler, Grant Wacker, and Randall Balmer, *Religion in American Life: A Short History* (New York: Oxford University Press, 2000); Harry S. Stout and D. G. Hart, eds., *New Directions in American Religious History* (New York: Oxford University Press, 1997); and Aliki Barnstone, Michael Tomasek Manson, and Carol J. Singley, eds., *The Calvinist Roots of the Modern Era* (Hanover, NH: University Press of New England, 1997).

78 Mark D. Jordan, *Blessing Same-Sex Unions: The Perils of Queer Romance and Confusions of Christian Marriage* (Chicago: University of Chicago Press, 2005).

79 *Obergefell v. Hodges*, 2015, 17.

80 Foucault is particularly interested in the ways in which the Catholic confessional is related to the secular process of psychoanalysis in producing the subject of sexuality. Foucault is very quiet on the question of Protestantism and the Reformation, but more recent scholarship has explored the possible connections. Ann Pellegrini has argued, for example, that Foucault's "chattering subject" is closer to the Protestant testimonial than the Catholic confessional in Ann Pellegrini, "Testimonial Sexuality; or, Queer Structures of Religious Feeling: Notes Towards an Investigation," *Journal of Dramatic Theory and Criticism* 20.1 (Fall 2005): 93–102. Molly McGarry has similarly noted, "If the confessional is one culturally specific space from which speech about the self was produced, the Protestant evangelical tent, revivalist meeting, or Spiritualist séance may be American corollaries." Molly McGarry, "'The Quick, the Dead, and the Yet Unborn': Untimely Sexualities and Sexual Hauntings," in Jakobsen and Pellegrini, *Secularisms*, 247–82.

81 Max Weber, *The Protestant Ethic and the Spirit of Capitalism*, trans. Talcott Parsons (New York: Charles Scribner's Sons, 1930).

82 Charles Taylor, "Sex and Christianity: How Has the Moral Landscape Changed?" *Commonweal: A Review of Religion, Politics and Culture* CXXXIV.16 (September 28, 2007), www.commonwealmagazine.org.

83 Cobb, *God Hates Fags*.

84 Ross Douthat, "The Crisis for Liberalism," *New York Times*, November 19, 2016, www.nytimes.com.

85 Josef Sorett, "Secular Compared to What?: Toward a History of the Trope of Black Sacred/Secular Fluidity," in *Race and Secularism in America*, ed. Vincent W. Lloyd and Jonathon S. Kahn (New York: Columbia University Press, 2016), 66.

86 Ibid., 68.

87 Josef Sorett, *Spirit in the Dark: A Religious History of Racial Aesthetics* (New York: Oxford University Press, 2016).

88 Ibid., 39.

89 Ibid., 52.

90 Nikki Young, "Queer Studies and Religion: Methodologies of Freedom," in "Queer/Religion," ed. Castelli, www.sfonline/barnard.edu.

91 Melissa M. Wilcox, *Queer Nuns: Religion, Activism, and Serious Parody* (New York: New York University Press, 2018), 2.

92 Melissa Sanchez, *Queer Faith: Reading Promiscuity and Race in the Secular Love Tradition* (New York: New York University Press, 2019), 1.

93 Ibid., chapter 2.

94 Mark Jordan, unpublished manuscript, paper for "Queer Life after DOMA: The Triumph of Gay Marriage in An Age of Family Values," Yale University, April 24, 2015, http://lgbts.yale.edu. Jordan produces his sense of heteroglossia through a reading of Samuel Delaney's novel *Triton: An Ambiguous Heterotopia* (1976).

95 Omise'eke Natasha Tinsley, *Ezili's Mirrors: Imagining Black Queer Genders* (Durham, NC: Duke University Press, 2018), 17. For an explanation of "masisi," "madivin," and related terms, see Roberto Strongman, *Queering Black Religious Traditions* (Durham, NC: Duke University Press, 2019).

96 Kahn argues that taking seriously the religious nature of many Black intellectual traditions also requires rethinking the nature of the public square. Specifically, the secular public need not mean a public sphere without religion. Jonathon Kahn, "When the Westboro Baptist Church Came to Vassar College: A Story of Success and Failure of the Secular Liberal Arts," unpublished manuscript.

97 Kahn, "Westboro Baptist Church" (quote at 21).

98 The ways in which noninstitutional religious expression and practice often does not count as "religious" has been documented by a number of scholars. See, for example, Winnifred Fallers Sullivan, *The Impossibility of Religious Freedom* (Princeton, NJ: Princeton University Press, 2005), and Robert Orsi, *Between Heaven and Earth: The Religious Worlds That People Make and the Scholars Who Study Them* (Princeton, NJ: Princeton University Press, 2004). As an example of the import of religious expression in popular culture, when religious studies scholar Erin Runions put out a call on Facebook for suggestions of videos and films referencing religion and queerness, she received answers across a wide range that included: *Hell House*, a documentary on a Christian-themed counter-Halloween attraction (see Ann Pellegrini, "'Signaling through the Flames': Hell House, Performance and Structures of Religious Feeling," *American Quarterly* 59.3 [2007]: 911–35); Richard Lindsay's essay on the queer elements in Christian-themed films like *The Ten Commandments* (Richard Lindsay, "Biblical Epics as High Camp," *Gay and Lesbian Review Worldwide* 23.4 [July/August 2016]: 48–49); a description of the religious themes engaged by the performance duo Kiki and Herb ("Kiki and Herb, and Grilled Cheezus" [blog post], October 11, 2010, https://apocalypsepuppy.blogspot.com); the memoir by Justin Vivian Bond, who performs as Kiki, which movingly explores the effects of a religious upbringing (*Tango: My Childhood, Backwards, and in High Heels* [New York: Feminist Press, 2011]); Christian references in AIDS activism in a salon in Columbia, South Carolina, as documented in Ellen Spiro's film *Diana's Hair Ego*, https://vimeo.com/ondemand/dianashairego (see also Anthony Petro, *After the Wrath of God: AIDS, Sexuality, and American Religion* [New York: Oxford University Press, 2015]); the pop singer Beyoncé's video album *Lemonade*, which has been read as including an engagement with the Yoruba goddess Oshun (Karmaria Roberts, "What Beyoncé Teaches Us about the African Diaspora in 'Lemonade,'" NPR, April 29, 2016, www.pbs.org); Madonna's "Like a Prayer" video (www.

youtube.com/watch?v=79fzeNUqQbQ); Lenny Kravitz's church-inspired trib-
ute to Prince at the Rock and Roll Hall of Fame, which opens with the question, "Can the congregation stand up?" as the lead-in to Prince's "When Doves
Cry" (www.youtube.com/watch?v=n1zQcsuOnJc); and Prince's very queer
halftime show at the 2007 Super Bowl, which includes the famous opening to
"Let's Go Crazy": "Dearly beloved, we are gathered here today to get through
this thing called life" (www.msn.com/en-ie/news/video/prince-super-bowl-
halftime-performance-purple-rain-2007/vp-AAyni8g). All of these queer religious engagements, both the queer readings of religiously themed culture and
the religious engagement of queer and popular culture, could be understood
as instantiations of a capacious religious *and* secular freedom.

    David K. Seitz brings a similarly sensibility to his reading of how under-
standings of queerness can be expanded through engagement with religiosity.
In *A House of Prayer for All People*, Seitz suggests that political engagement by
a queer Christian congregation that supports immigrants to Canada can move
the public away from its secular presumptions, disentangle religion from its
constitutive nationalism, and detach queerness from a specifically homosexual
identity, thus making conceptions of public action, religiosity, and queerness
all more expansive. David K. Seitz, *A House of Prayer for All People: Contesting
Citizenship in a Queer Church* (Minneapolis: University of Minnesota Press,
2017).

  99 Ann Braude, "Religion and Women's Political Mobilizations," in *Religion, the Secular and the Politics of Sexual Difference*, ed. Linell E. Cady and Tracy Fessenden
(New York: Columbia University Press, 2013), 69–77.

100 "While scholars need to subject to critique both secular and religious claims to
advance women's interests, we also need to be able to acknowledge both religious
and secular successes in fighting discrimination, whether on the basis of gender
or religion" (ibid., 75).

101 See Janice Fine, *Worker Centers: Organizing Communities at the Edge of the Dream*
(Ithaca, NY: Cornell University Press, 2006).

102 Jews for Racial and Economic Justice, "Employer Testimonials," in "Valuing Domestic Work," ed. Gisela Fosado and Janet R. Jakobsen, themed issue, *Scholar &
Feminist Online* 8.1 (Fall 2009), http://sfonline.barnard.edu.

103 A survey by the Public Religion Research Institute shows an increase in public
support between 2014 and 2019 for "religious freedom" as a basis for refusing
service to specific groups of people including LGBT people and African Americans and also to religious groups, particularly Jews and Muslims. Daniel Green-
berg et. al., "Increasing Support for Religiously Based Service Refusals," Public
Religion Research Institute, 2019, www.prri.org/research/increasing-support-for-
religiously-based-service-refusals.

104 *Trinity Lutheran Church of Columbia Inc. v. Comer*, U.S. Supreme Court No. 15–
577, argued April 19, 2017, decided June 26, 2017, https://casetext.com/case/trinity-
lutheran-church-of-columbia-inc-v-comer. Roberts wrote this in a footnote for

the majority opinion that received a lot of attention because the footnote limits the implications of the decision to the specific case.

105 Former attorney general Jeff Sessions similarly argued that religious freedom applied to religious people in a 2017 speech to the Alliance Defending Freedom, an organization of what the Federalist Society blog calls "Christian First Amendment lawyers." Sessions made the claim to be bolstering the freedom of religious persons even as he served as the Trump administration's point person with regard to the travel ban that administration officials widely acknowledged was based on Muslim majority populations. In other words, religious freedom applies to Christian citizens but not to Muslim immigrants. Jefferson Beauregard Sessions, "Prepared Remarks of the Attorney General to the Alliance Defending Freedom," *Federalist*, July 11, 2017, https://thefederalist.com. More recently, Missouri Senator Josh Hawley has made speeches arguing that not just religious freedom, but freedom itself should only be the purview of the righteous. Ed Kilgore, "Could Josh Hawley Be the Face of the Post-Trump Right?" *New York Magazine*, June 5, 2019, http://nymag.com.

106 The presumption that "religion" involves traditional—and masculinist—authority structures is part of the common sense of US public discourse. Take, for instance, the invocation of the importance of religion to working-class communities in J. D. Vance's *Hillbilly Elegy: A Memoir of a Family and Culture in Crisis* (New York: Harper, 2016). This book received widespread attention as offering background that explains the results of the 2016 elections. Vance is a perceptive observer of both the white working-class culture in which he grew up and the white, elite culture that he travels in after attending Yale Law School. But, he seems to have few analytic tools when thinking beyond the confines of these two cultures, and when he invokes the need for more support from religious communities, he speaks only of religious *institutions* that help "to keep the faithful on track." For Vance, "religion" as a category means that feelings of community, social support, and disciplinary authority must go together.

107 Lucinda Ramberg, *Given to the Goddess: South Indian Devadasis and the Sexuality of Religion* (Durham, NC: Duke University Press, 2014), 15–17.

108 Ibid., 219.

109 Ibid., 222.

110 Among scholars, political scientist Nandini Deo, for example, summarizes the understanding about religion and violence post-9/11 as follows: "Everyone agreed that religion mattered in understanding that attack and the resultant War on Terror, but few social scientists could explain how it mattered." Nandini Deo, ed., *Postsecular Feminisms: Religion and Gender in Transnational Context* (London: Bloomsbury Academic, 2018), 2. In a more recent example, the first version of Trump's "travel ban" included a requirement for a report on "the number and types of acts of gender-based violence against women, including so-called 'honor killings,' in the United States by foreign nationals" as part of the ban's stated goal of "protecting the nation." The inclusion of this provision was widely cited at the

time, including in legal action by the ACLU, as one indicator that the ban was an anti-Muslim ban, rather than a national security project. Kimberly Winston, "Trump Travel Ban Orders a Report on 'Honor Killings,'" *Religious News Service*, March 6, 2017, https://religionnews.com.

111 Tiloma Jayasinghe and Erin Ward, "Responding to Violence, Restoring Justice," *New Feminist Solutions* 10 (September 2018), http://bcrw.barnard.edu.

112 INCITE! Women of Color Against Violence, *Color of Violence: The Incite! Anthology* (Boston: South End Press, 2006), and Generation Five, "Toward Transformative Justice: A Liberatory Approach to Child Sexual Abuse and other forms of Intimate and Community Violence," www.generationfive.org. M. Jacqui Alexander also provides a theoretical framework for refusing to locate gendered and homophobic violence in religious "tradition." Alexander instead emphasizes regulatory practices "within three social formations: the colonial, the neocolonial and the neo-imperial." M. Jacqui Alexander, *Pedagogies of Crossing: Meditations on Feminism, Sexual Politics, Memory and the Sacred* (Durham, NC: Duke University Press, 2005), chapter 5.

113 For a critique of modern revolutionary ideals, see María Josefina Saldaña-Portillo, *The Revolutionary Imagination in the Americas and the Age of Development* (Durham, NC: Duke University Press, 2003). For a reworking of utopian possibility in a queer form, see Muñoz, *Cruising Utopia*.

114 William F. Fisher and Thomas Ponniah, eds., *Another World Is Possible: Popular Alternatives to Globalization at the World Social Forum* (New York: Zed Books, 2003); Susan George, *Another World Is Possible If . . .* (New York: Verso, 2004); Jee Kim et al., eds., *Another World Is Possible: Conversations in a Time of Terror* (New York: Subway Press, 2002).

CHAPTER 2. BECAUSE MORALITY, BECAUSE MATERIALITY

1 Thomas Frank, *Listen Liberal*, 245–46.

2 Although Frank criticizes Obama's policies throughout *Listen Liberal*, healthcare does not even appear in the index to the book, nor does the Affordable Care Act or Obamacare. In the election analysis Frank focuses on trade, which allows him to keep a clear division between "men in factories" and the policies of the Democratic Party.

3 Take an analysis of the 2020 election by Thomas B. Edsall, in which he promotes the idea that the Democratic Party was making gains by focusing on the "basic economic challenges" people face, but he quotes Jonathan Cowan, of the centrist organization Third Way as saying, "Going forward to 2020, there are lines that Democrats can't cross if they want to win nationally and hold the House and gain in the Senate. Medicare for All is one of those lines. But there are others like abolishing ICE, a guaranteed federal job, and certain climate proposals that ignore the economic circumstances of the interior of the country." Edsall does not explain how "Medicare for All" would not address people's "basic economic challenges," even as he frequently makes this type of argument. In February 2019, shortly after the Green New Deal made waves, Edsall reiterates what he sees as a longstanding

(yet somehow also deepening) split between "kitchen-table topics" on one side and race and "cultural permissive[ness]" on the other.

4 In building this analysis through the theoretical promiscuity of *The Sex Obsession*, I draw upon insights from the both Marxist traditions of materialism and new materialisms (which I take up more extensively in the next chapter).

5 A critique of coherence can be understood as correlative to a critique of the secularization narrative. In *Secularisms*, Ann Pellegrini and I connect the critique of the secularization thesis to a social analysis that can take into account the multiplicity of social formations that are simultaneously religious and secular.

6 Ilene Grabel, "Post-crisis Experiments in Development Finance Architectures: A Hirschmanian Perspective on 'Productive Incoherence,'" *Review of Social Economy* 73.4 (2015): 388–414. For Grabel, evidence for productive incoherence can be found by carefully tracing responses to major global events, such as the Asian financial crisis of the late 1990s and the global financial crisis of 2008. Grabel sees in the uneven responses to these crises the possibility for productive change toward "democratic, ethically viable development institutions" (388). For Grabel, the sense of a "productive" incoherence thus has a positive ethical valence. My use of the term understands that what is "produced" by the type of incoherent initiatives that Grabel describes may well not carry the positive ethical valence she asserts. On my reading, incoherence may be as likely to produce unequal hegemony as it is to lead to democratic development. (For example, the idea of "development" may itself be part of the infrastructure of hegemonic inequality.)

7 Zak Cheney-Rice, "The Sleight of Hand at the Heart of Trump's Appeal: Stephen Ross, Tucker Carlson, and How We Really Got Trump," *New York Magazine*, August 9, 2019, www.nymag.com.

8 In 2019, Representative Justin Amash left the Republican Party to become an Independent, but for the most part, even Republicans openly critical of President Trump, like former senator Jeff Flake, did not break with the party on major issues. Justin Amash, "Our Politics Is in a Partisan Death Spiral. That's Why I'm Leaving the GOP," *Washington Post*, July 4, 2019, www.washingtonpost.com.

9 Bell, *Ritual Theory, Ritual Practice*—see, especially, 104–6. Bell is drawing on Pierre Bourdieu, *Distinction: A Social Critique of the Judgement of Taste*, trans. Richard Nice (Cambridge, MA: Harvard University Press, 1984). In the first seven pages of *Distinction*, Bourdieu offers the following set of binaries: sacred/profane, beautiful/ugly, tasteful/vulgar, quality/quantity, form/substance, liberty/necessity, upper-class/lower-class.

10 Eve Kosofsky Sedgwick, *The Epistemology of the Closet* (Berkeley: University of California Press, 1990), 11.

11 Miranda Joseph brings forward the concept of the supplement as a means of explaining why the idea of "community" may be as likely to provide a politics that supports capitalism as one that opposes it (*Against the Romance of Community*).

12 Bernstein, *Brokered Subjects*, 20. For a journalistic discussion that is representative of popular discourse on neoliberalism, see Stephen Metcalf, "Neoliberalism:

The Idea that Swallowed the World," *Guardian*, August 18, 2018. www.theguard-
ian.com.

13 Roderick A. Ferguson and Grace Kyungwon Hong, "The Sexual and Racial
Contradictions of Neoliberalism," *Journal of Homosexuality* 59.7 (2012): 1057–64;
Howard Winant, *The New Politics of Race: Globalism, Difference, Justice* (Min-
neapolis: University of Minnesota Press, 2004); Elizabeth Bernstein, "Militarized
Humanitarianism Meets Carceral Feminism: The Politics of Sex, Rights, and
Freedom in Contemporary Antitrafficking Campaigns," *Signs: Journal of Women
in Culture and Society* 36.1 (2010): 45–72.

14 Inderpal Grewal makes a related argument that recognizes interconnection but
emphasizes particular histories of neoliberalism: "After many decades [of neolib-
eralism], we see an 'advanced stage,' that is also specific to each location a stage
that becomes the result of how neoliberalism manifested itself in its particularities." Inderpal Grewal, *Saving the Security State: Exceptional Citizens in Twenty-
First Century America* (Durham, NC: Duke University Press, 2017), 3. See also
Fernandes, "Toward a Feminist Analytic."
      Bernstein makes her argument through an "ethnography of a discourse"
that moves across governmental, nongovernmental, and corporate institutions.
While not a singular "global" phenomenon, neoliberal practices, such as antitrafficking initiatives tracked by Bernstein, have traveled from place to place.
These "travels in trafficking" are both enacted for specific reasons and in specific ways by local or national bodies and interconnected by larger discourses
located in international institutions like the United Nations or in the enforcement mechanisms the United States deploys internationally or in the practices
of transnational corporations (*Brokered Subjects*, 24–29).

15 Sonia Alvarez argues that neoliberalism has progressed through different stages
in different areas of the world. Sonia E. Alvarez, "Neoliberalismos y Trayectorias
de los Feminismos Latinoamericanos," *Revista América Latina en Movimiento*
489 (October 30, 2013), www.alainet.org. Kamala Kempadoo has argued that
neoliberal policies, like structural adjustment, which have come and gone in the
Caribbean can distract from the ways in which these policies continue the long
history of imperialism ("Sex, Migration, and Neoliberalism"). And Paul Amar has
suggested that practices of the security state are superseding neoliberal practices
across an archipelago of nations that includes Egypt and Brazil (*Security Archipelago*). Sasha Breger Bush argues that Trump's election in the United States
represents a shift away from globalism toward nationalism along with a continuation of neoliberalism, producing a "national neoliberalism." Sasha Breger Bush,
"Trump and National Neoliberalism."

16 Mario Pecheny, "Sexual Politics and Post-Neoliberalism in Latin America," in
"Gender, Justice, and Neoliberal Transformations," ed. Bernstein and Jakobsen,
http://sfonline.barnard.edu.

17 "We are the 99%" became the slogan of the Occupy Wall Street movement in Fall
2011, used in both press coverage about the movement and by activists online,

particularly through the Tumblr, "We Are the 99%," http://wearethe99percent.
tumblr.com. See Sarah Seltzer, "Where Are the Women at Occupy Wall Street?
Everywhere—and They're Not Going Away," *Nation*, October 26, 2011, www.
thenation.com.

18 David Harvey, *The Condition of Postmodernity: An Enquiry into the Origins of
Cultural Change* (New York: Wiley-Blackwell, 1991). The shift from Fordism
to flexible accumulation that Harvey traces in *The Condition of Postmodernity*
becomes the basis for his later analysis in *Brief History of Neoliberalism*.

19 Harvey, *Condition of Postmodernity*, 12–13.

20 Ibid., 171. There has been extensive debate within religious studies about whether
religious conservatives were, as Harvey claims, "not politically active" before the
formation of the Moral Majority, as well as whether religious activity has under-
gone a resurgence since the 1970s (*Brief History of Neoliberalism*, 49). See, for
example, Watt, *Antifundamentalism*, and Balmer, *Evangelicalism in America*.

21 One of the foundations for Harvey's argument is the idea that the institutions he
names (family, state, religion) and the values they institutionalize are stable and
coherent both within themselves and over time, but as I argued in chapter 1, religion and religious values are precisely sites of contestation, and the claim to tradition, stability and unchangeability is part of that contestation. It is also unclear
that all of the institutions Harvey names have been resurgent in the same way. In
the US, the "authority" of the state has, for example, been unevenly diminished as
anti-government discourses have risen in conjunction with an expansion of some
parts of the state, particularly the security apparatus.

22 "Neoliberalization required both politically and economically the construction
of a neoliberal market-based populist culture of differentiated consumerism and
individual libertarianism. As such it proved more than a little compatible with
the cultural impulse called 'postmodernism' which had been lurking in the wings
but could now emerge full-blown as both a cultural and an intellectual dominant"
(Harvey, *Brief History of Neoliberalism*, 42).

23 Harvey, *Brief History of Neoliberalism*.

24 Ibid., 49.

25 Ibid., 50.

26 There was, for example, an extensive argument on Twitter about the status of
intersectionality in the overall approach of the leftist online journal *Jacobin* in the
aftermath of the 2016 presidential election, https://twitter.com/jacobinmag/sta-
tus/843977991592054784.

27 Tax Policy Center Briefing Book, "Impact of the Child Tax Credit," Tax Policy
Center, Urban Institute and Brookings Institution, 2017, www.taxpolicycenter.org.

28 Chris Ladd, "Unspeakable Realities Block Universal Health Coverage in America,"
Forbes, March 13, 2017, www.forbes.com. For a related history of how govern-
ment action supported white homeownership and racial segregation, even as the
US Supreme Court fails to recognize that segregation is anything other than an

accident, see Richard Rothstein, *The Color of Law: The Forgotten History of How Our Government Segregated America* (New York: W.W. Norton, 2017).

29 Ladd traces this mechanism historically with regard to healthcare: "President Truman introduced his plan for universal health coverage in 1945. It would have worked much like Social Security, imposing a tax to fund a universal insurance pool. His plan went nowhere. Instead, nine years later Congress laid the foundations of the social welfare system we enjoy today, rejecting Truman's vision of universal private coverage in favor of a program controlled by employers while publicly funded through tax breaks. This plan gave corporations new leverage in negotiating with unions, handing the companies a publicly financed benefit they could distribute at their discretion. No one stated their intention to create a social welfare program for white people, specifically white men, but they didn't need to. By handing control to employers at a time when virtually every good paying job was reserved for white men the program silently accomplished that goal" ("Unspeakable Realities").

30 For example, political scientists John Sides, Michael Tesler, and Lynn Vavreck argue persuasively that neither economics nor identity alone can explain the voting patterns of the 2016 elections. They argue instead for an analysis of "racialized economics." This analysis leaves aside the role of misogyny in the Trump campaign (and, as chapters 3 and 4 will show, the movement between sexism and racism is a key aspect of kaleidoscopic common sense), but their analysis does break down the supposed opposition between "identity politics" and "economic interests." Putting racialized economics in the context of white familialism and Christian nationalism adds important additional nodes to the network they analyze. John Sides, Michael Tesler, and Lynn Vavreck, *Identity Crisis: The 2015 Presidential Campaign and the Battle for the Meaning of America* (Princeton, NJ: Princeton University Press, 2018).

31 Joseph E. Lowndes, *From the New Deal to the New Right: Race and the Southern Origins of Modern Conservatism* (New Haven, CT: Yale University Press, 2008), 4.

32 Barbara Foley, "Intersectionality: A Marxist Critique," *Science & Society: A Journal of Marxist Thought and Analysis* 82.2 (April 2018): 269–75. Foley's article is part of a symposium on intersectionality that provides a number of takes on the argument that while intersectionality may be helpful, class remains, as Lise Vogel says, "key" to social analysis. Lise Vogel, "Beyond Intersectionality," *Science & Society: A Journal of Marxist Thought and Analysis* 82.2 (April 2018): 275–87. Vogel makes the important point that a comparative analysis is not the most helpful approach to analyzing social difference, particularly when an assumption of comparability "leads to an interest in identifying similarities and parallels among the categories of difference, and a downplaying of particularities" (282). Vogel turns to social reproduction as a framework that can usefully integrate gender analysis while maintaining the idea that capitalism is a "unitary" system (283). See also Vogel's *Marxism and the Oppression of Women: A Unitary Theory* (New Brunswick, NJ:

Rutgers University Press, 1983). Vogel does not, however, take up the extensive discussion of racial capitalism, which has similarly worked to integrate a structural analysis of race and capitalism.

33 Foley, "Intersectionality," 272.

34 Here Foley refers to Gregory Meyerson, "Rethinking Black Marxism: Reflections on Cedric Robinson and Others," *Cultural Logic* 3.2 (2000).

35 Foley, "Intersectionality," 272. Foley's essay is helpful in its clarity and presents one among many versions of the argument that capitalism is "structural," whereas racism and sexism are "identities." Foley states clearly that gender, race, and class are all analytic categories but not of the same type. While I agree about the differences among categories, my concern with structuralist argument is not just the focus on causation that is actively maintained by Foley, but also that causation is often the only dynamic aspect of interrelation. The relation between domination and exploitation that I sketch below allows for multiple points of dynamic interaction.

36 Gayatri Chakravorty Spivak, "Scattered Speculations on the Question of Value," in *In Other Worlds: Essays in Cultural Politics* (New York: Methuen, 1987), 154–75. For a fuller reading of Spivak, see Janet R. Jakobsen, "Can Homosexuals End Western Civilization as We Know It?: Family Values in a Global Economy," in *Queer Globalizations: Citizenship and the Afterlife of Colonialism*, ed. Arnaldo Cruz-Malavé and Martin Manalansan (New York: New York University Press, 2002), 49–70. See also Amy Villarejo, *Lesbian Rule: Cultural Criticism and the Value of Desire* (Durham, NC: Duke University Press, 2003), 28–35, and Joseph, *Against the Romance of Community*.

37 Paying attention to the social relations that make human beings and create social values ensures that human bodies do not "simply disappear into labor power," in Mary Poovey's words. Mary Poovey, *Making a Social Body: British Cultural Formation, 1830–1864* (Chicago: University of Chicago Press, 1995), 31.

38 Spivak argues that the predication of the subject "can no longer be seen as the excess of surplus value over *socially* necessary labor" ("Scattered Speculations," 162, emphasis in original).

39 Richard Ohmann, *Selling Culture: Magazines, Markets, and Class at the Turn of the Century* (New York: Verso, 1996), 9.

40 Douglas V. Porpora, Alexander G. Nikolaev, Julia Hagemann May, and Alexander Jenkins, *Post-ethical Society: The Iraq War, Abu Ghraib, and the Moral Failure of the Secular* (Chicago: University of Chicago Press, 2013), 244.

41 Taylor, *From Pinochet to the Third Way*; Klein, *Shock Doctrine*.

42 The literature on anticolonialism, postcolonialism, and decolonization is now vast. Some helpful summaries are provided by Westad, *Global Cold War*; Robert J. C. Young, *Postcolonialism: An Historical Introduction* (Oxford: Wiley-Blackwell, 2001); and George J. Sefa Dei and Meredith Lordan, *Anti-colonial Theory and Decolonial Praxis* (New York: Peter Lang, 2016).

43 Duggan, *Mean Girl*.

44 Roderick A. Ferguson, "The Historiographical Operations of Gay Rights," in *After Legal Equality: Family, Sex, Kinship* (New York: Routledge, 2015), 161–62.

45 Anita Bryant formed the organization Save our Children originally to support a ballot referendum in the city of Miami dedicated to the repeal of a gay rights ordinance, and then, with the success of the referendum took her campaign into national cultural politics. Daniel K. Williams, *God's Own Party: The Making of the Christian Right* (New York: Oxford University Press, 2010), 148–49. The Briggs Initiative was a 1978 statewide ballot initiative in California, proposed by State Senator John Briggs, to purge all lesbian and gay teachers from public schools in the state. Although the initiative was defeated, it helped to promote the false idea of a connection between homosexuality and pedophilia, contributing to public conflicts that continued for decades. Jackie M. Blount, *Fit to Teach: Same-Sex Desire, Gender and School Work in the Twentieth Century* (Albany: SUNY Press, 2005). On Phyllis Schlafly and the campaign against the ERA, see Jane J. Mansbridge, *Why We Lost the ERA* (Chicago: University of Chicago Press, 1986).

46 For example, James Dobson founded Focus on the Family in 1976 and Jerry Falwell and Paul Weyrich founded the Moral Majority in June 1979. Williams, *God's Own Party*, 172–79.

47 On transnational Christian politics, see Doris Buss and Didi Herman, eds., *Globalizing Family Values: The Christian Right in International Politics* (Minneapolis: University of Minnesota Press, 2003); Melani McAlister, *The Kingdom of God Has No Borders: A Global History of American Evangelicals* (New York: Oxford University Press, 2018); and Bethany E. Moreton, "The Soul of Neoliberalism," *Social Text* 25.3 (Fall 2007): 103–23. For an excellent analysis of the complex interactions of capitalism and Christianity in a specific national context, see Eng-Beng Lim, *Brown Boys and Rice Queens: Spellbinding Performance in the Asias* (New York: New York University Press, 2014), chapter 2.

48 Marcus Taylor and Naomi Klein do not mention sexual politics, for example, while R. Marie Griffith focuses on moral conflict with little attention to economics or neoliberalism. The texts that I bring into conversation below are almost all singular in focus.

49 Stein's recognition that "the working-class" includes both working-class whites and people of color is not a small thing. Both labor historians and the popular press all too often focus on working-class whites as if they are representative of the working-class *tout court* or on the interests of working-class whites as if they are different than those working-class people of color. What distinguishes the interests of working-class whites from those of people of color other than their racial identity? And insofar as such distinctions are made—either in politics or by political analysts—how do they not reinforce white supremacy? Nonetheless, Stein accomplishes the connection of race and class by subsuming race into class, such that white racism across the class spectrum disappears. See, for example, an interview Stein did with *Jacobin* on the relation of race and class. The introduction

to the interview notes that Stein has been a leader in addressing race and class, particularly the history of Black workers and activism, including books like *Running Steel, Running America: Race, Economic Policy and the Decline of Liberalism*. But it also includes this summary of the overall question: "Contrary to today's liberals, Stein argues that it wasn't the racism of white workers that forced the Democratic Party to the right on economics. It was powerful political and business elites, who chose to abandon organized labor and turn the Party of Roosevelt into the Party of Clinton." Why can't it be both of these? Why weren't "elites" also part of or allied with the racism of white workers? Stein also makes a frequently reiterated assertion: "The current 'wages of whiteness' school reifies whiteness and makes it all-powerful, to counter a straw-man conception of Marxism that nobody even accepts anymore." Given the examples I offer herein, it seems that Marxists, like David Harvey, and liberals, like Thomas Frank and Thomas Edsall, and Jeffrey Sachs, do accept versions of Marxist or class analysis that separate class from race, sex, and nationalism. In other words, the strawman is regularly embodied across a range of positions.

50 Stein, *Pivotal Decade*, 17.

51 Ibid., 18.

52 Ibid., 22.

53 Robin D. G. Kelley offers this type of analysis in *Hammer and Hoe: Alabama Communists in the Great Depression* (Chapel Hill: University of North Carolina Press, 1990). Catherine Fosl also provides a moving account of cross-racial alliances in Southern working-class politics before the Civil Rights Movement in *Subversive Southerner: Anne Braden and the Struggle for Racial Justice in the Cold War South* (New York: Palgrave Macmillan, 2002).

54 Overall, the history of the "long civil rights movement" has provided an expansive grounding for reading civil rights as a movement of intertwined issues. See Jacquelyn Dowd Hall, "The Long Civil Rights Movement and the Political Uses of the Past," *Journal of American History* 91.4 (March 2005): 1233–63, and "The Long Civil Rights Movement Initiative," Southern Oral History Program, University of North Carolina, http://sohp.org.

55 Government-initiated infusions of purchasing power under conditions of increased global trade could stimulate increased imports as readily as increased manufacturing within the United States. There are other material shifts, including shifts supported by public policy that are also relevant to the effects of global trade, including the development of container shipping and the US interstate highway system to carry those containers across the United States. Adam Davidson, "Our Town," *New York Times Magazine*, May 1, 2016, 83.

56 Stein, *Pivotal Decade*, 203–4.

57 In response to the economic crisis of 2008, for example, Stein writes, "The President will not only have to regulate Wall Street, the President will have to discard the global agenda of Wall Street, which promoted the policies that hobbled production and wages" (ibid., 297).

58 Ibid., 61.

59 Jane Dailey, "Sex, Segregation, and the Sacred after *Brown*," *Journal of American History* (June 2004): 119–44. I thank Ann Pellegrini for bringing this article to my attention. In the 1970s, the courts did support racial justice and refused the idea that religious freedom was at stake in racial discrimination, but Dailey reports that, as late as 1984, "Mississippi senator Trent Lott insisted that the main issue in the Bob Jones case [in which Bob Jones University maintained its right to racially discriminate and still receive federal funding] was 'not a racial question, but a religious question'" (144).

60 Gillian Frank, "The Colour of the Unborn: Anti-abortion and Anti-busing Politics in Michigan, United States, 1967–73," *Gender & History* 26.2 (August 2014): 351–78.

61 Ibid., 351–52.

62 Ibid., 358.

63 Frank continues: "The MCC saw abortion as symptomatic of sexual chaos and instructed readers to ask legislators whether abortion reform legislation would, 'further devaluate [sic] human dignity and family life in a society already beset by pornography, violence and easy divorce.' . . . So prevalent were warnings of sexual chaos that MARC included in its pamphlets a standard response to the question, 'Won't legalizing abortion open the floodgates of sexual promiscuity?' Such discussions of permissiveness would fold into debates over liberalism and conservatism that animated national politics" (368).

64 "White working-class maternalism did significant political work in the struggle against racial integration as evidenced by the fact that Michigan's leading anti-bussing groups were composed and led by self-identified mothers and housewives. Likewise, the anti-busing correspondence received by politicians largely came from women who identified themselves as mothers or housewives. The silent majority, in other words, had a gendered and familial dimension as exemplified in the ubiquitous slogan of anti-bussers: 'This Family Will Not Be Bussed'" (Frank, "Colour of the Unborn," 356). It is clear that sex continues to be part of a wider set of religious concerns that include public prayer and the nation. See, for example, Ross Douthat, "Donald Trump's Christian Soldiers," *New York Times*, March 10, 2016. www.nytimes.com.

65 Frank, "Colour of the Unborn," 371.

66 For example, Frank writes: "The advertising firm [for an anti-abortion organization] explained this strategy as rooted in a suburban politics: 'None of the television commercials had blacks in them. That was preplanned because of the outstate antiblack thing. . . . A lot of whites look at blacks as baby factories.' Anti-abortion activism, in other words, depended upon making the foetus literally appear to be white in order for its child-saving rhetoric to work among white voters" ("Colour of the Unborn," 366). Activism against busing in Michigan also included a racialized understanding of welfare provision: "Some white constituents emphatically differentiated themselves . . . : 'We are the ones paying all the

high taxes and supporting all the welfare activities and we are the ones getting the royal shaft'" (354).

67 Lowndes, *New Deal to New Right*, 4.

68 Marisa Chappell, *The War on Welfare: Family, Poverty, and Politics in Modern America* (Philadelphia: University of Pennsylvania Press, 2010).

69 Robert O. Self, *All in the Family: The Realignment of American Democracy since the 1960s* (New York: Farrar, Straus and Giroux, 2012).

70 Ibid., 275.

71 See Miranda Joseph, "Family Affairs: The Discourse of Global/Localization," in *Queer Globalizations*, ed. Cruz-Malavé and Manalansan, 71–99.

72 Self, *All in the Family*, 343.

73 Williams describes how "[i]n an unprecedented showing of political and religious ecumenism, fundamentalist Protestants, socially conservative Catholics, right-wing organizations, and conservative legislators united in fighting sex education" (*God's Own Party*, 83).

74 Ibid.

75 Although the focus is often placed on gender and sex in narratives about the increasing political involvement of evangelicals, when Ronald Reagan could not realize proposals to restore Christian prayer in public schools and bans on abortion in the first term of his presidency, he maintained his moral legitimacy by returning to anticommunism. In 1984, his reelection year, Reagan gave a speech to the National Association of Evangelicals (NAE) that Williams terms "one of the most overtly religious speeches of his presidency," in which he reiterated his support for conservative positions against secularism and abortion and in favor of school prayer. But, he named opposition to a freeze on nuclear weapons as the most prominent political issue of his reelection campaign. For Reagan, the battle between capitalism and communism was the moral issue of the day, and he put the case in strongly religious terms: "'There is sin and evil in the world,' he declared, 'and we're enjoined by Scripture and the Lord Jesus to oppose it with all our might.' The Soviet Union was an 'evil empire,' he said, and the fight against communism was a 'struggle against right and wrong and good and evil'" (Williams, *God's Own Party*, 205).

76 And if one were producing a full analysis of the 1970s, one would need to continue to turn the kaleidoscope. I have not, for example, canvassed the importance of the 1970s as the lead up to the farm debt crisis that contributed significantly to urbanization and population shifts from the middle of the United States to the coasts through the second half of the twentieth century. Neil E. Harl, *The Farm Debt Crisis of the 1980s* (New York: Wiley-Blackwell, 1991); Kathryn Marie Dudley, *Debt and Dispossession: Farm Loss in America's Heartland* (Chicago: University of Chicago Press, 2002).

77 Stephanie Coontz, *The Way We Never Were: American Families and the Nostalgia Trap* (New York: Basic Books, 1993); Elaine Tyler May, *Homeward Bound: American Families in the Cold War Era* (New York: Basic Books, 1988).

78 John Stormer, *None Dare Call It Treason* (Florissant, MO: Liberty Bell Press, 1964), 124, as quoted in Lisa McGirr, *Suburban Warriors: The Origins of the New American Right* (Princeton, NJ: Princeton University Press, 2001), 157.

79 McGirr, *Suburban Warriors*, 163.

80 This shift was crystallized for Southern California suburban Christian activists in the campaign for the highly consequential Proposition 13, a 1978 ballot initiative that enshrined limits on taxation in the California state constitution. Proposition 13 was part of what became a national "tax revolt," beginning in the 1970s with movements to cut property taxes and over the decades leading to tax cutting as a central political issue, perhaps derailing the presidency of George H. W. Bush and representing the major legislative victory of the Trump administration. Historical sociologist Isaac William Martin argues that what he terms "the permanent tax revolt" began not as the movement for "small government" that it eventually became, but rather as a protection of "earned" government benefits for middle-class property owners. Tax reforms of the 1960s made the collection of property taxes fairer by, for example, standardizing the assessment of a property's value. In so doing these reforms also took away the discretion of tax assessors and left property tax payers subject to the vagaries of the ups and downs of the housing market. The response of tax payers, leading to ballot referenda in the 1970s, was to act to protect themselves. When Martin's analysis is read in conjunction with this chapter's focus on productive incoherence, it becomes clear that the tax revolt is much like the idea of "small government" activists wanting the government to "keep its hands off my Medicare." The idea that government standardization was unfair to home owners if it left them at the mercy of the market could end up conjoined with the idea that taxes themselves are unfair and the market should take over many government functions is clearly incoherent. But, it is an incoherence made all the more productive because the benefit that was being protected— home ownership as a source of financial security—could be configured as the result of hard work and often accrued to white middle-class families. Isaac William Martin, *The Permanent Tax Revolt: How the Property Tax Transformed American Politics* (Stanford, CA: Stanford University Press, 2008).

81 Bethany Moreton makes a similar point about the connections between a commitment to the free market and a commitment to sexual conservatism in her important book *To Serve God and Walmart: The Making of Christian Free Enterprise* (Cambridge, MA: Harvard University Press, 2009).

82 Grabel, "Productive Incoherence," 392.

83 Ibid., 408.

84 K. Ravi Raman, "Transverse Solidarity: Water, Power, and Resistance," *Review of Racial Political Economics* 42.2 (2010): 251–68.

85 Ibid., 256.

86 For a history of the connections between financialization and local politics, see Kim Moody, *From Welfare State to Real Estate: Regime Change in New York City, 1974 to the Present* (New York: New Press, 2007).

87 Neferti X. M. Tadiar, *Things Fall Away: Philippine Historical Experience and the Makings of Globalization* (Durham, NC: Duke University Press, 2009); Melissa Wright, *Disposable Women and Other Myths of Global Capitalism* (New York: Routledge, 2013).

CHAPTER 3. BECAUSE THE SOCIAL

1 Steven Greenhouse, "The 1992 Campaign: The Economy; Despite Recession's End, Bush May Face Unusually Harsh Judgment," *New York Times*, May 11, 1992, www. nytimes.com.

2 Thomas B. Edsall, "Can Hillary Clinton Manage Her Unruly Coalition?": "The controversies generated by the Trump campaign have pushed offstage many of the conflicts that divide the contemporary upstairs-downstairs Democratic coalition, including housing integration. But the Republican Party has been most successful when it has been able to drive a wedge between competing Democratic constituencies, each with its own legitimate interest—tax payers versus tax beneficiaries, voters who resent the regulatory power of government versus voters who welcome it, environmentalists versus the construction trades, those seeking autonomy and self-expression versus those struggling paycheck to paycheck; investors and property owners versus those without wealth or assets." The oppositions Edsall outlines seem like common sense—they are part of the loosely coherent fabric of political discourse in the US. But take the supposed opposition between "tax payers" and "beneficiaries": Who benefits from government services, subsidies, and outright cash gifts? Mostly corporations, wealthy individuals, particularly real estate developers and hedge fund owners, and then middle-class families that receive the bulk of tax credits (mortgage deduction, earned income tax credit) and entitlements (Social Security and Medicare). In other words, those who pay the most in taxes—middle-class and wealthy people—are also the greatest beneficiaries. They are the same people, not two opposing groups. Similarly, with regard to "autonomy and self-expression" versus "those struggling paycheck to paycheck": How do these two concepts relate to each other such that we should think of them as "versus"? In fact, aren't the people usually placed on the self-expression side of this opposition also those less likely to have economic power—to be struggling paycheck to paycheck: people of color, white women, LGBQTI people, immigrants?

3 Bill Clinton's popularity with African American voters in the 1990s is much discussed and often posited as having been based on a sense of cultural ease as much as on policy positions. Danielle Kurtzleben, "Understanding the Clintons' Popularity with Black Voters," NPR, March 1, 2016, www.npr.org. There has been much debate about Toni Morrison's comment in the *New Yorker* that Clinton was America's "first black president," with both Morrison and Ta-Nehisi Coates arguing that it was not so much about Clinton's sense of "blackness" or his ease with Black culture as the way in which he was treated discursively as someone who, because of his background as the poor child of a single mother, was always, already

guilty. Toni Morrison, "The Talk of the Town: Comment," *New Yorker*, October 5, 1998, www.newyorker.com; Ta–Nehisi Coates, "It Was No Compliment to Call Bill Clinton the First Black President," *Atlantic*, August 27, 2015, www.theatlantic. com.

4 Pew Research Center, "Welfare Income by Race and Ethnicity: 2013," March 11, 2013, www.pewhispanic.org.

5 As noted in my detailed discussion below, Senator Bill Bradley from New Jersey explicitly called out his colleagues for participating in a "coded" racial discourse. *Congressional Record*, August 1, 1996, S9367.

6 "President Bill Clinton: Remarks to Progressive National Baptist Convention," Charlotte, NC, August 9, 1995, quoted in Traci West, "The Policing of Poor Black Women's Sexual Reproduction," in *God Forbid: Religion and Sex in American Public Life*, ed. Kathleen Sands (New York: Oxford University Press, 2000), 142.

7 Bill Clinton, "Radio Address of the President of the Nation," January 4, 1997, quoted in West, "Policing of Poor Black Women," 138.

8 Bill Clinton, "Speech on Affirmative Action," July 19, 1995, washingtonpost.com; "President Clinton Announces New Equal Pay Initiative," press release, January 24, 2000, https://clintonwhitehouse4.archives.gov.

9 Crenshaw, "Demarginalizing the Intersection."

10 Edward Wong, "U.S. Expands Anti-abortion Policies with New Overseas Funding Rules," *New York Times*, March 26, 2019, www.nytimes.com.

11 Bruce Frederick and Don Stemen, "The Anatomy of Discretion: An Analysis of Prosecutorial Decision Making," Vera Institute of Justice, December 17, 2012, www.vera.org.

12 Jeffrey Toobin, "The Milwaukee Experiment," *New Yorker*, May 11, 2015, www. newyorker.com.

13 Ibid.

14 Ibid.

15 Theda Skocpol, *Protecting Soldiers and Mothers: The Political Origins of Social Policy in the United States* (Cambridge, MA: Harvard University Press, 1992).

16 Maureen Fitzgerald, *Habits of Compassion: Irish Catholic Nuns and the Origins of New York's Welfare System, 1830–1920* (Champaign: University of Illinois Press, 2006).

17 Chappell, *The War on Welfare*.

18 Eileen Boris and Jennifer Klein, *Caring for America: Home Health Care Workers in the Shadow of the Welfare State* (New York: Oxford University Press, 2012), 5.

19 Mol, *Body Multiple*. For an earlier reading of this material, see Jakobsen, "Economic Justice after Legal Equality."

20 Mol is here working in the actor-network theory school of thought, which is often associated with Latour, *Reassembling the Social*.

21 In learning how to analyze discontinuous (and even contradictory) relations, which nonetheless come together to produce a hegemonic social fabric, I have also been influenced by Jasbir Puar's convincing use of a Deleuzian version of "as-

semblage." Puar's approach to assemblage provides a means of tracing the interactions among categories in relation to the instability of the categories themselves. Intersectionality and assemblage are sometimes read as contradicting each other, but as Puar argues in the essay "I'd Rather Be a Cyborg than a Goddess," an intersectional approach is needed along with assemblage because these categories of analysis or identity are "not simply legal 'fictions' or means of analysis, but rather they have continuing effects in the world." The combination of intersectionality and assemblage allows for a shifting emphasis in reading between the solidity and instability of materialization.

22 Like many of those who use "new materialist" approaches, the multiplicity Mol records is not merely an epistemological representation of an underlying, ontological unity. Mol is clear about her ontological claims in relation to questions of epistemology but is less clear about the relationship between ontology and phenomenology—is the fact of multiplicity an ontological fact of being in itself or a phenomenological fact of our world as it is perceivable? Instead of making ontological claims (as does Mol), I remain at the level of phenomenology as the level of reality to which perception—whether in the form of ethnography or of scientific observation—has access. I am open to the type of interaction and engagement between observation and reality described by thinkers like Mol, but I would argue that the reality with which we interact is a phenomenological one. In this approach I leave room for empirical analysis while also resisting empiricist claims that would separate fact from interpretation, being from knowing.

23 Mol identifies multiple mechanisms that create coherence out of disjunction. While I focus on "coordination" and "distribution," Mol also names "inclusion," which holds disparate realities together through the incorporation of one reality into another.

24 As Mol writes elsewhere with John Law, "And this is what many of the debates concerning complexity are about: does order expel, produce, or suppress the complex, and if so, how?" Annemarie Mol and John Law, "Introduction," in *Complexities: Social Studies of Knowledge Practices* (Durham, NC: Duke University Press, 2002), 5. For an early critique of additive epistemologies, see Elizabeth Spelman, *Inessential Woman: Problems of Exclusion in Feminist Thought* (Boston: Beacon Press, 1980).

25 Mol, *Body Multiple*, 96.

26 Ibid., 114. The factors that make some enactments dominant in relation to others can change over time: the institutional power of particular actors (medical doctors or physical therapists, for example), the technologies available (shifting from X-rays to sonograms), the articulateness and predilections of individual patients, and movements for less invasive healthcare and patients' rights all may affect which enactment is dominant, or even possible, in a given instance. These factors are dynamically interrelated—underdetermined—but they are not all simply equal. Repeated enactments that favor one approach can make that enactment more likely to be dominant. If a friend's pain is relieved through surgery, another

patient may join surgeons in the sense that pain, vessel obstruction, and surgical treatment should align.

27 Ibid., 117.

28 Ibid., 120.

29 Richard L. Burke, "Fulfilling '92's Promise; Capturing a '96 Issue," *New York Times*, August 1, 1996; Peter T. Kilborn and Sam K. Verhovek, "Clinton's Welfare Shift Ends Tortuous Journey," *New York Times*, August 2, 1996, www.nytimes.com.

30 Z. Fareen Parvez, "Women, Poverty and Welfare Reform," Sociologists for Women in Society, August 15, 2002, www.socwomen.org.

31 This analysis was developed in part through a joint project with Elizabeth Bernstein sponsored by the United Nations Research Institute for Social Development, www.unrisd.org, and Elizabeth Bernstein and Janet R. Jakobsen, "Gender Equality in the U.S.," *Third World Quarterly* 31.6 (2010) (translated and reprinted as "Politique du sexe aux États-unis: le poids des communautés religieues," *Cahiers du Genre* [2012]: 183–201). See also "Family Values and Working Alliances: The Question of Hate and Public Policy," in *Welfare Policy: Feminist Critiques*, ed. Elizabeth Bounds, Pamela Brubaker, and Mary Hobgood (New York: Pilgrim Press, 1999), 109–32.

32 Mimi Abramovitz, *Regulating the Lives of Women: Social Welfare Policy from Colonial Times to the Present* (Boston: South End Press, 1988); Gwendolyn Mink, *Whose Welfare?* (Ithaca, NY: Cornell University Press, 1999).

33 *Congressional Record*, July 22, 1996, S8419.

34 *Congressional Record*, July 19, 1996, S8366.

35 *Congressional Record*, August 1, 1996, S9366.

36 Ibid., S9360.

37 Ibid., S9366.

38 Ibid., S9367.

39 Anna Marie Smith, *Welfare Reform and Sexual Regulation* (Cambridge: Cambridge University Press, 2007).

40 "The Negro Family: The Case for National Action," Office of Policy Planning and Research, 1965, www.dol.gov.

41 Coontz, *The Way We Never Were*.

42 Two decades later Bill Moyers, who had worked on the original report, reiterated its thesis in a television special: CBS Reports, *The Vanishing Family: Crisis in Black America* (New York: Carousel Flim & Video, 1986). The airing of this special once again produced numerous refutations from feminist scholars and activists. See, for example, Patricia Hill Collins, ed., "Black Feminists Respond," *Nation* (1989). And, another ten years after that, William Bennett, secretary of education in the Reagan administration, explicitly invoked the Moynihan Report in his 1995 testimony before the House subcommittee considering "welfare reform."

43 *Congressional Record*, July 18, 1996, S8074.

44 West, "Policing Black Women,"142–43. In his testimony in favor of the legislation economist Glenn C. Loury, also promoted an alliance between religious moralism

and neoliberal economics. Loury is a self-described "born-again Christian" who is African American and who had focused much of his career on "fundamental failures in Black society," including "unwed pregnancies," before shifting toward a more progressive approach. Adam Shatz, "Glenn Loury's About Face," *New York Times Magazine*, January 20, 2002, www.nytimes.com.

45 Clinton Foundation, "Remarks by the President," 1996, 1997, 1998, 1999.

46 *Congressional Record*, July 18, 1996, S8074.

47 Moynihan acknowledged the strong connection that both legislators and the Clinton administration made between out-of-wedlock births and welfare and did not deny that these linkages were relevant. His only tempering intervention was to argue that we do not know enough about the causal relations involved ("The basic model of this problem in the minds of most legislators, and most persons in the administration, is that since we first had welfare and then got illegitimacy, it must be that welfare caused illegitimacy. And they may be right. I do not know. But neither do they").

48 Teresa Kominos, *Journal of Civil Rights and Economic Development* 21.3 (2007): 915–49: "(1) '[P]rovide assistance to needy families so that children may be cared for in their homes or in the homes of relatives,' (2) 'end the dependence of needy parents on government benefits by promoting job preparation, work and marriage,' (3) 'prevent and reduce the incidence of out-of-wedlock pregnancies and establish annual numerical goals for preventing and reducing the incidence of these pregnancies' and, (4) 'encourage the formation and maintenance of two parent families'" (917–18). See also Vee Burke, "Welfare Reform: An Issue Overview," Congressional Research Service, Library of Congress, October 14, 2003, 9, http://digitalcommons.ilr.cornell.edu.

49 The law also codified the connection between religion and the provision of services to needy families by permitting states to 'administer and provide services' through contracts or vouchers redeemable with charitable, religious, or private organizations. This provision came to be known as "charitable choice" and was later added to a number of laws related to welfare state benefits, including food stamps, Medicaid, Community Services Block Grants and substance abuse programs. The initiative was further institutionalized by the George W. Bush administration as the Office of Faith-Based and Community Initiatives, by Obama as the Office of Faith-Based and Neighborhood Partnerships, and eventually broken into offices within various administrative departments of the federal government.

50 H.R. 3355, Pub.L. 103–322.

51 Congressional Research Service, "The Violence Against Women Act (VAWA): Historical Overview, Funding, and Reauthorization," November 19, 2018, https://fas.org.

52 Vera Institute of Justice, "Justice in Focus: Crime Bill @ 20," http://crimebill20.vera.org.

53 Movement for Black Lives, "End the War on Black People," 2016, http://policy.m4bl.org.

54 Michelle Alexander, "Why Hillary Clinton Doesn't Deserve the Black Vote," *Nation*, February 10, 2016, www.thenation.com.

55 Peter Beinart, "Hillary Clinton and the Tragic Politics of Crime," *Atlantic*, May 1, 2015. www.theatlantic.com.

56 Division C of Pub.L. 104–208, 110 Stat. 3009-546.

57 Chandan Reddy, *Freedom with Violence: Race, Sexuality, and the U.S. State* (Durham, NC: Duke University Press, 2011), 158–59.

58 Ibid., 160.

59 Associated Press, "New Rules to Deny Green Cards to Many Legal Immigrants," *New York Times*, August 12, 2019, www.nytimes.com.

60 Adam Liptak, "Immigrants Facing Deportation Must Be Detained after Release from Criminal Custody, Justices Rule," *New York Times*, March 19, 2019; Jason Zengerle, "How America Got to 'Zero Tolerance' on Immigration: The Inside Story," *New York Times Magazine*, July 16, 2019, www.nytimes.com.

61 The racism of Trump's focus on immigration is all too evident, not just in his remarks and tweets, but in his focus on Latinx immigrants even as many wealthy Russians are reported to be living in Trump properties in Florida specifically to provide US citizenship to their children. Josh Dawsey, "Trump Derides Protections for Immigrants from 'Shithole' Countries," *Washington Post,* January 12, 2018, www.washingtonpost.com; Katie Zavadski, "Russians Flock to Trump Properties to Give Birth to U.S. Citizens," *Daily Beast*, September 6, 2017, www.thedailybeast.com.

62 The entire text of the speech can be found at the Avalon Project at Yale Law School, http://avalon.law.yale.edu/21st_century/gbush2.asp.

63 Laura Bush first expressed her great support for women's well-being in Afghanistan in November 2001 by giving the weekly presidential radio address on this topic. See introduction, n40. In 2005, Mrs. Bush made her first visit to Afghanistan, where she spent six hours and extolled women's education. Carlotta Gall, "Laura Bush Carries Pet Causes to Afghans," *New York Times*, March 31, 2005, www.nytimes.com.

64 The Bush administration invested heavily in marriage promotion and reinstated the "global gag rule" to suspend US funding to reproductive health organizations if they provided any access to abortion. At one point, the president advocated amending the US Constitution to prevent same-sex marriage from being legalized. Robert Pear and David D. Kirkpatrick, "Bush Plans $1.5 Billion Drive for Promotion of Marriage," *New York Times*, January 14, 2004; David Stout, "Bush Backs Ban in Constitution on Gay Marriage," *New York Times*, February 24, 2004, www.nytimes.com.

65 For an extended reading of the mutual constitution between sexual politics and the "war on terrorism," see Jakobsen, "Sex, Secularism, and the 'War on Terror.'"

66 When the Bush administration first agreed to support generic drug distribution in Africa through PEPFAR, many activists saw the program as a breakthrough, although the eventual results were decidedly mixed because of the move away

from support for prevention through the use of condoms. For important background on evangelicals' embrace of AIDS as an issue leading up to and following on Bush's institution of PEPFAR, see Petro, *After the Wrath of God.*

67 Françoise Girard, "Global Implications of U.S. Domestic and International Policies on Sexuality," International Working Group on Sexuality and Social Policy Working Papers, No. 1, June 2004. I thank Rebecca Jordan-Young for directing me to this extremely useful essay.

68 Girard reports that in 2002 the CDC first removed a page titled "Programs That Work," which described a variety of sexual education curricula and then removed "Facts about Condoms and Their Use in Preventing HIV Infection" ("Global Implications," 7). See also Russell Shorto, "Contra-Contraception," *New York Times Magazine,* May 7, 2006, 48.

69 As an example of the US press's failure to remark on the broader conservative implications of the Bush administration's AIDS policies, see Frank Rich, "The Gay Old Party Comes Out," *New York Times,* October 15, 2006, WK 13. In this column, the usually critical Rich found one (and only one) positive thing about the Bush administration policies on sex: its efforts around AIDS, arguing that for all of its gay bashing, "the effort to eradicate AIDS [ironically] led by a number of openly gay appointees like Dr. [Mark] Dybul, may prove to be the single most beneficent achievement of this beleaguered Administration." Rich finds it ironic that what he sees as one of the best achievements of a homophobic administration should be led by an openly gay person, but if we take seriously the effects of the administration's AIDS policies, it is also possible to locate the irony in the fact that an openly gay person should be leading an initiative with such a conservative sexual agenda and with such possibilities for disastrous results from diminishing both condom use and education for prevention.

70 Esther Kaplan, *With God on Their Side: How Christian Fundamentalists Trampled Science, Policy, and Democracy in George W. Bush's White House* (New York: New Press, 2004), 218.

71 Ellen Chirwa, Address Malata, and Kathleen Norr, "HIV Prevention and Awareness Practices among Married Couples in Malawi," *Malawi Medical Journal* (June 2011): 32–33.

72 For some of the debates over the effects of policy-shifts in Uganda, see Human Rights Watch, "The Less They Know, the Better: Abstinence-Only HIV/AIDS Programs in Uganda," March 2005, www.hrw.org; Will Ross, "The Battle over Uganda's AIDS Policy," BBC News, April 12, 2005, http://news.bbc.co.uk; and Christine Cynn, "AIDS Policy," lunchtime lecture, BCRW, April 5, 2007. The British AIDS organization Avert also has a helpful website detailing the history of AIDS policy in Uganda and the current debates: www.avert.org/aidsuganda.htm. For analyses of AIDS policy in Africa as part of a larger assemblage of neoliberal policy, see Colleen O'Manique, *Neoliberalism and AIDS Crisis in Sub-Saharan Africa* (New York: Palgrave Macmillan, 2004), and Vinh-Kim Nguyen, *The Republic of Therapy: Triage and Sovereignty in West Africa's Time of AIDS* (Durham, NC:

Duke University Press, 2010). After the Bush administration, the focus of PEPFAR moved away from ABC, and the results in Uganda improved again, particularly with the introduction of anti-retroviral drugs. M. Kate Grabowski et. al., "HIV Prevention and the Incidence of HIV in Uganda," *New England Journal of Medicine* 377 (November 30, 2017): 2154–66, doi: 10.1056/NEJMoa1702150.

73 White House, "President Addresses United Nations High-Level Plenary Meeting," press release, September 14, 2005, www.whitehouse.gov.

74 Cornel West, "Pity the Sad Legacy of Barack Obama," *Guardian*, January 9, 2017, www.theguardian.com; interview by Audie Cornish, "Cornel West Doesn't Want to Be a Neoliberal Darling," *New York Times*, November 29, 2017, www.nytimes.com.

75 In thinking about the ways in which the Obama administration dealt with sexual politics, it is also necessary to think about the relation between the fact that something truly historic had taken place with Obama's election *and* that his election would not in and of itself fundamentally change the nature of politics in the United States. Given the ways in which electoral politics in the United States remains bound to the legacy of slavery, the election of a Black man as president is a truly astonishing accomplishment. As legal scholar Paul Finkelman has argued from his survey of the historical record of the Constitutional Convention, part of the reason the Constitution institutes the use of an electoral college, rather than direct popular vote, to elect the president of the United States was to protect the interests of the slave states by including the extra representation of Southern states accorded by the "three-fifths" rule of counting slaves who could not themselves vote. Finkelman argues that "significantly the most vocal opposition to [direct] election [of the president] by the people came from three southerners: Charles Pinckney, George Mason, and Hugh Williamson." Paul Finkelman, *Slavery and the Founders: Race and Liberty in the Age of Jefferson* (New York: M.E. Sharpe, 2001), 22.

76 Jodi Kantor, "The Obamas' Marriage," *New York Times Magazine*, November 1, 2009, www.nytimes.com.

77 Critics of Obama's centrism, like Cornel West, have displayed their own ambivalence and conservatism on gender and sexuality. West wrote a deeply conservative book on family structure with centrist feminist Sylvia Ann Hewlett. Sylvia Ann Hewlett and Cornel West, *The War against Parents: What We Can Do* (New York: Houghton Mifflin, 1998). Robin D. G. Kelley's *Yo' Mama's Disfunktional!* provides an important alternative to the culture wars approach used by Hewlett and West.

78 This reading is based on Jakobsen, "Perverse Justice."

79 White House, "Obama Announces Office of Faith-Based and Neighborhood Partnerships," press release, February 5, 2009, www.whitehouse.gov. For an analysis of the early working of the office by Melissa Rogers who became its executive director in Obama's second term, see Melissa Rogers, "Continuity and Change: Faith-Based Partnerships Under Obama and Bush," Brookings Institution, December 13, 2010, www.brookings.edu. And for an analysis of Trump's use of an official coun-

cil of evangelical Christian advisors rather than the formal multifaith advisory council of the Obama years, see Jack Jenkins, "Trump Is Dismantling Obama's Religion Initiatives," *ThinkProgress*, October 10, 2017, https://thinkprogress.org.

80 White House, "Obama Announces," press release, 2009, www.whitehouse.gov.

81 The administration continued this focus on "responsible fatherhood" throughout Obama's two terms in office, developing a "responsible fatherhood pledge" in 2010, and creating an interagency initiative and major report on "responsible fatherhood," in 2012. White House, "Promoting Responsible Fatherhood," June 2012, www.whitehouse.gov.

82 In the end, Obama's hope that "abortion reduction" could be a point of compromise did not materialize. In a preview of the hyperbole that President Obama would face throughout his administration, Newt Gingrich claimed, "I think the president's position has been the most radical, pro-abortion of any American president"—this despite the fact of Obama's careful rhetoric on abortion reduction and attempt to find common ground. Katharine Q. Seelye, "Obama's Notre Dame Visit Is Still Drawing Criticism," *New York Times*, May 11, 2009, www.nytimes.com.

83 In his inaugural address Obama also tied this conservative emphasis on responsible fatherhood directed mainly toward the poor—those who might need to "get off the streets"—with an aspiration toward accountability across the economic spectrum, calling on Wall Street executives to be similarly responsible in their financial dealings. "President Barack Obama's Inaugural Address," January 21, 2009, www.obamawhitehouse.archives.gov.

84 President Bush used the language of "crusade" in remarks at the White House on September 16, 2001, as he announced a turn from a period of mourning over the loss of life in the September 11 attacks to a period of war: "We need to go back to work tomorrow and we will. But we need to be alert to the fact that these evil-doers still exist. . . . This is a new kind of—a new kind of evil. And we understand. And the American people are beginning to understand. This crusade, this war on terrorism is going to take a while." Bush tried to walk back this language the next day by visiting the Islamic Center of Washington and speaking briefly on the distinction between war against Islam and war on terrorism. Controversy over Bush's attitude toward Islam was revived in the 2016 presidential election campaign when commentators began to point to his tolerance of Islam in contradistinction to the 2016 Republican candidates, particularly Donald Trump, who directly called for registration of Muslims. Jamelle Bouie, "George W. Bush Needs to Speak to His Party," *Salon*, November 20, 2015; Paul Blest, "The False Resurrection of George W. Bush: Don't Be Fooled by Calls to Reassess His Loathsome Legacy," *Salon*, November 25, 2015, www.salon.com.

85 Even traditionally progressive and thus skeptical outlets like the *Guardian* and the *Nation* heard Obama's Cairo speech as "a world away" from the approach of the Bush administration. Jonathan Freedland, "Barack Obama in Cairo: The Speech

No Other President Could Make," *Guardian*, June 4, 2009, www.theguardian. co.uk. The editor of the *Nation*, Katrina vanden Heuvel, simply called the Cairo speech "magnificent." Katrina vanden Heuvel, "Obama: Reset and Refocus," *Nation*, June 23, 2009, www.thenation.com.

For a report that puts transnational interreligious relations definitively within the realm of national security, see "Engaging Religious Communities Abroad: A New Imperative for U.S. Foreign Policy," report of the Taskforce on Religion and U.S. Foreign Policy, Scott Appleby and Richard Cizik, co-chairs, Thomas Wright, project director, Chicago Council on Global Affairs, 2010, www.thechicagocouncil.org. The press release for this report positions it as "the next step" after Obama's Cairo speech "in developing a strategy to engage religious communities of all faiths in addressing foreign policy challenges."

86 Sullivan, *Impossibility of Religious Freedom*. In particular, the dialogue model for interrelation across religious difference claims to be based in equality and openness but is actually framed by a Christian understanding. The model of interfaith dialogue offers negotiation among different "faiths," a view of religion that mirrors the Christian emphasis on belief as definitive of religion. If, however, practice or land is the basis for one's religion, then dialogue might not be the way to approach conflict. For interfaith dialogues, the issue is talking through beliefs, rather than, say, negotiating about land rights. As with the secular calendar, which is at once used across cultures and specifically Christian, these assumptions make the Office of Faith-Based and Neighborhood Partnerships' claim to be open to working with community activists "no matter [their] political or religious beliefs" into a claim that is simultaneously universalist and Christian.

87 As both the *Guardian* and CBS News reported, many commentators in the US and elsewhere widely regarded the award to President Obama as a counterpoint to President Bush's approach to foreign policy and war. See "World Reacts to Obama's Nobel Peace Prize," CBS News, October 9, 2009, www.cbsnews.com, and Chris McGreal and Gwladys Fouché, "Barack Obama 'Surprised' and 'Humbled' by Nobel Peace Prize," *Guardian*, October 9, 2009, www.guardian.co.uk.

For a discussion of secularism as a state of feeling, see Pellegrini, "Feeling Secular," *Women and Performance* 19.2 (July 2009): 305–18.

88 Eric Schmitt, "Obama Issues Orders for More Troops to Afghanistan," *New York Times*, November 30, 2009, www.nytimes.com.

89 Niebuhr was, in the mid-twentieth century, exceptionally influential. He was on the cover of *Time* magazine in 1948, interviewed on television by Mike Wallace in 1958, and repeatedly quoted by President John F. Kennedy and his advisors in the early 1960s. Both a video and a transcript of this interview (April 27, 1958) are available at www.hrc.utexas.edu/multimedia/video/2008/wallace/niebuhr_reinhold_t.html.

90 Kathy Kiely, "Surprise! Palin Likes Obama's Nobel Speech," *USA Today on Politics*, http://content.usa.today.com; Andrew Sullivan, "The Tragedy of Hope," *Atlantic*, December 11, 2009, www.theatlantic.com; George Packer, "Peace and War," *New*

Yorker, December 21, 2009, www.newyorker.com; David Brooks, "Obama's Christian Realism," *New York Times*, December 14, 2009, www.nytimes.com.

This praise for Obama's speech across the political spectrum is reflective of something of a Niebuhr revival in academic and policy circles. In a review of one of the many Niebuhr studies published during the Obama administration, Jordan Michael Smith describes the revival in the following terms: "Indeed, Niebuhr has somehow become the go-to thinker in the age of terrorism. He has been invoked for various purposes by the neoconservative columnist David Brooks, the liberal journalist Peter Beinart, and the isolationist professor Andrew Bacevich. Politicians have gotten in on the act too: Republican Sen. John McCain, then-New York Gov. Eliot Spitzer, and President Barack Obama have all cited Niebuhr to serve their needs in recent years." Jordan Michael Smith, "The Philosopher of the Post-9/11 Era: Why Have the Right and Left Resurrected Reinhold Niebuhr?," *Slate*, October 17, 2011, www.slate.com.

91 Jakobsen and Pellegrini, *Secularisms*, 2008. See also Jakobsen and Pellegrini, "Bodies- Politics."

92 Sullivan had earlier provided this type of reasoning when arguing on behalf of the US invasion of Afghanistan in 2001. Andrew Sullivan, "This *Is* a Religious War," *New York Times Magazine*, October 7, 2001, 44–53. For a more extensive reading of Sullivan's argument, see Janet R. Jakobsen, "Is Secularism Less Violent than Religion?," in *Interventions: Activists and Academics Respond to Violence*, ed. Elizabeth A. Castelli and Janet R. Jakobsen (New York: Palgrave Macmillan, 2004), 53–67. After promoting this position from 2001 through the Obama administration, Sullivan eventually changed his views on the US wars in Afghanistan and Iraq, arguing that they had been "useless" and admitting that he had been prowar in the run-up to Iraq, but not acknowledging either his avid support for the invasion of Afghanistan, nor his approval of President Obama's decision to extend the US mission there in 2009. Andrew Sullivan, "The Establishment Will Never Say No to a War," *New York Magazine*, December 21, 2018, www.nymag.com.

93 Gary Dorrien, *The Soul in Society: The Making and Renewal of Social Christianity* (Minneapolis: Fortress Press, 1995), 89ff.

94 As Ann Pellegrini and I document, Niebuhr himself was a sometimes-fierce advocate of gender and sexual normativity. Jakobsen and Pellegrini, "Bodies-Politics."

95 As just one among any number of possible example, in 2019 in the middle of his administration, Trump returned to criticism of Senator John McCain for voting against the repeal of the Affordable Care Act (President Obama's signature accomplishment), despite the fact that McCain himself had died several months before and the Democrats had racked up sweeping victories in the 2018 midterm elections in part by emphasizing their support for Obamacare. Maggie Haberman, Annie Karni, and Michael Tackett, "Months after John McCain's Death, Trump Keeps Feud with Him Alive," *New York Times*, March 20, 2019, www.nytimes.com.

96 Adam Behsudi, "Trump's NAFTA Changes Aren't Much Different than Obama's," *Politico*, March 30, 2017, www.politico.com.

97 Sasha Breger Bush, "Trump and National Neoliberalism."

98 Various commentators have tried to provide a coherent rationale for Trump's foreign policy, e.g., Richard Goldberg, "Trump Has an Iran Strategy: This Is It," *New York Times*, January 24, 2020, www.nytimes.com. Overall, though, Trump's actions remain incoherent. Max Fisher, "What Is Trump's Iran Strategy? Few Seem to Know," *New York Times*, January 6, 2020; David E. Sanger, "Trump's Iran Strategy: A Cease-Fire Wrapped in a Strategic Muddle," *New York Times*, January 8, 2020, www.nytimes.com. Early in his administration, Trump authorized a covert mission in Yemen, and it seemed as though he might extend military operations as Obama had done. Eric Schmitt and David E. Sanger, "Raid in Yemen Risky from the Start and Costly in the End," *New York Times*, February 1, 2017, www.nytimes.com. The Trump administration has also sustained and expanded the program of drone warfare that was the signature of the Obama administration. Allegra Harpootlian, "How the Presidency Seized Control of Drone Strikes," *Nation*, January 14, 2020, http://thenation.com. Despite these commitments to continuing or expanding US military action, Trump also claimed the position of a nationalist, withdrawing troops suddenly from Syria with the claim that fighting there was no longer in America's interest and then partially reversing course, and making erratic efforts to bring the war in Afghanistan to an end. Julian E. Barnes and Eric Schmitt, "Trump Orders Withdrawal of U.S. Troops from Northern Syria," *New York Times*, October 13, 2019; Eric Schmitt, "U.S. Resumes Large-Scale Operations against ISIS in Northern Syria," *New York Times*, November 25, 2019; Lara Jakes, Thomas Gibbons-Neff, and Eric Schmitt, "Will a New Plan End the War in Afghanistan?," *New York Times*, August 9, 2019, www.nytimes.com.

99 Trump's "travel ban" included a requirement for a report on "the number and types of acts of gender-based violence against women, including so-called 'honor killings,' in the United States by foreign nationals." The inclusion of this provision was interpreted in legal action, including by the ACLU, as one indicator that the ban was anti-Muslim rather than being a national security project. Kimberly Winston, "Trump Travel Ban Orders a Report on 'Honor Killings,'" *Religious News Service*, March 6, 2017, https://religionnews.com.

100 Azadeh Moaveni, "How the Trump Administration Is Exploiting Iran's Burgeoning Feminist Movement," *New Yorker*, July 9, 2018, www.nytimes.com.

101 Katherine M. Marino, "How Mike Pompeo's New Commission on 'Unalienable Rights' Butchers History," *Washington Post*, August 15, 2019, www.washingtonpost.com.

102 Lara Jakes, "Peace Road Map for Afghanistan Will Let Taliban Negotiate Women's Rights," *New York Times*, August 16, 2019, www.nytimes.com.

103 Here's how Mol describes the promise of her multiple approach to understanding reality: "For a long time, and in many places, science held (or continues to hold) the promise of closure through fact-finding. In ethics, the promise of closure, or at least temporary consensus, through reasoning is widely shared. In an attempt to disrupt these promises, it may help to call 'what to do?' a political question. The

term politics resonates openness, indeterminacy. It helps to underline that the question 'what to do' can be closed neither by facts nor by arguments. That it will forever come with tensions—or doubt. In a political cosmology 'what to do' is not given in the order of things, but needs to be established. Doing good does not follow on finding out about it, but is a matter of, indeed, doing. Of trying, tinkering, struggling, failing and trying again" (*Body Multiple*, 177).

CHAPTER 4. BECAUSE STASIS

1 My initial description of mobility for stasis can be found in Jakobsen, "Different Differences" (see introduction).

2 Siegel, "The Rule of Love" (see introduction).

3 Kyle Crowder and Maria Krysan, "Moving beyond the Big Three: A Call for New Approaches to Studying Racial Segregation," *City and Community* 15.1 (March 2016): 18–22. Crowder and Krysan summarize the current state of segregation in the US as follows: "Despite declines in average levels of segregation and the increasing prevalence of multiethnic neighborhoods, overall levels of segregation between black and white Americans remain high by most measures, and are especially pronounced in cities with the largest black populations. Levels of segregation between Latinos and whites, and between Asians and whites, have changed very little in recent decades" (18). Gary Orfield, John Kucsera, and Genevieve Siegel-Hawley, "E Pluribus . . . Separation: Deepening Double Segregation for More Students," Civil Rights Project, September 19, 2012, https://civilrightsproject. ucla.edu; Emmanuel Felton, "The Department of Justice Is Overseeing the Resegregation of American Schools," *Nation*, September 8, 2017, www.thenation.com.

4 Douglas S. Massey, "The Legacy of the 1968 Fair Housing Act," *Sociological Forum* 30.51 (June 2015): 571–88. "Under these circumstances, the most reasonable prediction for the future is more of what we have seen in the past. Black segregation will probably continue to fall, on average, but will be characterized by a growing divergence between smaller metropolitan areas with less restrictive zoning regimes and smaller, more affluent black populations, on the one hand, and large metropolitan areas with restrictively zoned suburbs and large, poor black communities, on the other hand. Whereas the former will continue to desegregate at a steady pace, the latter will increasingly come to be comprised of a distinct set of hypersegregated areas in which little movement toward integration occurs. Hispanic segregation, meanwhile, can be expected to creep upward and neighborhood isolation to increase as Hispanic population growth continues." See also Alexander Astin and Leticia Oseguera, "The Declining 'Equity' of American Higher Education," *Review of Higher Education* 27.3 (Spring 2004): 321–41; Susan Choy, "Students Whose Parents Did Not Go to College: Postsecondary Access, Persistence, and Attainment," National Center for Education Statistics, 2001, https://nces.ed.gov.

5 Will Stancil, "Segregation Is Not a Myth," *Atlantic*, March 14, 2018, www.theatlantic.com.

6   Miles Corak, "Economic Mobility," Stanford Center on Poverty and Inequality, 2016, https://inequality.stanford.edu.

7   Linda Hirshman, *Victory: The Triumphant Gay Revolution* (New York: Harper, 2013); Empire State Pride Agenda, "Important News," October 22, 2015, www.prideagenda.org; Jesse McKinley, "Empire State Pride Agenda to Disband, Citing Fulfillment of Its Mission," *New York Times*, December 12, 2015, www.nytimes.com.

8   The North Carolina anti-trans bathroom bill was passed by the state legislature in 2016, touching off a long-running controversy and much back and forth on the status of the legislation that was finally settled in 2019, when a US court overturned the part of the law that barred transgender people from using public bathrooms that matched their gender. But, the settlement let stand that part of the law that prohibited municipalities in North Carolina from creating their own laws to prevent discrimination against LGBTQ people. Reuters, "North Carolina 'Bathroom Bill' Settlement Approved," July 23, 3019, www.nytimes.com.
    On Trump's anti-trans initiatives, see Helene Cooper and Thomas Gibbons-Neff, "Trump Approves New Limits on Transgender Troops in the Military," *New York Times*, March 23, 2018, and Robert Pear, "Trump Plan Would Cut Back Health Care Protections for Transgender People," *New York Times*, April 21, 2018, www.nytimes.com.

9   Once in office, President Trump moved to provide full exemptions for both religious and moral objections to the provision of contraception. Robert Pear, Rebecca R. Ruiz, and Laurie Goodstein, "Trump Administration Rolls Back Birth Control Mandate," *New York Times*, October 6, 2017; Linda Greenhouse, "On Contraception, It's Church over State," *New York Times*, October 11, 2017, www.nytimes.com. The Trump administration also moved rapidly on the question of abortion: Julie Hirschfeld Davis and Maggie Haberman, "Trump Administration to Tie Health Facilities' Funding to Abortion Restrictions," *New York Times*, May 17, 2018; Jeremy W. Peters, "Under Trump an Office Meant to Help Refugees Enters the Abortion Wars," *New York Times*, April 5, 2018; Julie Hirschfeld Davis, "Trump Signs Law Taking Aim at Planned Parenthood Funding," *New York Times*, April 13, 2017, www.nytimes.com.

10 An example of how people experience progress as happening and not happening would be this speech by activist and actor Jesse Williams at the 2016 BET awards ceremony naming continuing state violence against African American people: "Yesterday would've been young Tamir Rice's 14th birthday, so I don't want to hear anymore about how far we've come when paid public servants can pull a drive-by on a 12-year-old playing alone in a park in broad daylight, killing him on television and then going home to make a sandwich. Tell Rekia Boyd how it's so much better to live in 2012 than 1612 or 1712. Tell that to Eric Garner. Tell that to Sandra Bland. Tell that to Darrien Hunt." BET Awards 2016, www.bet.com.

11 I first came to this topic because I was scheduled to give a paper for a graduate student workshop on queer studies and religion at Vanderbilt Divinity School in

2013 shortly after this series of decisions, and their interrelation was so striking as to be unavoidable. I thank Rebecca Alpert and Emilie M. Townes, as well as the participating graduate students for their helpful exchanges in relation to that initial paper.

12 Also note that affirmative action in college admissions and employment has focused on gender, as well as race, and that both access to college education and to professional employment have increased most for white women in the period since the institution of such policies. Sally Kohn, "Affirmative Action Has Helped White Women More than Anyone," *Time*, June 17, 2013, http://ideas.time.com.

13 June Jennings, "The Psychology of the Affirmative-Action Backlash," *Nation*, December 9, 2015, www.thenation.com.

14 Tamar Lewin, "Appeals Panel Upholds Race in Admissions for University," *New York Times*, July 15, 2014; Adam Liptak, "Supreme Court to Weigh Race in College Admissions," *New York Times*, June 29, 2014, www.nytimes.com. After a rehearing of the *Fisher* case in the circuit court, a new appeal returned the case to the Supreme Court in the 2015–16 session. The circuit court once again affirmed the Texas program, and the further appeal returned the case to the US Supreme Court.

15 Adam Liptak, "Supreme Court Upholds Affirmative Action Program at University of Texas," *New York Times*, June 23, 2016, www.nytimes.com.

16 Fisher v. University of Texas at Austin et al. Certiorari to the United States Court of Appeals for the Fifth Circuit, No. 14–981, argued December 9, 2015, decided June 23, 2016, cite as: 579 U. S. ____ (2016). Justice Alito, with whom the Chief Justice and Justice Thomas join, dissenting, p. 1, www.supremecourt.gov/opinions/15pdf/14-981_4g15.pdf.

17 It is also clear that court cases challenging affirmative action programs at other universities will continue to be brought before the courts. As the *New York Times* reported: "Roger Clegg, the president of the Center for Equal Opportunity, which supports colorblind policies, said the decision, though disappointing, was only a temporary setback. 'The court's decision leaves plenty of room for future challenges to racial preference policies at other schools,' he said. 'The struggle goes on.'" Liptak, "Supreme Court Upholds Affirmative Action."

Carol Anderson presented a strong argument that the Fisher case and the repeated attacks on affirmative action of which it is a part were central to President Trump's agenda of deepening white resentment by repeatedly finding "a new target for its ire." Carol Anderson, "The Policies of White Resentment," *New York Times*, August 5, 2017, www.nytimes.com; Jelani Cobb, "In Trump's World, Whites Are the Only Disadvantaged Class," *New Yorker*, August 4, 2017, www.newyorker.com.

In 2017 the issue of affirmative action once again returned to high profile public conversation, and the specific instance for the renewed focus is also important as it was based on an effort to reexamine a 2015 complaint filed with the Education and Justice Departments that challenged the affirmative action program at Harvard University for discriminating against Asian Americans. Charlie Savage, "Justice Dept. to Take on Affirmative Action in College Admissions," *New York Times*, August 1, 2017; Charlie Savage, "Asian-Americans' Complaint Prompted Justice Inquiry of College Admissions," *New York Times*, August 2, 2017, www.nytimes.com. For a thoughtful essay on the complexities of this case, see Jeannie Suk Gersen, "The Uncomfortable Truth about Affirmative Action and Asian-Americans," *New Yorker*, August 20, 2017, www.newyorker.com.

18 As law professor Richard L. Hasen summarized in the *New York Times*, Chief Justice John Roberts "is famous for saying, 'the way to stop discrimination on the basis of race is to stop discriminating on the basis of race.' Colorblindness is fast becoming his signature issue." Richard L. Hasen, "The Chief Justice's Long Game," *New York Times*, June 26, 2013, www.nytimes.com.

19 The Century Foundation's self-description is available at https://tcf.org. See also Richard D. Kahlenberg, "A Better Affirmative Action: State Universities That Created Alternatives to Racial Preferences," Century Foundation, February 25, 2014, http://tcf.org. Justice Alito took up this tack in his dissent from the final decision, arguing that the Texas program supported well positioned students of color over impoverished students of all races (*Fisher v. University of Texas, Austin,* Alito dissent, 32).

20 The 2019 college admissions scandal in which wealthy parents paid bribes and otherwise cheated to ensure admission for their children at elite schools once again highlighted the various ways (both legal and illegal) in which rich parents ensure that a college degree will reinforce existing class and race hierarchies. Daniel Golden, "The Curious Story behind Jared Kushner's Admission to Harvard," *ProPublica*, November 18, 2016, www.propublica.org; John Eligon and Audra D. S. Burch, "'What Does It Take?': Admissions Scandal Is a Harsh Lesson on Racial Disparities," *New York Times*, March 13, 2019, www.nytimes.com; Nicholas Lemann, "Want to Fix College?: Admissions Aren't the Biggest Problem," *New Yorker*, March 20, 2019, www.newyorker.com.

21 Patricia J. Williams, "Racism Remains Alive and Well," Room for Debate, *New York Times*, May 13, 2013, www.nytimes.com. Sherilyn Ifill presented a similarly strong defense in response to the Trump administration's moves to undercut affirmative action policies. Sherilyn A. Ifill, "Racial Justice Demands Affirmative Action," *New York Times*, August 2, 2017, www.nytimes.com.

22 Joshua Freeman, *American Empire: The Rise of a Global Power, the Democratic Revolution at Home* (New York: Penguin, 2013), 23.

23 Kathleen Frydl reports that the cost of the education portion of the GI Bill surpassed that of the Marshall Plan in Europe. Kathleen Frydl, *The GI Bill* (New York: Cambridge University Press, 2009), 3.

24 Ira Katznelson, *When Affirmative Action Was White: An Untold History of Racial Inequality in Twentieth-Century America* (New York: W.W. Norton, 2006). Katznelson reiterated this argument in the *New York Times* in response to the Trump administration's inquiries into affirmative action policies. Ira Katznelson,

"Making Affirmative Action White Again," *New York Times*, August 12, 2017, www. nytimes.com.

25 See Noel Ignatiev, *How the Irish Became White* (New York: Taylor & Francis, 1996).

26 Ginsburg continues: "See House Research Organization, Bill Analysis, HB 588, pp. 4–5 (Apr. 15, 1997) ('Many regions of the state, school districts, and high schools in Texas are still predominantly composed of people from a single racial or ethnic group. Because of the persistence of this segregation, admitting the top 10 percent of all high schools would provide a diverse population and ensure that a large, well qualified pool of minority students was admitted to Texas universities.'). It is race consciousness, not blindness to race, that drives such plans." 570 U. S. ____ (2013), 1, Ginsburg, J., Dissenting, Supreme Court of the United States, No. 11–345, Abigail Noel Fisher, Petitioner v. University of Texas at Austin, et al., on Writ of Certiorari to the United States Court of Appeals for the Fifth Circuit [June 24, 2013], p. 2, www.supremecourt.gov/opinions/12pdf/11-345_l5gm.pd.

27 "Percentage plans encourage parents to keep their children in low-performing segregated schools, and discourage students from taking challenging classes that might lower their grade point averages." 579 U. S. ____ (2016), Supreme Court of the United States, No. 14–981, Abigail Noel Fisher, Petitioner v. University of Texas at Austin, et al., on Writ of Certiorari to the United States Court of Appeals for the Fifth Circuit, June 23, 2016. See also Richard Primus, "Affirmative Action in College Admissions Here to Stay," *New York Times*, June 23, 2016, www.nytimes. com.

28 The controversy over the relation between race and class-based affirmative action programs has continued to expand in the years since the *Fisher* decision, and the Century Foundation remains a leading voice. David Leonhardt, "The Leading Liberal against Affirmative Action," *New York Times*, March 9, 2013, http://econo-mix.blogs.nytimes.com; Letters, "Should Race Be a Factor in Affirmative Action," *New York Times*, December 24, 2015, www.nytimes.com. See also Richard Kahlenberg, *The Remedy: Class, Race and Affirmative Action* (New York: Basic Books, 1997), and *The Future of Affirmative Action: New Paths to Diversity in Higher Education after Fisher v. University of Texas* (Washington, DC: Century Foundation, 2014).

Over against this argument for class-based affirmative action replacing race-based programs, a number of commentators argue that those places that have banned race-based affirmative action in favor of programs focused only on class have lost racial diversity. The California university system has, for example, not reached the levels of racial and ethnic diversity in its student body that existed before the passage of Proposition 209 in 1996. Julianne Hing, "Class-Based College Admissions Are No Magic Wand for Keeping Schools Diverse," *Guardian*, April 23, 2014, www.theguardian.com. See also Sigal Alon, *Race, Class and Affirmative Action* (New York: Russell Sage Foundation, 2015).

29 Kahlenberg, "A Better Affirmative Action," 3.

30 *Grutter v. Bollinger*, 539 U.S. 306—Supreme Court 2003, 39. "It has been 25 years since Justice Powell first approved the use of race to further an interest in student body diversity in public education. Since that time the number of minority applicants with high grades and test scores has indeed increased. See Tr. of Oral Arg. 43. We expect that 25 years from now, the use of racial preferences will no longer be necessary to further the interest approved today."

31 Take, for example, the public reactions to President Obama's very personal statement of his own experiences of racism in response to the not-guilty verdict in the case of the shooting of Trayvon Martin, an unarmed African American teenager who was stalked and shot by a white man in the community where his father lived. One public response as quoted in the newspaper *USA Today* was that even by speaking of racism in his own experience, Obama was "fanning the flames; it's time to move on." "A Post-Racial America? Your Say," *USA Today*, July 22, 2013; Catalina Camia, "GOP Rep on Zimmerman Verdict: Get Over It," *USA Today*, July 17, 2013, www.usatoday.com.

32 Gary May, *Bending toward Justice: The Voting Rights Act and the Transformation of American Democracy* (Durham, NC: Duke University Press, 2014); Ari Berman, *Give Us the Ballot: The Modern Struggle for Voting Rights in America* (New York: Farrar, Straus and Giroux, 2015).

33 Jonathan Weisman, "Underachieving Congress Appears in No Hurry to Change Things Now," *New York Times*, December 2, 2013; Eric Lichtblau, "Why the Justice Department Will Have Fewer Watchdogs in Polling Places," *New York Times*, October 24, 2016, www.nytimes.com.

34 Tomas Lopez, "'Shelby County': One Year Later," Brennan Center for Justice, July 24, 2014; Kevin Morris, "Voter Purge Rates Remain High, Analysis Finds," Brennan Center for Justice, August 1, 2019, www.brennancenter.org.

35 United States v. Windsor, Executor of the Estate of Spyer, et. al. Certiorari to the United States Court of Appeals for the Second Circuit, No. 12–307, argued March 27, 2013, decided June 26, 2013, p. 45. www.supremecourt.gov/opinions/12pdf/12-307_6j37.pdf.

36 The Court also refused to rule on an earlier, lower court decision (*Hollingsworth v. Perry*) that had struck down a California ban on same-sex marriage passed by ballot referendum, Proposition 8. In allowing this earlier court ruling to stand, the US Supreme Court allowed same-sex marriage in California to once again be legal.

37 "An Act to Defend and Protect the Institution of Marriage," HR 3396, 1, www.congress.gov.

38 *United States v. Windsor*, 22.

39 Liptak, "Supreme Court Upholds Affirmative Action."

40 On the magazine's website (www.advocate.com), the article now appears as "Gay Is the New Black?"; in the academic database Omnifile, it appears under the title "Pride and Prejudice." Ellis Cose, "Don't Compare Gay Rights, Civil Rights," *USA Today Forum*, http://usatoday30.usatoday.com.

41   On the right, both Justice Alito (p. 101) and Justice Thomas (p. 88) in their dissents from the *Obergefell* majority opinion criticize any connection between
     arguments over interracial marriage and same-sex marriage. In popular culture
     on the right, Mike Huckabee stated in a radio interview that to "equate same-sex
     marriage" to a "civil right" was an "insult" to African Americans, who were "truly
     discriminated against." Mike Huckabee interview, 1150 WJBO Baton Rouge News-
     Radio, June 30, 2015.
         The conversation in more progressive sites has included longstanding critiques of the use of analogies, including Jakobsen, *Working Alliances,* chapter 4,
     and Janet Halley, *Don't: A Reader's Guide to the Military's Anti-gay Policy* (Durham, NC: Duke University Press, 1999). On the other hand, some longtime
     civil rights activists like John Lewis and Julian Bond have been arguing that
     building on the work of Black activists was important both because many Black
     people are also gay people and because the work of the Civil Rights Movement
     was an expansive resistance to many forms of discrimination. Karen Grigsby
     Bates, "African Americans Question Comparing Gay Rights Movement to Civil
     Rights," NPR, July 2, 2015, www.npr.org.

42   Roderick A. Ferguson argues that the narrative of linear progress on which claims
     for gay rights are made is a form of power/knowledge that is "at once the constitution of a community and the delimitation of what belongs within and outside that
     community." Roderick A. Ferguson, "The Historiographical Operations of Gay
     Rights," in *After Legal Equality: Family, Sex, Kinship,* ed. Robert Leckey (Milton
     Park: Routledge, 2015), 153. As part of making this argument, Ferguson provides
     a reading of *Windsor* in relation to *Shelby County* (159). Meg Wesling makes a
     related argument that the relation between *Shelby County* and *Windsor* highlights that "when Justice Kennedy evokes the stigma that accompanies the denial
     of marriage recognition to same-sex couples, and the 'humiliat[ion] of tens of
     thousands of children now being raised by same-sex couples,' he relies on a vision
     of marriage as the scene of protection for white bourgeois domesticity" (178). Meg
     Wesling, "The Unequal Promise of Marriage Equality," *American Quarterly* 66
     (2014): 171–79.

43   Jakobsen, *Working Alliances,* chapter 4.

44   Brennan Center for Social Justice, "Voting Laws Roundup 2013," December 9,
     2013, www.brennancenter.org.

45   This narrative also fails to recognize that both DOMA at the federal level and
     California's Proposition 8 are relatively recently imposed forms of discrimination (passed in 1996 and 2008, respectively). They are treated as if they simply
     represent an anachronistic, millennially old form of discrimination that is finally
     being removed by an enlightened court. Alternatively, these legal actions could be
     interpreted as new instantiations of battles that make sexual politics repetitively
     important in US policy even as that import is also repetitively dismissed.

46   Binyamin Appelbaum, "What the Hobby Lobby Decision Means for America,"
     New York Times Magazine, July 22, 2014, www.nytimes.com; Dana Milbank, "In

Hobby Lobby Ruling the Supreme Court Uses a 'Fiction,'" *Washington Post*, June 30, 2014, www.washingtonpost.com; Carrie Halperin, "Health Care Law's Other Challenges," *New York Times*, June 30, 2014, www.nytimes.com.

47 David Firestone, "The Political Repercussions of the Hobby Lobby Decision," *New York Times*, June 30, 2014, http://takingnote.blogs.nytimes.com; Karen Finney, "Hobby Lobby Opens a New Front in the 'War on Women,'" MSNBC, July 13, 2014, www.msnbc.com.

48 Linda Greenhouse, "Reading Hobby Lobby in Context," *New York Times*, July 9, 2104, www.nytimes.com.

49 Justice Alito continues: "RFRA, however contemplates a 'more focused' inquiry: It 'requires the Government to demonstrate that the compelling interest test is satisfied through application of the challenged law 'to the person'—the particular claimant whose sincere exercise of religion is being substantially burdened.'" *Burwell v. Hobby Lobby Stores, Inc.*, Supreme Court of the United States No. 13–354, decided June 30, 2014.

50 *United States v. Windsor*, 2014, 52.

51 Alito writes, "The University still has not identified with any specificity the interests that its use of race and ethnicity is supposed to serve" (*Fisher v. University of Texas, Austin*, Alito dissent, 32). As Adam Liptak summarized in the *New York Times*: "Justice Alito described those goals—concerning 'the destruction of stereotypes,' promoting 'cross-racial understanding' and preparing students 'for an increasingly diverse work force and society'—as slippery and impervious to judicial scrutiny." Adam Liptak, "Supreme Court Upholds Affirmative Action Program at University of Texas," *New York Times*, June 23, 2016, www.nytimes. com. See also Christina Sterbenz, "Justice Alito Spent 50 Pages Railing against Affirmative Action in College Admissions—These Are His Main Points," *Business Insider*, June 23, 2016, www.businessinsider.com.

52 Almost immediately upon taking office, President Trump moved to fulfill his campaign promise to enact a "total and complete shutdown of Muslims entering the United States," with an executive order, which he termed a "ban" on travel from seven Muslim-majority countries (Iraq, Syria, Iran, Libya, Somalia, Sudan, and Yemen). Jenna Johnson, "Trump Calls for 'Total and Complete Shutdown of Muslims Entering the United States,'" *Washington Post*, December 7, 2015, www. washingtonpost.com; David Savage, "Trump Undercuts His Lawyers with Tweets about Travel Ban," *Los Angeles Times*, June 5, 2017, www.latimes.com. The initial ban was struck down in court, and the administration followed up with a second iteration, which was also struck down, and a third "proclamation" with a stated basis in national security, a claim supported by dropping Iraq, Sudan, and Chad and adding North Korea and Venezuela to the countries involved. Steve Almasy and Darran Simon, "A Timeline of President Trump's Travel Bans," CNN, March 30, 2017, www.cnn.com. In *Trump v. Hawaii*, the Court upheld the administration's action and its claim to be using "national security" concerns, rather than anti-Muslim animus, as its basis.

53 Roberts writes, "Finally, the dissent invokes *Korematsu v. United States*, 323 U. S. 214 (1944). Whatever rhetorical advantage the dissent may see in doing so, Korematsu has nothing to do with this case. The forcible relocation of U. S. citizens to concentration camps, solely and explicitly on the basis of race, is objectively unlawful and outside the scope of Presidential authority. But it is wholly inapt to liken that morally repugnant order to a facially neutral policy denying certain foreign nationals the privilege of admission. See post, at 26–28. The entry suspension is an act that is well within executive authority and could have been taken by any other President—the only question is evaluating the actions of this particular President in promulgating an otherwise valid Proclamation. The dissent's reference to *Korematsu*, however, affords this Court the opportunity to make express what is already obvious: *Korematsu* was gravely wrong the day it was decided, has been overruled in the court of history, and—to be clear—'has no place in law under the Constitution.'" 323 U. S., at 248 (Jackson, J., dissenting). *Trump v. Hawaii*, 38. Roberts's statement here formalized that *Korematsu* can no longer serve as a basis for precedent, but, as noted below, Sotomayor found this important step inadequate to the issues of the current moment. Charlie Savage, "Korematsu: Notorious Supreme Court Ruling on Japanese Internment Is Finally Tossed Out," *New York Times*, June 26, 2018, www.nytimes.com.

54 Catie Edmondson, "Sonia Sotomayor Delivers Sharp Dissent in Travel Ban Case," *New York Times*, June 26, 2018, www.nytimes.com.

55 *Trump v. Hawaii*, Justice Sotomayor dissenting, with whom Justice Ginsburg, www.supremecourt.gov/opinions/17pdf/17-965_h315.pdf. Sotomayor writes: "The majority holds otherwise by ignoring the facts, misconstruing our legal precedent, and turning a blind eye to the pain and suffering the Proclamation inflicts upon countless families and individuals, many of whom are United States citizens. Because that troubling result runs contrary to the Constitution and our precedent, I dissent" (1). In the argument that follows, she lays out her position in detail: "Although the majority briefly recounts a few of the statements and background events that form the basis of plaintiffs' constitutional challenge, ante, at 27–28, that highly abridged account does not tell even half of the story. See Brief for The Roderick & Solange MacArthur Justice Center as Amicus Curiae 5–31 (outlining President Trump's public statements expressing animus toward Islam). The full record paints a far more harrowing picture, from which a reasonable observer would readily conclude that the Proclamation was motivated by hostility and animus toward the Muslim faith" (4). And she goes on to list instances in which the president expressly stated that the "travel ban" was directed toward Muslims (4–10).

56 "Notably, the Court recently found less pervasive official expressions of hostility and the failure to disavow them to be constitutionally significant. Cf. Masterpiece Cakeshop, Ltd. v. Colorado Civil Rights Comm'n, 584 U. S. ___, ___ (2018) (slip op., at 18)" (*Trump v. Hawaii*, Sotomayor dissent, 12).

57 Sotomayor concludes her dissent as follows: "Today's holding is all the more troubling given the stark parallels between the reasoning of this case and that of *Korematsu v. United States*, 323 U. S. 214 (1944). . . . Although a majority of the Court in Korematsu was willing to uphold the Government's actions based on a barren invocation of national security, dissenting Justices warned of that decision's harm to our constitutional fabric. Justice Murphy recognized that there is a need for great deference to the Executive Branch in the context of national security, but cautioned that 'it is essential that there be definite limits to [the government's] discretion,' as '[i]ndividuals must not be left impoverished of their constitutional rights on a plea of military necessity that has neither substance nor support.' 323 U. S., at 234 (Murphy, J., dissenting). Justice Jackson lamented that the Court's decision upholding the Government's policy would prove to be 'a far more subtle blow to liberty than the promulgation of the order itself,' for although the executive order was not likely to be long lasting, the Court's willingness to tolerate it would endure. Id., at 245–246.

"In the intervening years since Korematsu, our Nation has done much to leave its sordid legacy behind. See, e.g., Civil Liberties Act of 1988, 50 U. S. C. App. §4211 et seq. (setting forth remedies to individuals affected by the executive order at issue in Korematsu); Non-Detention Act of 1971, 18 U. S. C. §4001(a) (forbidding the imprisonment or detention by the United States of any citizen absent an Act of Congress). Today, the Court takes the important step of finally overruling Korematsu, denouncing it as 'gravely wrong the day it was decided.' Ante, at 38 (citing Korematsu, 323 U. S., at 248 (Jackson, J., dissenting)). This formal repudiation of a shameful precedent is laudable and long overdue. But it does not make the majority's decision here acceptable or right. By blindly accepting the Government's misguided invitation to sanction a discriminatory policy motivated by animosity toward a disfavored group, all in the name of a superficial claim of national security, the Court redeploys the same dangerous logic underlying Korematsu and merely replaces one 'gravely wrong' decision with another. Ante, at 38. Our Constitution demands, and our country deserves, a Judiciary willing to hold the coordinate branches to account when they defy our most sacred legal commitments. Because the Court's decision today has failed in that respect, with profound regret, I dissent" (27–28).

58 On some of the complex interrelations and confusions between race and religion with regard to Islam, see Edward E. Curtis IV, *Muslims in America: A Short History* (New York: Oxford University Press, 2009), and *Islam in Black America: Identity, Liberation and Difference in African-American Islamic Thought* (Albany: SUNY Press, 2002); Zareena Grewal, *Islam Is a Foreign Country: American Muslims and the Global Crisis of Authority* (New York: New York University Press, 2013); and Puar, *Terrorist Assemblages*.

59 Chakrabarty, *Provincializing Europe*, 8.

60 Ibid., 253.

61 Take, for example, the way in which editorials in the *New York Times* regularly talk about Muslims as if they are somehow behind the times of secular, Western democracies. Here is an exemplary excerpt from columnist David Brooks in an essay addressed to Muslims: "We in the West were born into a world that reflected the legacy of Socrates and the agora. . . . Our mind-set is progressive and rational. Your mind-set is pre-Enlightenment." David Brooks, "Drafting Hitler," *New York Times,* February 9, 2006, A27. Note Brooks here is not expressing opposition to all religion, only to that religion which doesn't place itself within the broader framework of European history and secularism.

62 Evolution has been a common term of analysis in religious studies. See, for example, Robert Bellah's early essay "Religious Evolution," in *Beyond Belief: Essays on Religion in a Post-Traditional World* (New York: Harper & Row, 1970), 20–50, and his final book, *Religion in Human Evolution: From the Paleolithic to the Axial Age* (Cambridge, MA: Harvard University Press, 2011).

63 For a recent iteration of this narrative, see Mark Lilla, *The Stillborn God: Religion, Politics, and the Modern West* (New York: Knopf, 2007).

64 David Kazanjian, *Colonizing Trick: National Culture and Imperial Citizenship in Early America* (Minneapolis: University of Minnesota Press, 2003).

65 Immanuel Kant, *Religion within the Limits of Reason Alone*, trans. Theodore M. Greene and Hoyt H. Hudson (New York: Harper, 1960). See also Immanuel Kant, *Religion within the Boundaries of Mere Reason and Other Writings*, trans. and ed. Allen Wood and George di Giovanni (New York: Cambridge University Press, 1998).

66 Stuart Hall, "The West and the Rest: Discourse and Power," in *The Formations of Modernity,* ed. Bram Gieben and Stuart Hall (Cambridge: Polity Press, 1992), 275–332.

67 The Poor People's Campaign: A National Call for Moral Revival, www.poorpeoplescampaign.org.

68 Here, I diverge from some readings of Chakrabarty, such as that offered by Ann Braude, which suggest that his critique makes the possibility of doing history (or social analysis more generally) "fatally hampered as an academic project" (Braude, "Religion and Women's Political Mobilizations," 69). I read Chakrabarty's argument as undoing a sense of an overarching or coherent "social," such as one might find in the genealogy of Durkheimian social analysis, but throughout this book I explore methods of social analysis that do not depend on this approach.

69 Chakrabarty, *Provincializing Europe*, 107.

70 Jakobsen and Pellegrini, *Secularisms*, 2008.

71 Premilla Nadasen and Tiffany Williams, "Valuing Domestic Work," *New Feminist Solutions* 5 (2010), http://bcrw.barnard.edu; Gisela Fosado, "Women and Work: Feminists in Solidarity with Domestic Workers" (video), BCRW, 2009, http://bcrw.barnard.edu.

72 By 2019, domestic workers bills of rights had been passed in nine states: California, Connecticut, Hawaii, Illinois, Massachusetts, Nevada, New Mexico, New

York, and Oregon. Senator Kamala Harris (a candidate for the 2020 Democratic Party presidential nomination) and Representative Pramila Jayapal are working with NDWA to introduce legislation for a Domestic Workers Bill of Rights at the federal level, www.domesticworkers.org.

73 DAMAYAN Migrant Workers Association and the Urban Justice Center with the assistance of Ninotchka Rosca, "Doing the Work That Makes All Work Possible: A Research Narrative of Filipino Domestic Workers in the Tri-state Area," Community Development Project, October 23, 2010, www.cdp-ny.org.

74 *Obergefell v. Hodges*, 2015, 8.

75 As Ann Pellegrini and I document in *Love the Sin*, Chief Justice Warren Burger made these claims about the "ancient roots" and universal history of opposition to sodomy in the Court's 1983 decision to uphold sodomy laws. Although that decision was overturned, the appeal to the unchanging status of marriage over millennia is apparently more persistent (30–31).

   Chief Justice Roberts, in his dissent, makes similar claims to the history of marriage throughout "human society": "As a result, the Court invalidates the marriage laws of more than half the States and orders the transformation of a social institution that has formed the basis of human society for millennia, for the Kalahari Bushmen and the Han Chinese, the Carthaginians and the Aztecs. Just who do we think we are?" (42). Similarly, Justice Thomas argues that "[t]he traditional definition of marriage has prevailed in every society that has recognized marriage throughout history" (88). Justice Thomas makes this argument in response to claims that the one man–one woman definition of marriage entered US law at some points through laws against interracial marriage under slavery. In disputing this claim, he returns to the ground of universality for this definition, despite the historical (whether in ancient societies or the nineteenth-century US) and contemporary evidence for polygamy as at least one alternative definition of marriage.

76 Sarah Barringer Gordon, *The Mormon Question: Polygamy and Constitutional Conflict in Nineteenth-Century America* (Chapel Hill: University of North Carolina Press, 2002).

77 Henry Abelove, "Some Speculations on the History of 'Sexual Intercourse' During the 'Long Eighteenth Century' in England," in *Nationalisms and Sexualities*, ed. Andrew Parker et al. (New York: Routledge, 1991), 335–42. See also Cott, *Public Vows*. Cott also testified as an expert witness in the California trial over Proposition 8, before that issue reached the Supreme Court for which she also provided an expert affidavit, www.glad.org.

78 Michael Cobb, "The Supreme Court's Lonely Hearts Club," *New York Times*, June 30, 2015, www.nytimes.com. See also Cobb, *Single*.

79 Joseph N. DeFilippis, Lisa Duggan, Kenyon Farrow, and Richard Kim, eds., "A New Queer Agenda," themed issue, *Scholar & Feminist Online* 10.1–2 (Fall 2011–Spring 2012), http://sfonline.barnard.edu.

80 Lisa Duggan and Richard Kim, "Preface to 'A New Queer Agenda,'" in 'A New Queer Agenda,' ed. DeFilippis et al., http://sfonline.barnard.edu/a-new-queer-agenda.

81 Lisa Duggan, "After Neoliberalism? From Crisis to Organizing for Queer Economic Justice," in "A New Queer Agenda," ed. DeFilippis et al., http://sfonline.barnard.edu.

82 For a description of Queer Survival Economies, see http://queersurvivaleconomies.com.

CONCLUSION

1 Josh Gerstein, "Sparks Fly over Trump Tweets at Travel Ban Court Arguments," *Politico*, December 18, 2017, www.politico.com.

2 See, for example, Tourmaline, Dean Spade, and Hope Dector, "Prison Abolition + Prefiguring the World We Want to Live In" (video), released January 7, 2014, http://bcrw.barnard.edu/videos/reina-gossett-dean-spade-part-1-prison-abolition-prefiguring-the-world-you-want-to-live-in, and CeCe McDonald, Tourmaline, and Dean Spade, "Prisons Aren't Safe for Anybody" (video), BCRW, April 21, 2014, http://bcrw.barnard.edu/videos/cece-mcdonald-reina-gossett-and-dean-spade-prisons-arent-safe-for-anybody.

3 McDonald, Tourmaline, and Spade, "Prisons Aren't Safe for Anybody."

4 Craig Willse, *The Value of Homelessness: Managing Surplus Life in the United States* (Minneapolis: University of Minnesota Press, 2015).

5 Cecilia Varela, "Gender, Justice, and Neoliberal Transformations," comments, Working Group Meeting, Danish Institute for International Studies, May 29, 2017.

6 For an expansive consideration of the breadth of the claim for abolition, see abolition.org.

7 This insight builds on the long-standing analysis of feminist antiviolence activists that understands violence as a means used to solve problems—rather than, for example, an inevitable aspect of human nature or an inexplicable aberration. Many of the leaders in the prison abolition movement developed their analyses in the context of women of color feminism, particularly through the development of INCITE! Women of Color Against Violence, as leaders of Critical Resistance, and through the collaboration between the two groups. INCITE!–Critical Resistance Statement, "Gender and the Prison Industrial Complex," 2001, www.incite-national.org.

8 BCRW, "Ky Peterson."

9 So-called "hate crimes" laws provide a prime example here. A spate of laws passed in the 1990s and early 2000s promised to "protect" LGBTQ people from street violence by instituting harsher penalties when hate speech or other expressions of hateful intent accompanied the violence. These laws, of course, do not protect anyone; they instead involve harsher punishment *after* violence has been committed. And, often these laws are enforced through violence that is surprisingly similar to the "hateful" crimes they are supposed to prevent. Janet R. Jakobsen,

"Tolerating Hate? Or Hating Tolerance?: Why Hate Crimes Legislation Isn't the Answer," *Sojourner: The Women's Forum* 24.12 (August 1999): 9–11; Kay Whitlock and Michael Bronski, *Considering Hate: Violence, Goodness, and Justice in American Culture and Politics* (Boston: Beacon Press, 2015).

10 On the effectiveness in US political discourse of focusing on some people as if they are always already criminal see, for example, comments by Barry Goldwater, the "father" of new right conservatism in the Republican Party. As documented by Allan J. Lichtman in *White Protestant Nation* through confidential campaign memos from Goldwater's 1964 presidential campaign, "The [campaign] used carefully coded language to tap into white fear of black crime and sexuality, without directly stirring racial antagonism." Lichtman quotes Goldwater as making this converse connection between sexuality and crime just as directly as the connection that makes Black sexuality (always already) criminal: "On the campaign trail, Goldwater charged, 'The moral fiber of the American people is beset by rot and decay. . . . It is on our streets that we see the final, terrible proof of a sickness which not all the social theories of a thousand social experiments have even begun to touch. Crime grows faster than population, while those who break the law are accorded more consideration than those who try to enforce the law" (254).

11 Tourmaline, Spade, and Dector, "Prison Abolition."

12 Abigail Boggs, Eli Meyerhoff, Nick Mitchell, and Zach Schwartz-Weinstein, for example, offer a manifesto for taking an abolitionist perspective on issues of higher education that were raised in chapter 4. Abigail Boggs, Eli Meyerhoff, Nick Mitchell, and Zach Schwartz-Weinstein, "Abolitionist University Studies: A Manifesto," *Abolition: A Journal of Insurgent Politics* (August 27, 2019).

13 McDonald, Tourmaline, and Spade, "I Use My Love to Guide Me."

14 Dean Spade, "Impossibility Now" (video and slideshow), in "Gender Justice and Neoliberal Transformations," ed. Bernstein and Jakobsen, http://sfonline.barnard.edu.

15 Tourmaline, "Making a Way Out of No Way," keynote address at Scholar and Feminist Conference 41: Sustainabilities, February 27, 2016, http://bcrw.barnard.edu.

16 Melissa Wright, *Disposable Women and Other Myths of Global Capitalism* (New York: Routledge, 2006); Neferti Tadiar, "Life-Times of Disposability within Global Neoliberalism," *Social Text* 31.2 (2013): 19–48.

17 Janet Mock, "Celebrating Living Trans Women on Transgender Day of Remembrance," November 22, 2013, http://janetmock.com.

18 Trans Life and Liberation Art Series, http://translifeandliberation.tumblr.com. Many of these portraits also appear in the animated short film about the life of Miss Major Griffin-Gracy, directed by Tourmaline, "The Personal Things," BCRW, November 20, 2016, https://vimeo.com/192223519. See also Tamara Best, "Black Queer Brooklyn on Film Focuses on Diverse Voices," *New York Times*, June 7, 2017, www.nytimes.com.

19 Braude, "Religion and Women's Political Mobilizations."

20 Muñoz, *Cruising Utopia*.

21 Angelika Bammer, *Partial Visions: Feminism and Utopianism in the 1970s* (New York: Routledge, 1991); Tracy Fessenden, "Disappearances: Race, Religion and the Progress Narrative of U.S. Feminism," in *Secularisms*, ed. Jakobsen and Pellegrini, 139–61.

22 Sara Ahmed, *The Promise of Happiness* (Durham, NC: Duke University Press, 2010), 3; quoting Simone de Beauvoir, 28. Jeanette Winterson, *Why Be Happy When You Could Be Normal?* (London: Jonathan Cape, 2011).

23 For examples of what such utopias might look like, see Davina Cooper, *Everyday Utopias: The Conceptual Life of Promising Spaces* (Durham, NC: Duke University Press, 2013).

24 Cindy Milstein, ed., *Rebellious Mourning: The Collective Work of Grief* (Chico, CA: AK Press, 2017).

25 Martha Nussbaum, *Frontiers of Justice: Disability, Nationality, Species Membership* (Cambridge, MA: Belknap Press, 2007); John Rawls, *A Theory of Justice* (Cambridge, MA: Harvard University Press, 1971).

26 Nussbaum, *Frontiers*, 108ff.

27 Che Gossett provides a means of grounding animal justice in the genealogy of "Black radical imaginings of abolition" (rather than the liberal tradition of expanding democracy). Che Gossett, "Blackness, Animality, and the UnSovereign," *Verso* (blog), September 8, 2015, www.versobooks.com.

28 Gayle Rubin uses the metaphor of the "charmed circle" of sexuality to describe the persistence of social hierarchies based on sex. She notes that married people remain at the center, while those whose sexual practices don't fit well with wedded bliss are excluded. The symbolic enclosure of the circle remains unchanged, with married couples on the inside and everyone else on the outs. Gayle Rubin, "Thinking Sex: Notes for a Radical Theory of the Politics of Sexuality," in *The Lesbian and Gay Studies Reader*, ed. Henry Abelove, Michèle Aina Barale, and David M. Halperin (New York: Routledge, 1993 [1984]), 13.

29 Ernesto Laclau and Chantal Mouffe, *Hegemony and Socialist Strategy*, trans. Winston Moore and Paul Cammack (London: Verso: 1985). For a more extensive reading of the limits of claiming equivalences, see Jakobsen, *Working Alliances*, conclusion.

30 David M. Halperin, *Saint Foucault: Towards a Gay Hagiography* (New York: Oxford University Press, 1997).

31 Anna Lowenhaupt Tsing, *Friction: An Ethnography of Global Connection* (Princeton, NJ: Princeton University Press, 2005); David L. Eng and David Kazanjian, eds., *Loss: The Politics of Mourning* (Berkeley and Los Angeles: University of California Press, 2003).

32 On the complexities of this commitment, see, for example, Catriona Mortimer-Sandilands and Bruce Erickson, eds., *Queer Ecologies: Sex, Nature, Politics, Desire* (Bloomington: Indiana University Press, 2010).

33 Clare, *Brilliant Imperfection*.
34 Jakobsen, "Queer Is? Queer Does?"
35 Henry Abelove has made clear the value of keeping this simultaneous activity in mind. In particular, it allows for recognition of the import of *both* claims to the centrality of sex to politics in the United States *and* a recognition of the ways in which sexuality is marginalized as a public concern. In an essay in his collection *Deep Gossip*, on the prominent Harvard professor of American Studies, F. O. Matthiessen, Abelove's meticulous research and exactitude of statement show how eroticism subtends Matthiessen's field-establishing book, *American Renaissance*. At the same time, Abelove shows the ways in which sexuality is or can be articulated with critical activism that challenges the modern nation and its states. Abelove, *Deep Gossip*, 56–69.
36 Amber Hollibaugh, Catherine Sameh, and Janet R. Jakobsen, "Desiring Change," *New Feminist Solutions* 7 (August 2011), http://bcrw.barnard.edu.
37 My earlier consideration of this question can be found in Jakobsen, "Perverse Justice."
38 Herbert Marcuse, *An Essay on Liberation* (Boston: Beacon Press, 1969), ix.
39 Karl Marx, *Capital: A Critique of Political Economy*, trans. Ben Fowkes, vol. 1 (New York: Penguin Books, 1976), 125; Herbert Marcuse, *Eros and Civilization: A Philosophical Inquiry into Freud* (Boston: Beacon Press, 1955), 100.
40 Antonio Negri, *The Politics of Subversion: A Manifesto for the Twenty-First Century* (Cambridge: Polity Press, 2005).
41 Roderick Ferguson, *Aberrations in Black: Toward a Queer of Color Critique* (Minneapolis: University of Minnesota Press, 2003).
42 Ferguson, "Of Our Normative Strivings," and Villarejo, "Tarrying with the Normative."
43 Miranda Joseph and David Rubin have argued that complicity with capital does not, in itself, signal a lack of moral value. Rather, the pursuit of economic justice does not necessarily require continuing the search for that which is purified of capital's touch (whether the search is conceived in terms of an outside to capital or an unrealized future). Miranda Joseph and David Rubin, "Promising Complicities: On the Sex, Race, and Globaliztaion Project," in *Companion to Lesbian, Gay, Bisexual, Transgender, and Queer Studies,* ed. Haggerty and McGarry, 430–51.
    Moreover, a number of theorists have also suggested the search for a purified outside or a future entirely free from capitalism entails ascribing to contemporary capitalist systems a totality and wholeness to which capital aspires but which it certainly has not achieved. And, in so doing critics miss noncapitalist practices in the current moment. See Paul Smith, *Millennial Dreams: Contemporary Culture and Capital in the North* (London: Verso, 1997), and J. K. Gibson-Graham, *The End of Capitalism (As We Knew It): A Feminist Critique of Political Economy* (Cambridge: Blackwell, 1996).

44 David Ruccio, "Failure of Socialism, Future of Socialists?," *Rethinking Marxism* 5 (Summer 1992): 18. For a broader reading of this material, see Jakobsen, "Perverse Justice."

45 Ruccio, "Failure of Socialism," 19. The idea that a coherent community is not the natural alternative to the capitalist individual is particularly important because, as Miranda Joseph has so convincingly shown, community is not the romantic antidote to capitalism, but its effective supplement, leading to a need to consider possibilities beyond the "romance of community." (*Against the Romance of Community*).

46 Ruccio, "Failure of Socialism," 17: "The same society that creates the conditions for the formation of individual subjectivity that serves to reproduce the relations of commodity exchange may also give rise to other types of subjectivity—including collective subjectivity—which challenge and seek to move beyond the 'objective dependency relations' characteristic of the existing system of money and exchange."

47 Jakobsen and Pellegrini, *Love the Sin*.

48 Janet R. Jakobsen and Elizabeth Lapovsky Kennedy, "Sex and Freedom," in *Regulating Sex*, ed. Elizabeth Bernstein and Laurie Schaffner (New York: Routledge, 2004), 247–70.

49 Elizabeth Freeman, "Time Binds, or, Erotohistoriography," in "What's Queer about Queer Studies Now?," ed. Eng, Halberstam, and Muñoz, 59.

50 For a rundown of such grassroots efforts in a number of areas of the world, see the Alliance for Youth Achievement, www.allforyouth.org.

51 See www.healthgap.org.

52 See www.tac.org.za. As Richard Kim has noted, even queer-identified organizations like ACT UP in the US are connecting sexual politics to questions of economic justice. Richard Kim, "ACT UP Goes Global," *Nation*, July 9, 2001, www.thenation.com.

53 Mary Hawkesworth has criticized Hardt and Negri's proposal for its failure to recognize gender difference. Michael Hardt and Antonio Negri, *Multitude: War and Democracy in the Age of Empire* (New York: Penguin Press, 2004).

54 Chela Sandoval, *Methodology of the Oppressed* (Minneapolis: University of Minnesota Press, 2000). See also Chela Sandoval, "U.S. Third World Feminism: The Theory and Method of Oppositional Consciousness in the Postmodern World," *Genders* 10 (Spring 1991): 1–24.

55 Laura Levitt makes this argument about the challenges of maintaining secular Judaism when Judaism is understood as a religion. Laura Levitt, "Other Moderns, Other Jews: Revisiting Jewish Secularism in America," in *Secularisms*, ed. Jakobsen and Pellegrini, 107–38.

56 Sandoval, "U.S. Third World Feminism," 16.

57 "Moreover, differential consciousness makes more clearly visible the equal rights, revolutionary, supremacist, and separatist forms of oppositional consciousness,

which when kaleidoscoped together comprise a new paradigm for understanding oppositional activity in general" (ibid.).

58 Dean Spade, "Methodologies of TransResistance," in *A Companion to Lesbian, Gay, Bisexual, Transgender and Queer Studies*, ed. George E. Haggerty and Molly McGarry (Oxford: Blackwell, 2007), 237–61. See also Spade, *Normal Life*.

59 This is one of the concerns Patricia Williams raises in *The Alchemy of Race and Rights: Diary of a Law Professor* (Cambridge, MA: Harvard University Press, 1992). In thinking about and working toward social justice for Black people in the United States, Williams understands that sometimes an alchemical transformation of narrowly established and argued contract law expands into a redrawn social contract—legal reform is sometimes part of revolutionary change.

60 On the complexity of reforming drug enforcement, see Kerwin Kaye, *Enforcing Freedom: Drug Courts, Therapeutic Communities, and the Intimacies of the State* (New York: Columbia University Press, 2019).

61 Tarso Ramos, Political Research Associates meeting, May 11, 2017. Ramos also served as an activist-in-residence at BCRW 2016–18, www.bcrw.barnard.edu.

62 Sandoval, "U.S. Third World Feminism," 1.

63 Ibid., 15.

64 See, for example, Bender and Klassen, *After Pluralism*; Roderick A. Ferguson, *The Reorder of Things: The University and Pedagogies of Minority Difference* (Minneapolis: University of Minnesota Press, 2012); and Sara Ahmed, *On Being Included: Racism and Diversity in Institutional Life* (Durham, NC: Duke University Press, 2012).

65 For my specific critique of diversity politics, see Jakobsen, *Working Alliances*, and "Ethics after Pluralism."

66 Kafer, *Feminist, Queer, Crip*, 155–56.

67 Grace Chang argues that both domestic workers and disabled people cared for by domestic workers are treated as non-workers whose lives become extremely precarious in the face of neoliberal policies: "Certainly immigrant women of color are 'always and already' seen as noncitizens, regardless of immigration status— just as disabled people, poor people, and prisoners are seen as sub-citizens. These groups are all viewed by society not as citizens, workers or consumers, but alternately as 'charity cases' or 'welfare cheats' helpless souls or dangerous menaces to society—thus deserving of only pity, punishment or rehabilitation instead of fair wages for their 'nonlabors.'" Grace Chang, "Inevitable Intersections: Care, Work, and Citizenship," in *Disabling Domesticity*, ed. Michael Rembis (New York: Palgrave Macmillan, 2017), 186.

68 Hand in Hand Domestic Employers Network, History, domesticemployers.org. Hand in Hand is also part of the broader advocacy network Caring Across Generations, https://caringacross.org.

69 Elizabeth Freeman, *Time Binds: Queer Temporalities, Queer Histories* (Durham, NC: Duke University Press, 2010), xiii.

70 Ibid., xiv.

71 Ibid., xv.

72 One of the many responses to Christina Sharpe's *In the Wake: On Blackness and Being* (Durham, NC: Duke University Press, 2016) has been a renewed emphasis on an ethics of care and on the relation between justice and care. See also Christina Sharpe, "'And to Survive,'" *Small Axe* 22.3 (2018): 171–80. For my earlier reading of the relation between justice and care, see Janet R. Jakobsen, "Feminist Ethics in a World of Moral Multiplicity: Dimensions and Boundaries," in *Making Worlds: Metaphor and Materiality in Feminist Texts*, ed. Susan Aiken et al. (Tucson: University of Arizona Press, 1998), 205–14.

INDEX

Abelove, Henry, 155, 195n20, 223n71, 263n77, 266n28, 267n35
abolition, 204n62, 221n49, 265n12, 266n27; animal justice in, 168, 266n27; in prison, 31, 42, 103, 113, 161–63, 180, 254n7, 261n57, 264n7, 269n67
abortion, 4, 89–90, 203n57, 237n63 237n66; global gag rule on, 102, 245n64; Obama on, 3, 120–21, 248n82; political battles over, 132, 253n9; women and, 9, 46, 113, 126, 143–44, 152–54, 262n72. *See also* contraception; reproductive justice
actor-network theory, 213n89
Affirmative Action, 20, 90, 134, 135–39, 142–44, 147
Affordable Care Act, 143, 229n2, 250n95
Ahmed, Sara, 165–66, 204n61, 266n22, 269n64
AIDS policy, 117–18, 177–79, 245n66, 246nn68–69
Alito, Samuel, 133–35, 143–45, 147, 173, 258n41, 259n49; on education and race, 254n16, 255n19, 259n51
Alpert, Rebecca, 194n5, 225n12, 254n11
anticommunism, 17, 91–92, 238n75
antiracism, 101–2
assemblage, 22, 105, 210n81, 212n86, 222n53, 241n21

Barnard Center for Research on Women (BCRW), 64, 161–62, 269n61
Berlant, Lauren, 16, 201n45, 204n61, 206n67, 230n36

Bernstein, Elizabeth, 73, 198n29, 208n71, 209n74, 230n12, 232n13, 253n31
binary oppositions, 94–95, 172–74, 179–80, 184, 268n57; common sense and, 71–72, 230n9; domination by, 58, 63, 84; of gender, 58, 121; in religion and secularism, 85, 180
biopolitics, 45–47, 53, 179, 219n33, 222n59
Blacks, 57–58, 84, 102, 226n96, 236n53, 266n27; legal reform benefiting, 180–81, 269n59; Moynihan Report on, 110–11, 243n42, 244n47; Obama election and, 119, 247n75, 247n77; prison abolition and, 103, 113, 180; progress narrative on, 134, 253n10; reproduction and women as, 46–47, 222n59; Voting Rights Act of 1965 influencing, 133–34, 138–39, 146, 150, 173
Bordowitz, Gregg, 188, 191
Brady, Mary Pat, 206n67
Braude, Ann, 61, 65, 164, 227n99, 262n68, 265n19
Burger, Warren, 263n75
Burnham, Linda, 2, 193n4
Bush, George W., 14–15, 102, 116, 118–19, 200n40, 245nn63–64; AIDS policy of, 117, 245n66, 246nn68–69; on crusade, 121–22, 248n84
Bush, Laura, 14–15, 116, 200n40, 245n63
busing, 4, 88–90, 101, 237n64
Buttigieg, Pete, 9, 197n26

ABOUT THE AUTHOR

Janet R. Jakobsen is Claire Tow Professor of Women's, Gender, and Sexuality Studies at Barnard College, Columbia University, where she has also served as Director of the Center for Research on Women and Dean for Faculty Diversity and Development. She is the co-author, with Ann Pellegrini, of *Love the Sin: Sexual Regulation and the Limits of Religious Tolerance.*